The Big Turnoff

The Big Turnoff

Confessions of a TV-Addicted Mom Trying to Raise a TV-Free Kid

by

Ellen Currey-Wilson

ALGONQUIN BOOKS OF CHAPEL HILL   2007

Published by
ALGONQUIN BOOKS OF CHAPEL HILL
Post Office Box 2225
Chapel Hill, North Carolina 27515-2225

a division of
WORKMAN PUBLISHING
225 Varick Street
New York, New York 10014

To protect the privacy of people mentioned in this book, characters
have been combined and situations disguised, and certain names,
places, and other identifying characteristics have been changed.

Library of Congress Cataloging-in-Publication Data
Currey-Wilson, Ellen.
    The big turnoff : confessions of a TV-addicted mom trying to
raise a TV-free kid / Ellen Currey-Wilson. — 1st ed.
        p. cm.
    ISBN-13: 978-1-56512-539-1; ISBN-10: 1-56512-539-8
    1. Currey-Wilson, Ellen.   2. Television and family — United
States — Case studies   3. Parenting — United States — Case
studies.   4. Parents — United States — Biography.   I. Title.
HQ520.W55 2007
302.234508973 — dc22   2006049893

10 9 8 7 6 5 4 3 2 1
First Edition

For Bob and Casey

And in memory of my mother
Virginia Currey

May the best of her live on in me

Contents

1 Grandiose Goals 1

2 The Final Push 19

3 High Need 38

4 Cell Mates 57

5 Bag Lady 78

6 Doing Dishes 101

7 Kid Friendly 124

8 Sex Fiends and Shooters 149

9 Passion Is Everything 165

10 Cocktail Hour 194

11 A Lovely Offer 210

12 Forest Friends 241

13 A First Time for Everything 271

14 Pandora's Box 296

15 "I'm Fine, Mom!" 313

16 Leaving TV Land 331

Epilogue 335

Acknowledgments 341

The Big Turnoff

1

Grandiose Goals

I am walking to the car with my husband, Bob. We are in the parking lot of one of those gourmet natural food stores dotting the Oregon landscape. It's Saturday in Portland and, in spite of the rain, the lot is almost full and a line is forming at the Starbucks next door. An old maroon Volvo station wagon is parked next to us. Bob brings our cart to a stop and points to a faded KILL YOUR TELEVISION bumper sticker plastered to the Volvo's rear windshield.

"Don't you want one of those for your car?" he asks.

I put a bag of groceries into the trunk of our Nissan, looking around to make sure the owner of the Volvo is not within earshot.

"That car," I say matter of factly, "belongs to a zealot." I keep my voice down, thinking that maybe the owner of the car wouldn't want to be called a zealot. My husband stares at me.

"But that's what you are," he says, not bothering to keep *his* voice down. "You think our child will be an absolute moron if he watches television."

He is pointing his finger at me, which is highly annoying, and I'm about to push it away from my face if he doesn't stop. We have been married for eleven years and although we have successfully rid each other of many annoying habits, this pointing thing of his has persisted. He puts the rest of the groceries in the trunk and shuts it firmly.

"I just don't want our child to sit in front of a screen in a mindless stupor," I tell him, trying not to sound defensive. Turning into a zealot is one of my biggest fears. I think of those Hare Krishnas who hang out at the airport, passing out literature, sure in their belief that they have found the one way to God. I could be one of them.

"I just want our child to have an imagination, and a social life with real people in it," I tell him. "I want him to know those around him better than he knows the cast of *Friends*. That doesn't make me a zealot."

We are speaking about our child as if we have one. Actually we don't. I am three months pregnant, though, and we have already begun to think of ourselves as a family of three, complete with arguments about how our offspring should be raised. Bob has grown weary of the television topic, but unfortunately I never feel that I've convinced him of anything until he is completely exhausted. I throw my damp polar fleece jacket into the backseat, fasten my seatbelt, and say what I have already said at least twenty times since I found out I was pregnant.

"I just want to make sure we are all connected, that we talk. I want us to have more in common than a desire to watch reruns together on Nickelodeon. I want our discussions to be about something more important than whether or not Gilligan will get off his island."

"We'll be connected," he assures me. His voice is softer now, gentler, the kind of voice I imagine he will use with our child. We have waited a long time to have kids, but not because I didn't think Bob would be a good father. Mostly, I was scared of screwing the whole thing up. What if I brought the next Charles Manson or Timothy McVeigh into the world?

Bob pauses to look behind him as he backs out of the parking lot. "We'll be fine," he says emphatically, "unless, of course, *you* can't stop watching television."

I turn to stare out of the window. We're on Dosch and it is a windy road, lined with the large evergreens that characterize the West Hills of Portland. Bob doesn't say anything else because he knows he's hit a nerve, he of little faith. He understands only too well that I know not only that Gilligan never gets off the island but also every ridiculous way in which he tries. Even as a kid I considered it one of the stupidest shows on television. But I watched it as much as I watched the shows I liked, simply because it was on. The theme songs for *The Courtship of Eddie's Father* and *The Beverly Hillbillies* are embedded in my brain, and I can name every guest character on *Batman,* from the Penguin to the Riddler. While this information might be useful in a television trivia game, it mostly proves how much I don't know, what I didn't learn, and the connections to others I never had. And that's what I don't want for our baby.

"I can stop watching TV," I say, turning to look at him.

"Without getting rid of it?" He scoffs, not taking his eyes off the road.

I remind him that the plan I've been devising does not require us to get rid of the television. The plan is to raise our child with the bare minimum of television.

"When he's little, he can watch on special occasions, like if someone is landing on the moon again, that sort of thing. Then after he's six, he will get two hours a week. That way television won't be a forbidden fruit and he won't have to feel left out."

I don't bring up the fact that I often felt left out when I was a kid even though I watched loads of television. I haven't quite figured out that part, but I don't mention this, lest I weaken my argument.

"So the television will stay?" he says.

"We will show our child that we can exist with a television in our house, and that it is available to be used wisely."

"I see," he says blandly, and I can tell that he isn't pleased. Although he has never watched nearly as much television as I have, he doesn't want to be without it when something he likes is on. That's why we haven't ever gotten rid of it and why he has rarely complained about my excessive watching. He also knows that if I weren't watching television he might feel obligated to engage in conversation, and this would be difficult for him, as he is more self-contained than most people. Asking him to utter over two sentences at a time is like asking a short-order cook to make a soufflé every night.

"Will I at least get to watch some of the NFL play-offs?" he asks at last.

"You won't need to watch the play-offs," I say. "You'll get to watch the baby!"

He gives me a fake smile, the one he wears at parties when he is being introduced to people who sell Herbal Life for a living.

"Listen to this," I say. I pick up one of the many articles I have been collecting in order to make my point, as much to myself as to Bob. I keep them with me in the car, because Bob is my captive audience here.

"The average child will have seen 16,000 murders on TV by age eighteen. And for every hour a day that a preschooler watches television, his chance of becoming a bully in grade school increases by 9 percent!"

"Amazing," he says, but his voice is monotone. I recite more statistics, darker and scarier ones.

"The majority of kids ages four to six would rather watch television than spend time with their fathers. That's you!" I say, and flash the article in front of him.

"Hey, I'm driving!" He waves the article away.

We are rounding a curve and I am afraid of getting carsick if I read from the next article, so I set it aside and sum it up as best I can. "More than 60 percent of the reported cases of obesity in children are linked to excessive TV viewing. And almost half of all families eat in front of the television," I tell him.

Bob looks restless, but I'm on a roll. "Kids don't talk with their parents. And it's not because they're reading. It's because they're watching TV, and the more they watch, the less likely they'll be able to read at all! In fact, children who have watched the most television between ages five and fifteen are the least likely to graduate from high school or college!"

"Aren't you supposed to be collecting baby blankets and nursing bras?" he asks.

"This is more important," I say. "I want you to see how television is wreaking havoc on the lives of children and how our child thankfully will be spared."

He nods, now attempting to humor me in what he clearly sees as my latest obsession. "And you think we're going to be able to do this without getting rid of the television?"

"Yes," I say.

He sighs, probably mourning the play-offs he'll be missing.

"Television will be for us what alcohol is for Sam on *Cheers,*" I tell him. "Even though Sam used to be an alcoholic, he still chooses to work in a bar."

"Doesn't he own the bar?" Bob asks.

"In the first four years of the show," I say exasperated. "Then he loses ownership when Rebecca replaces Diane. Of course, later on he regains ownership." Bob is nodding but I can tell that he has lost interest. I raise my voice because that's one of the things I do when someone isn't paying enough attention to me. "We'll prove that it's possible to keep a television in our house without having it on all the time. It will only be available to be used wisely."

I'm beginning to repeat myself. I realize this as I consider the plan. It really sounds so simple. I picture our little family sitting together at the dinner table, discussing what our two hours of television for the week will consist of. We might consult the TV guide together or a list of movies available on video. Our child will be cheerful and agreeable about our way of life because I, as a good mother, will have easily modeled nonaddictive behavior, sometimes even forgetting that we own a set. In addition, we will effortlessly limit computer time for him to maybe no more than thirty minutes a week. Video games will also be drastically limited, if not nonexistent.

While the concept of being without television requires a good imagination on my part, it's not far away from Bob's experience growing up in Arizona. Every summer he and his family went to a ranch outside of Flagstaff and spent three months of the year there without television. He and his siblings actually found ways to entertain themselves without *The Brady Bunch* and *Bewitched*. It's one of the best parts of his childhood, he says, and one of the things that attracted me in the first place. "But what did you do in the evening?" I asked him on our first date. "We played together and we read a lot," he said. "Oh," I said in amazement, "you were like the Waltons and the Ingallses on *Little House on the Prairie*."

"Well, sort of," he said smiling, "but none of us played a musical instrument."

I later learned that hardly anyone in his family can hold a tune either, but at least he grew up without television every summer, which is more than I can say for myself.

It is because of his own upbringing that Bob doesn't doubt his ability to be without television if he has to. He just doubts mine.

"Do you really think you can do this?" he asks me as we turn onto our street. "I mean, you haven't exactly taken care of anyone else's kids without television."

"That doesn't matter," I say, quickly brushing aside the truth. When I was in college, I wouldn't take a childcare job without television. On Friday nights I babysat for a family near campus and the evenings always revolved around TV. After watching *The Love Boat,* I would put the baby in bed just before *Dallas* came on, my favorite show at the time. Then, with the three-year-old and five-year-old on either side of me, I began to explain the last episode to them, why J.R. was sleeping with a bimbo from the office instead of his wife and why this was a bad idea. "You see, Sue Ellen has only slept with someone other than her husband once, and it was with a cute college student who was tutoring her son," I tell little Ainsley. "That was a terrible move on her part, because J.R. then planted an illegal drug called cocaine on him and got him arrested."

The strange thing is that I don't recall thinking that I was anything but a good babysitter. The children liked watching shows with me and the family never told me to restrict television viewing.

Later, when I became an aunt, I turned to Disney videos and PBS kid programs to entertain my nieces. Although the content was an improvement over my college babysitting days, the effect was the same. Even if my nieces were watching *Sesame Street,* they were still in a passive, hypnotic state that Bob and I came to depend on. We prided ourselves on being fun relatives, taking the kids to the zoo and the park, but when we were home, we couldn't think of how else we might fill the time with them.

As we turn into our driveway, I reach into the backseat to grab my jacket.

"Things will be different because this will be our child," I tell Bob.

I believe this, too. I am like the character played by Holly Hunter in the movie *Raising Arizona.* She and her husband are about to adopt a baby (actually, steal a baby), and she tells her husband that once they become parents, they have to straighten up and fly right, or something like that. I imagine that a lot of people when they become parents are finally able to make the changes they wanted to make for years. They quit drinking or taking drugs because they know they can't be good parents if they are drunk and stoned all the time.

Unfortunately, for some other people, becoming a parent leads them to drink and take drugs more than ever before. This seems to be what happened to my mother.

"I just hope you don't become too intense about this is all," Bob says, turning to look at me for a second or two. We are sitting in the car and he has turned off the motor.

"I'm not like that," I say, trying to keep from sounding too intense.

Bob thinks I'm going to go off the deep end, as people in my family have tended to do, particularly while pregnant. He probably remembers what it was like when my sister was expecting her first child, the first of the two girls she now has, ages twelve and seven. She phoned to wake me up at six one morning for what she called an emergency family meeting at her house. We lived in Eugene a few blocks away from her at the time. I rushed over and, still without breakfast, sat waiting with her closest friends, whom she had also awakened. She was five months pregnant and she patted her belly and spoke softly but importantly as soon as everyone had arrived.

"I believe I am carrying a girl and she will become the next Buddha," she announced. "She will lead us into the true age of enlightenment." She raised her hands toward the heavens. I looked around the room. No one broke into laughter, or even so much as rolled their eyes. She continued, watching her captivated audience.

"As an ascended master, this child must remain at all times unpolluted by the American diet. Therefore, I've decided that after she is weaned, she must eat only fruits, nuts, seeds, and sprouts. Eventually, I hope she will be able to transcend the need for food altogether and become a breatharian." She smiled the smile of a visionary and, upon seeing the looks of confusion on some of our faces, added, "She will subsist on air alone."

She then invited us all to become coparents, a grand design that would require each of us to spend one day a week caring for this future savior of humankind.

"She will be ours together," she said, her eyes shining, "and her last name will be OceanMoon. As coparents, you may each give her a first name that expresses her divineness as you see it." I smiled, glad that I had something useful to do. I would definitely choose a mainstream name, something completely different from Red Corn and Light Spirit, the names my sister liked. When I first came to Oregon, my sister, who had changed her name to Sapphire, wanted me to change mine to Emerald. She lived in a house with ten people, including two women named Diamond and Ruby. "Together we would be Diamond, Ruby, Sapphire, and Emerald," she said.

"But I don't want to be named after a gem," I told her.

I don't mention Sapphire to Bob right now. Besides, I don't think my goal of raising our child without television is as extreme as my sister's goal was for her offspring. But my feelings about television are as powerful. I wish I could throw our set out of a ten-story building. Unfortunately, it isn't that simple for me. I recognize that the rest of the world is immersed in the medium and so my child needs at least to be aware of it. As much as I want him to be television free, I also don't want to keep him from having friends and feeling a part of his school, his neighborhood and community. I'm not sure how I'll do this.

We get out of the car and I wave to Peggy, the neighbor across the street. She's a skinny woman with four oversized kids and they all watch television. I know because last Christmas I saw her carrying a giant Scooby-Doo into her house. "It's Noah's favorite show," she said. She sounded a little apologetic about it. That's because this is a neighborhood filled with liberal, well-educated people who might have a sense that watching *Scooby-Doo* isn't the most enriching activity for their children. We've lived on this street for only a year, but as I look around me, I wonder if there is anyone raising their kids without television.

At least I'm not too old to be pregnant here. Unlike women in the suburbs and the rural areas outside Portland, where most women are married and pregnant in their early twenties, the women in our urban neighborhood often wait until they are at least thirty-five to start their families. I've been checking around and remember now to tell Bob my latest findings about our neighbor next door.

"Olivia will be forty-one when she has her baby," I tell him happily, as we carry the groceries into the house. We set the bags on the counter.

"What about Gordon?"

"He's forty-five," I say gleefully.

At thirty-six, we take comfort in finding parents who are older than us. Probably when our child graduates, we will take comfort in knowing that while other parents have arthritis and heart disease, we are dealing only with stronger prescriptions for our reading glasses.

At least Bob has the advantage of looking younger than he is. People think he has sandy blond hair, but he actually has red hair with so much white in it that it appears blond. His face is relatively unlined—only a year ago he was carded when he ordered a beer at a local pub. I like to think that I look really young for my age as well—but no one has asked me for my ID in about ten years.

It wasn't just fear of having a Charles Manson that made me wait to start a family. Unlike those people who say they had no idea how much having kids would change their lives, I had an idea. And I didn't want to resent my child because I could no longer work my way up the ladder to success and professional fulfillment. Unfortunately, I never got very far up that ladder. It might have helped if I'd ever actually worked at the same place for more than two years. And, of course, if I hadn't watched so much television.

Besides, I always assumed I could wait until forty to have a baby. But then I watched *Oprah* and saw these women weeping about their declining fertility. I threw away our condoms and one month later I was pregnant and making plans about how to keep television from ruining our lives.

"I'm going to make enchiladas with verde sauce," Bob tells me as I finish putting the groceries away. "Does that sound okay?" He has taken out a large casserole pan and fresh bell peppers have been put in a bowl.

"Sounds delicious!" I try to be enthusiastic about whatever he makes. Bob is the kind of cook everyone dreams of marrying. I fell in love with him the first time I tasted the pumpkin pie he made at Thanksgiving. We met at a restaurant where we both worked. He was a chef. I waited tables. Cooking is a creative activity to him, not the chore it is to me. He loves perusing cookbooks and he is at home using words like *sauté* and *poach*. I'm more comfortable with the words *reheat* and *take out*.

I turn on the set in the family room. Finding something to watch on Saturday has always been a bit of a challenge, as I don't like to watch sports or obscure shows about fishing. Weekday television is better, but I'm now working as a teaching assistant and don't have as much time in the morning. I used to teach elementary school but the assistant position is easy to do while pregnant and it still allows me to keep my teaching certificate current. I stop on channel 49, where there is often a Saturday movie. Usually, it's pretty stupid, aimed at adolescents, something such as *I Was a Teenage Werewolf*. But today it's *All of Me* with Lily Tomlin and Steve Martin. It's a great movie, even if the ending is silly and far-fetched. I just can't picture anyone wanting to live out the rest of her life as a horse just to avoid prison. But it's the best thing on, and I don't even care that it started twenty minutes ago.

"When exactly are you going to start this grand plan of not watching TV?" Bob asks after a few minutes. He is stirring a tomato sauce and isn't interested in the movie.

"After the baby is born," I say. "At that point, we'll watch two hours a week as planned."

"I thought we were starting right away."

"We were, but this is helping me understand more than ever that watching television is not the right thing for the baby."

Bob's right that I was planning to stop watching right away, but the way I see it is I don't really have that much time left to veg out.

I'm like one of those people who finishes every cookie in her house on New Year's Eve because she plans to start a diet the next day.

"I don't think this is such a good sign," Bob says.

"Have a little confidence," I say, not averting my eyes from the screen. Steve Martin has just discovered that Lily Tomlin is planning to carry on with her life in the body of a blond bombshell.

After the movie is over I grab a pad of paper and a pencil in hopes of reassuring Bob of my commitment.

"This is the plan," I say. "Starting tomorrow I'll watch no more than fifteen hours a week. By month seven, I'll get it down to ten hours a week. And a month before the due date, I'll watch only five hours a week," I announce proudly. "By the time the baby is born, I'll be down to two hours, the desired number."

I post the chart on the bulletin board in our study and write "We are free of TV" at the top of the chart. I've always believed in the power of positive affirmations. Dieters who put pictures of morbidly obese people on their fridge have it all wrong. Envision your goal, not your worst nightmare.

"We are free of TV," I say aloud.

Bob looks skeptical. He's not so convinced about the power of affirmations.

BOB AND I ARE on our way to my amniocentesis appointment. I am four months pregnant and sick with worry. My doctor said that women my age have eggs that are practically ancient and the possibility that something could be wrong with the baby frightens me almost as much as the thought of losing the baby from having this procedure itself. I wish I were twenty. I am not reassured when I find that our appointment is with a Dr. Austin, who is actually a dentist. JIM AUSTIN, DMD reads the sign on his door.

We step inside and I see another pregnant woman, who is shifting uncomfortably in her seat. "We must be in the right place," I say.

"Why do you think he does this if he's a dentist?" Bob asks me.

"Well," I say irritably, "maybe one day he was in middle of jacking open someone's jaw, when he realized that he might have more fun sticking a giant needle into the uterus of a pregnant woman who has been asked to drink a quart of water and not pee for at least an hour."

"Maybe he'll give you a root canal, too, if you ask him."

I don't laugh. I look around for a television but don't see one. I pick up a *Newsweek* and remind myself that this dentist comes highly recommended and his rate of miscarriage with this procedure is phenomenally low.

We wait for fifteen minutes before we are called back into a small, well-lit room, where I reluctantly lie down on the examining table. I close my eyes to avoid seeing the needle he is using. I am as still as stone, barely breathing.

"Just relax," the dentist says. I hate when men tell me to relax. I count to myself slowly.

When the needle is out, I gasp for air. I look at the dentist, checking his face for signs of distress, hoping he isn't about to launch into a talk about how a child really can live well with just one leg and limited brain capacity.

"Everything looks fine," he says. "We'll have the results in a week or so." He hands us a list of instructions. "I want you to take it easy for forty-eight hours, just as a precaution to prevent miscarriage," he says. "Don't engage in rigorous activity."

Bob is looking over the instruction sheet as we leave the office, zeroing in the important points. "They just don't want us to have sex."

"We'll survive," I tell him as we leave the office, "but I'll need funny movies, lots of them."

I wait in the car in front of Blockbuster, keeping movement to a minimum. I've always been somewhat of a hypochondriac. If I read about a possible complication or side effect, I can't help but imagine I have it. If an unknown bump appears, my first thought is cancer. Before I was married, I used to get myself checked for sexually transmittable diseases all the time.

When we get home, I slowly head upstairs and wait there while Bob moves the television set from the family room into the bedroom. I prop up pillows. Bob puts the first movie in: *Annie Hall.* An old Woody Allen movie is sure to do the trick.

I know other mothers-to-be might feel guilty lying around watching TV all weekend. If they had to stay in bed, they would still be knitting little booties or writing cards to relatives, enclosing copies of the ultrasound pictures. Or they would reread *War and Peace.* But I have one purpose and one purpose only, which is not to worry about miscarrying, and watching TV is the only way I know to avoid worrying.

One of the things I have always liked best about television is that it keeps me from thinking about or feeling anything unpleasant. If I'm sad, depressed, or anxious, I turn on the television. Afraid, nervous, bored, I turn on the set. It's a long list of emotions and situations I have trouble with, but television is always the answer.

Up until now I've been successfully watching just fifteen hours a week, as planned, but some situations simply demand lots of television. After *Annie Hall* is over, I watch *Animal House, Tootsie,* and *Sleepless in Seattle,* one after the other.

Bob makes my favorite meals and by Sunday night I'm confident that our little one is happy where he is. I look at the ultrasound picture. I can tell where the head is, but the rest resembles a mollusk. I'm glad my little mollusk is staying put.

A WEEK LATER the television is still in our bedroom. "Shouldn't we be getting it out of here?" Bob asks me. He's standing in the doorway. "I thought it was just supposed to be in here for two days during the amnio recovery."

I consider this, but I'm still feeling a little tense.

"We'll move it out after we hear the results from the dentist."

I'm sprawled out on the bed watching a *Mary Tyler Moore* weekend marathon on Nickelodeon. Bob shuts the door behind him. He isn't interested in joining me, even though this is a really good episode. Ted has just been offered a job as a game show host and might actually quit being a newscaster. I smile to myself, amused by this enough to keep watching even though I have already been at it for five hours, getting up only for a few snack breaks. At this point I'm vaguely aware that I need to go to the bathroom but the episode is almost over. I wait until it ends and then make a run for it before the next one starts.

I stand at the sink quickly washing my hands in a way the health department would not characterize as true hand-washing and think to myself that I knew all along that Lou would want to keep Ted as an anchor, however incompetent he is. They couldn't get rid of him because he's important for comic relief and it would be weird to bring in a replacement. When I was nine and they brought in a different husband for Samantha on *Bewitched,* it was alarming. How could Samantha pretend that this was the same old husband she'd been sleeping with for years? After a few weeks, though, I did get used to him. The same way I'm getting used to seeing cropped pants and sport utility vehicles. You can sell a TV addict on almost anything. Why else would parents give their kids Kool-Aid?

I settle back down on the bed, pulling the comforter up to my shoulders in time to hear "Who Can Turn the World on with Her Smile" for the twelfth time today. I watch Mary throw her hat up into the air knowing, as the song tells us, she's going to make it after all. She makes it look fun, throwing her hat up like that. I would try it sometime, if I looked good in hats. Unfortunately, my hair looks flat or misshapen if I wear any hat for more than five minutes. Besides, I spend too much of my life watching these marathons to have time to go around tossing a hat into the air. It works for Mary because she is perky and productive. I'm better at remaining in relatively the same position for up to six hours at a time, which is how long I watch this marathon before I finally click off the set.

THE DENTIST CALLS Bob at his office the next day with the amnio results. Bob calls me immediately.

"Our baby is fine and he's a boy."

"A boy is wonderful," I say, and I mean it, even though I had wanted a girl. This is mostly due to my experience with my little brother, who had tended to be on the uncontrollable side. I wasn't sure I could handle a boy like that. I mean, I handled my brother all right by beating him up until he was bigger than I was, but I didn't think that would be a sound child-rearing strategy.

On the other hand, with a girl I'd be likely to project onto her every minute childhood misery I'd ever experienced until she crumpled under the weight of my fear and grief. She wouldn't survive unless she proved to be especially resilient and could say things like, "Really, Mother, I don't mind wearing the purple top even though the other girls are wearing blue ones."

A boy could be a good thing for me. It will be much harder for me to make assumptions about a child of the opposite gender. And Bob, as a male, will be required to take on a greater role in understanding him. By the time Bob comes home in the evening, I'm ready to embrace him and our male progeny. Bob moves the television into the bonus room, the room above our garage, which we have been using mostly for storage. The TV is now near the back of the room and there are two worn out chairs we can sit in while we watch. There really isn't any reason to go into this room other than to watch television or retrieve a stack of old *Sunset* magazines.

This is a big step, moving the television, almost as big as getting rid of the portable, which we did last month. But the biggest change is that we can't have cable in the bonus room, or at least not without calling someone to hook it up. This means no more USA Network, Lifetime, WGN, and TNT.

Bob is resigned.

"I'll miss seeing the Tour de France," he says.

"We'll go to France," I say.

"People smoke a lot there. You won't like it."

That night I missed watching David Letterman in bed, but as I fell asleep I pictured our little boy sleeping next to us. I saw myself reaching out to hold him, no remote in sight. This boy will matter to us, and he will know it.

2

The Final Push

A lot of people don't really know how much television kids watch. You ask a mother or father about it and they'll typically say something like, "The children hardly ever watch. We're all just too busy."

But when I became a school teacher, I started giving the kids surveys about their TV viewing. The answers the kids gave were quite different from what their parents led me to believe.

"First I watch *Beavis and Butt-Head, The Nanny,* and *Full House* after school," a fifth grader revealed to me. "Then I have to do my homework, but I get to watch *Family Ties* and *Seinfeld* while my mom makes dinner. Then if my homework is done, we watch *Jeopardy!* and *Wheel of Fortune* until my favorite programs are on."

"How many of those do you watch?" I asked, my tone friendly and nonjudgmental.

"Well, it depends on what day it is. On Wednesday, I have four programs in a row that I watch. If it's Monday, I usually play video games until I have to go to bed. On Saturday, I always watch cartoons."

The mother of this same child told me, "He watches a few educational shows. That's all."

It hardly seemed right to reprimand her, though, when I had spent the last week showing her child and his classmates four hours of films. If she had asked me if I thought this was a bit excessive, I would have shown her the school-approved catalog in which I had found them all and told her, "These are educational films."

Showing films was the only way I could cope as a teacher, which is another reason I decided to work as a teaching assistant this year instead of being a full-time teacher. I work a few blocks from home. And this job gives me an opportunity to continue my surveys.

I used to think I was prying until I listened to the teacher next door to me at the school where I used to teach. He was a divorced man in his forties, handsome in a disheveled sort of way. He liked to flirt with the female teachers, who outnumbered the male teachers there six to one.

"How many of your parents sleep together in the same bed?" I heard him ask his fifth-grade class once. I moved closer to his door to listen. My class was watching a film on the Revolutionary War, so I had to strain to hear him. "That's not too many," he said, and I assumed he was counting hands. Then he began talking about the sleeping customs in other cultures. A clever way, I thought, to find out how many moms might be ripe for sleeping with him.

Well, I can be indirect, too. Today I'm asking the fourth graders in my reading group to make a plan for completing their chapter books.

"You'll need to finish reading the book by Monday," I say.

"We won't have time," Evan complains.

"Let's see if I can help you make the time," I say. I whip out a pad of paper, write down the kids' names, and proceed to question them about their television habits. I pull out a television schedule, too, in case they need to refer to it.

"Just list the programs or videos that you watch in the columns here, and you can put video games in this column," I tell the group. "Then add up the minutes or hours on this side," I say.

"But what if we sometimes fall asleep with it on so we don't really know how much we watch?" Joe asks. "I always watch *Married . . . with Children* on the TV in my room."

"Does it count if my mom is the one watching and I only look at it for a few minutes, like when there was a show about transsexuals?"

"I saw that, too," Mark pipes in. "Wasn't it cool when they showed the before and after pictures?"

Brian, a freckled child who watches at least thirty hours a week, prefers to turn his survey into a paper airplane. We talk about how much time they will actually have for doing their homework if they can simply eliminate a few programs.

"It's not that easy," Lenny says.

"Of course it isn't," I say, wondering if I will forgo watching *Friends* tonight.

I tuck the surveys into my bag to tabulate the results later.

Emma is the winner with one show a week. She is a bright little girl with curly black hair and dark brown skin. She is liked by her peers and her two best friends, Elizabeth and Shauna. "I have an art room," she says. "Elizabeth comes over and we make things together."

Emma's parents are soft-spoken and friendly. I scrutinize their appearance, their mannerisms, their speech. This is what intelligent parents are like, I tell myself. They are giving me the strength to uphold my convictions. Emma is not ostracized by her peers because she spends more time making collages than watching

Rugrats. She is helping me stay on course, and I'm giving myself time to get there, to make this drastic change in my life. I remind myself of this as I head home in time to watch *Matlock*.

AS MONTH SEVEN rolls around, I look unmistakably pregnant. No one is afraid to comment on it and everyone does. Yesterday a stranger put her hand on my belly.

I look at my schedule and realize I'll have to cut out five more TV hours. I'm hoping Bob will forget about the schedule. I'm tempted to take it off the bulletin board.

"You'll just have to pick a program and stop watching it," he says when he comes home and finds me watching *Wheel of Fortune*.

"That's not the way it works," I tell him. He doesn't understand. I watch when I need to watch no matter what is on. If I'm going to quit, I'll have to learn how to deal with not watching even when I feel the need.

I glance at the stack of child-rearing books beside me that I haven't read. There's still time, I tell myself. At least I make time for exercise. I walk every day up into the hills high above our house. My legs are strong, my belly massive. I will watch ten hours a week now, I affirm to the hills in the distance. I will take good care of you, I tell my baby.

EVERYONE AT WORK gives me a shower the last week of the school year.

"When are you planning to come back?"

"I don't know," I say.

I don't tell them that I'm not coming back. Not to teaching, not to working for anyone else for a long time, if I can help it. But

I don't want to offend anyone, women and men who would never consider quitting their jobs to be at home with their kids, and parents who would quit if only they could afford it. I think of the women who were raised by mothers who stayed at home and hated it, moms who took out their anger on their kids, who didn't have money and a profession of their own, who resented their husbands and raised daughters who vowed never to be like their mothers.

Then there are those like me who felt the other way didn't work out very well either. My mother went back to work a week after I was born. "It was either that or get fired," she said. She was a political science professor back in the days when pregnancy in the workplace was an anomaly and paid maternity leave wasn't an option. She knew plenty of moms who stayed home and ended up living on Valium. Which way is right? I have no idea.

By staying home with my baby, I'll be putting myself to a difficult test when it comes to television. I've always dealt with my unscheduled time the same way, by watching TV. It's the way I handle isolation, and however poor of a tool it has been, it is familiar.

My time will be my own until this baby arrives, I think to myself as I pack up on my last day of school.

THE NEXT DAY I wake up at ten o'clock and linger in bed. I'm getting used to sleeping on my side, and in spite of my needing to make a snack at three a.m., I slept pretty well. I consider watching some of my favorite morning shows, *AM Northwest* or *Family Feud,* shows I've been missing because of work.

Instead I steer myself away from the bonus room and make breakfast. I'm halfway through cooking oatmeal when the phone rings. It's Bob, calling from work.

"My parents are coming. They want to buy us what we need for the baby."

I drop the spoon I'm using to stir my oatmeal.

"When?" I ask.

"Next week!"

I forget about the television schedule, along with the parenting books I'd hoped to read, knowing that as the days of this pregnancy dwindle away, I'll be getting the house ready for my in-laws and then going on a frantic buying spree with them when they arrive.

Bob's parents are good at buying us things, and luckily, I'm good at receiving. "Oh, no, you shouldn't have" is not a phrase that has ever rolled off my tongue. After having spent too many hours of my childhood wandering through warehouses with my mother picking out smoke-damaged clothing and being told "That's too expensive," it was a welcome relief to meet Bob's parents and hear the words "Of course, you can have that. Have two! Have as many as you want."

I feel a childlike glee whenever we're with them. Even if we aren't intending to shop, I need only to mention an item that might be fun to have and that's all it takes to change the direction for our day.

The first time they came for a visit, I saw a giant terra-cotta pot of geraniums outside a restaurant downtown and commented that it might be nice to have something like that for our patio at home. Before I knew what was happening, we were at the nursery loading up the trunk and backseat with enough terra-cotta pots and flowers to fill five patios. On the way home, we passed a health club, and I mentioned that Bob and I really ought to be getting more exercise. Thirty minutes later, we had five-year memberships there. And that was when Bob and I were only living together.

When we became engaged, they took us to look at china patterns and silverware. They wanted to be sure we registered for real silver. The only silver I knew growing up was hocked by my brother when he was sixteen.

"If you don't get all of the settings, we'll buy you the rest," Bob's dad said. With this in mind, I was as excited as a child at Christmas. We sat down with a bridal registration clerk and listened to her helpful suggestions. "You might want to get matching linen napkins with that stoneware." I felt like I was on *Let's Make a Deal.* Surely, I could go for door number three and get the grand prize? Why just ask for napkins and casserole pans when we could be getting the things we really need for our home?

"What about patio furniture?" I asked. "Could we ask for patio furniture?"

"Why not ask for a couch and loveseat, too?" Bob asked in a sarcastic tone.

"Can we ask for that, too?" I ignored Bob's fingers digging into the side of my leg. I guess he wasn't comfortable with my ostentatious display of greed.

By now I'm a seasoned shopper. Bob is wary when we arrive at Baby Depot with his parents.

"We don't need to let them buy everything, you know," he whispers to me as we get out of the car.

I nod and attempt to look sincere. Then I join his parents, leaving Bob to push the cart behind us. Bob's parents are in their sixties and are still able to keep up with me. I quickly pick out a changing table, some cotton T-shirts with little snaps, and a stroller, which takes another thirty minutes to learn to open and close. I consider telling Bob's parents that we really won't need a crib, and that our doctor thinks it's fine for the baby to sleep with us, but I decide to say nothing.

I figure I'll set up a nursery and then when people come over, they'll assume that our baby sleeps there. They'll be glad that we aren't like those weirdoes they might have heard about who think that it's okay to sleep with babies.

It's the same way with the television. I want to be able to say, "Yes, we have a television in our house. You see, we're just like you."

We throw some changing table pads and a baby backpack into the cart, a front pack and a car seat into a second cart.

"Here are the bottles," Bob's mother says.

"Thanks, but I'll only need them if I decide to pump," I say nervously. "I plan to breastfeed for a long time, at least a year or two. That's what my doctor recommends." I'm making a point of mentioning my doctor so she will sound like the extremist instead of me. The truth is that my doctor is as much of a zealot about breastfeeding as I am about being TV-free. She nursed her last child for two and a half years. I'm used to seeing babies on television raised on Evenflo, so I was shocked when she told me that she nursed that long.

Fortunately my mother-in-law doesn't look shocked. She just nods and listens politely. I've always liked that about Bob's mother. I could tell her that Bob and I are planning to raise our child in a nudist colony and she would smile and nod.

My father-in-law on the other hand has already walked away. Hearing the word *breastfeed* was difficult enough for him, but discussion of breast pumps and nursing toddlers put him over the edge. He comes back a few minutes later with a large baby swing, something he can comfortably discuss with me.

"This one has three settings," he says.

I smile. If my doctor is right, my baby is going to like my breasts a lot more than that swing.

WHEN I WAS in elementary school, I played a game with my brother and sister. The game was designed to find out what each of us was willing to do if the price was right. "Would you take off all of your clothes and run down to Collins Street if I gave you a million dollars?"

"Yes, I would. Definitely!" I said. We all agreed.

"Would you be willing to stay locked up in a tower with only crackers to eat for a week if you were given two million dollars?" my sister asked.

"No," my brother answered, but I hesitated.

"Would I be allowed to have television?" I asked. "Because if I was locked up alone and living on crackers, I could survive if I had a television on the whole time."

And so it was that much of my life I did have it on. By the time I was in elementary school, I had the TV schedule memorized. Television was a stronger influence on me than either of my parents, although my dad didn't have much of a chance to influence me since he died when I was five and a half.

"I WON'T BE USING drugs for my labor and delivery, if I can help it," I tell Peggy, my neighbor across the street. Her straight black hair is pulled back with a rubber band. I am entering the ninth month.

"Well, I felt the same way, but then I changed my mind when it felt as if a Mack truck was slamming into my back."

But I was there when my cousin gave birth. She demanded

that labor be induced, and then received one intervention after another, until she could only lie there stuck on the hospital bed trying to push her baby out. Finally, the doctor used a vacuum device to suck the baby out of her.

I talk to Bob about my plan to deliver naturally and remind him that my sister did it that way.

"I was there for Trillium's birth. Sapphire did it at home without any drugs."

"You said she smoked pot during the entire labor."

"Well, she did it without the *usual* drugs. And she didn't smoke anything the last few hours," I tell him in her defense. I don't like it when he insults her. No one has the right to do that but me. Besides, with or without pot, my sister proved to be hearty enough at giving birth, although at a certain point, both she and my cousin wanted to give up. "I don't want to do this anymore," they both had pleaded. They wanted to change the channel and, from what I've seen, birth isn't like that. The only way out of the pain is to go through it.

Besides, if I want to raise my child without the numbing effects of television, handling the rigors of childbirth without drugs feels like a good place to start. *Spoken like a real zealot,* Bob would say.

My doctor believes in me. She had her own babies at home even though she delivers other people's babies in the hospital. I'm feeling confident as I enter the final phase. It's the next twenty years that scare me: the actual raising of this child.

It is August and almost ninety degrees in Portland. Bob takes me to the coast. There's a small pool at the rustic hotel where we're staying. I'm possessed with a strange desire to do flips in the pool the way I did when I was at Girl Scout camp and our troop did a water ballet performance.

I swim out into the eight-foot depth, doing the breaststroke, my large belly no longer a heavy weight beneath me. I quickly curl my head under, bending at the waist while keeping my legs perfectly straight. I may be pregnant, but I execute a perfect flip, and it thrills me that I can still perform this way in the water. No one else is around to applaud, no camp counselor or sister scouts. Maybe if someone had been there they would have told me that pregnant women aren't supposed to be turning somersaults in the water. But I'm alone with my baby and it's on the second front curl that he makes his presence known. I feel him turn. He does his own little flip. I am stunned. I quickly do the flip again hoping he will flip back over, but I can tell that he's found a new position. I try the flip again and again, but he's apparently staying this way.

Bob is waiting in the room. I don't look at him. I say nothing. I am too worried, too mad at myself to speak. I open the cabinet where the television has been hiding.

"What are you doing?"

I channel surf, not answering him. *The Terminator* is on. It will do. I sink onto the carpet, still unable to tell Bob what has happened.

"What's the matter?"

I'm sitting cross-legged on the carpet, and there is a heaviness that wasn't there before. My baby is sitting up straight. His head is up like mine. Maybe his legs are crossed, too.

"I'll tell you later," I say. Arnold Schwarzenegger has entered the police station.

I try to concentrate on the death and mayhem.

Bob stalks out of the room. I don't want him to leave, but I don't have the energy to ask him to stay.

When he finally comes back, the movie is almost over.

"Are you okay?"

"Not really," I say, and then I tell him, my voice shaking as I try to explain what happened. By the time I finish, Arnold Schwarzenegger is reborn from a pile of scrap metal.

Bob calls the doctor's office and the nurse tells us to come back into town.

"Someone will see us tomorrow," he says. "Maybe you're mistaken."

"Maybe," I say. But I know I'm not mistaken. I know he has turned.

I watch *Ellen* and *X-Files,* but nothing helps. I'm supposed to be down to five hours a week, but Bob doesn't say anything.

The next morning we drive back to Portland. My ankles begin to swell in the ninety-five-degree weather. The air conditioner can't seem to muster the strength it needs to do the job. I know the feeling.

"YOU'RE RIGHT," THE NURSE practitioner says. "He's breech."

We are staring at the ultrasound picture and I can actually see what she's looking at. "Come back the day after tomorrow to see Dr. Hapfield. Maybe she can get him to turn. He isn't due for three more weeks."

I fall asleep on the carpet that night in the bonus room watching *Manhattan.* I don't wake up until nine a.m. As I make my way to the bathroom, water spurts out of me.

"Maybe you've just peed in your pants," the nurse says when I call her.

"I didn't pee in my pants. I'm not even wearing pants," I tell her. I'm holding a towel under my crotch because so much water is gushing out of me.

I call Bob's office and ask to have his meeting interrupted.

"The baby is coming," I say dramatically to his secretary, hoping she's picturing me in the later stages of labor. "Bob needs to come home now!"

The doctor on call confirms that the baby is still breech and tells me I will need a cesarean section. She looks at me cheerfully. "You can check into the hospital and have your baby in your arms in a couple of hours." She says this as if I'm about to get a new puppy. I am speechless. She's not my real doctor and I'm not ready to have this baby in two hours. I haven't started reading the baby books or watched the videotape on breastfeeding that the midwife brought to the class that I missed! My real doctor, Dr. Hapfield, is at home with her own babies today, but she meets us fifteen minutes after we call her.

"You might not have to have a cesarean if you go to OHSU."

"Isn't that the place where the medical students experiment on you?" I ask.

"The students are supervised by Dr. Lin, and he's one of the best," she says.

I think of my mother always wanting me to go to the beauty college to save money. "The students can cut your hair just fine," she would say. "Cyndi works there." Cyndi was one of our neighbors and her hair looked like straw.

"It's not what we planned," I tell Bob.

"It's the only place with a doctor willing to do a vaginal delivery for a first-time mother with a breech baby," he says.

We check in twenty minutes later.

"You'll have to have an X-ray, but if everything looks all right you can deliver him naturally," my doctor had said.

I don't want the X-ray, but the alternative seems worse.

The midwife arrives a few hours later at the hospital. She is a busty hippie with three children of her own at home. She has brought coffee with her and a scone from Starbucks.

"How are you feeling?"

"I'm having menstrual cramps," I tell her.

"You're in labor," she says.

I consider this. If this is labor, then it's more annoying than anything else. I was prepared for deep pain and drama, not this crampy feeling that makes me want to pull the pink and purple flower out of the midwife's hair. Mostly, though, I'm irritable because I must push this baby out bottom first.

We are moved to a dingy room overlooking a Dumpster where I'm free to move around. My doctor has called ahead and talked with Dr. Lin, the supposed expert here whom I've never met, but who will be delivering the baby. He comes in a few minutes later. He has short black hair and unlined skin, but he's probably at least forty, considering his level of expertise.

"I understand you don't want an epidural or an episiotomy," he says. "I want you to know that delivering a breech baby makes it difficult."

"Have you ever delivered a breech without an epidural and an episiotomy?" my husband asks.

"Never with a first-time mother."

"Well, I'm not really a first-time mother," I say.

Bob stares at me, wondering what little secret I have hidden from him for all these years. I smile.

"It's a past life thing," I say. "I've had babies in my other lifetimes. That's why it feels so familiar to me."

Dr. Lin gives me a pained look, the kind of look people give my sister when she tells them why she will never let her children's hair be cut. It's a break in the energy flow, she says.

"I'll check back with you," Dr. Lin says.

"Past lives?" Bob says when the doctor is out of sight.

"At least I have a sense of humor," I say, but I'm not laughing. The midwife comes back in.

"They're going to leave you alone for a while, and it's going to be a while," she says as she crosses the room to turn on the television. I see Daryl Hannah half naked roaming through the woods in *The Clan of the Cave Bear*. I always wanted to see this movie, but right now, as the contractions are getting more intense, I feel angry that the midwife didn't even ask me if I wanted to watch television.

"Turn it off," I bark at her.

"I just thought it might help," she says.

"Well, it doesn't," I say, and I'm surprised to hear myself say it. Here I am in pain stuck in this drab room and a movie I've always wanted to see is on. Daryl Hannah is crouching beside a boulder. I've been told that her legs are unshaven in this movie, a Hollywood first, but I don't care at the moment and this fact alone I find astonishing. Maybe it's a sign. *We will be TV-free*, I tell myself before the next contraction starts.

The midwife turns off the set. I don't like her very much right now. She's probably a TV addict, used to delivering babies with *Home Improvement* on in the background.

LABOR GOES SLOWER than I expected it would, at least in the beginning. When I finally reach six centimeters, I find that it's best to grip Bob around the shoulders as hard as I can with each contraction.

"Why don't you try gripping this instead," the midwife says, pointing to an orange vinyl chair. "I think you're hurting Bob."

I glare at her and move away from the chair. I'm starting to despise her. "Bob's feelings aren't exactly my number one priority right now," I tell her. I grip him harder with the next contraction and she winces. I glare at her again and she goes away.

Good riddance as far as I'm concerned. Let her go to another room to stare at Daryl Hannah's unshaven legs. I grip Bob again. He doesn't complain. Then, as the contractions become more intense, I instinctively press my short hospital gown against my crotch, hoping to keep any of my bodily fluids from dripping onto the floor. I shudder each time I do this, and I'm taken by surprise, the same kind of surprise I experienced when I was nine and I climbed up and down the metal poles on the grade school playground. I press again with the next contraction and it happens again. So little is required, and it happens over and over.

I lose track of the time as each contraction brings another orgasm, and with each orgasm I know I am getting closer and closer to having my baby. Who needs a big-screen TV? I doubt Daryl Hannah can have this many orgasms in an hour.

Bob and I get in the shower together before another nurse can come in to check on me again. I kiss him forcefully after so many orgasms and so much pain. Natural childbirth is not for the prissy.

When we come out of the bathroom, the midwife checks me again.

"You're fully dilated. They're going to want to move you to the operating room now."

I don't like that they call it the operating room.

At ten centimeters, I'm ready to push the baby out in the way that feels natural for me, squatting like the South American women I saw in the childbirth film my sister gave me. But my baby is breech and therefore considered high risk and I'm at a learning hospital. They don't want me to do this myself. I'm told I must lie flat on my back while twelve student doctors file in to stare at my vagina.

Unfortunately, as soon as I am on my back, I lose the urge to push. I feel almost nothing.

I look up at the midwife.

"It's up to you now to push anyway, when we tell you, whether you feel like it or not." I look around at the faces of the young men and women with their scrubs, ready to don masks. They're kids really, kids who have probably never been in this room with a woman who wasn't drugged and made ready for surgery.

I will myself to push, but it doesn't seem to be enough.

"Try again when I tell you," the midwife says.

I stare at the doctor leaning over me. I look at the clock and know that time is running out. They will C-section me. That's what they do here. They warned me. I will have a big ugly scar and will have to lie around convalescing for weeks.

What about my past lives? What about all the body memory stuff? Where is my ancestral help when I need it? The problem is that I'm holding back. It's because I'm scared, but not of having a baby. I'm scared of becoming a mother once he's here. That's why I started doing flips in the water. That's why he turned. That's why I can't get him out now. I'm still not ready. He wasn't due for three more weeks. I didn't get a chance to read all those books about how to raise the perfect child or pick another name for him besides Casey. I didn't even get a chance to get used to being without television.

I want to explain to the doctor that I'm holding back because I'm having a boy and it terrifies me. I look into his eyes. They are dark brown and piercing. He meets my gaze and I know he is not thinking about his next game of golf the way other doctors do. He is thinking about me and this baby. I clutch his arm.

"Did you have a good relationship with your mother?" I ask him.

He looks surprised but his gaze remains steady. "I had a great relationship with my mother," he says matter of factly. "I still do. We get along well."

I let go of his arm and take a deep breath as I let his words sink in. He gets along well with his mother. That means that he probably never sold her belongings without her permission or used her house for a methamphetamine lab the way my brother did with our mother. He probably moved away from home before he was twenty-eight, too, and not because he had to go to prison.

I close my eyes and take another deep breath. "Come on, Casey," I say. "It's time to come out."

I push with all of my strength and courage, knowing that when this baby comes out, he might tear me open, but I'm getting him out because we're going to make it. We're going to be okay together. And we won't need Daryl Hannah or *Sesame Street* to do it.

CASEY ARRIVES AT 7:05 in the morning, blue eyed with delicate blond hair that is sticking straight up. I can barely contain my joy. He is perfect and I know it absolutely. I stroke his tender back and long to hold him forever, but no sooner do I feel him against my chest than he is whisked away from me. Another horde of student doctors poke and prod him before they finally give him back to me an hour later, declaring us both to be fine. He latches on to my breast perfectly and nurses as though his life depended on it, and I believe it does.

We stare at each other, love at first sight, and as they wheel me down the hall, I am still looking into his eyes. I look away only for a second when we enter my room, long enough to catch a glimpse of *The Price Is Right* on the set that my roommate is watching. But it doesn't interest me in the slightest because I already have my prize.

3

. . . .

High Need

Casey is the most lovable boy in the world and he's also the best looking. I know that everyone says that all babies are beautiful, but it isn't true. Many are so skinny that they look like old men, and most don't have any hair to speak of. But Casey is even better looking than the babies on television. He has just the right amount of baby fat and has at least an inch of fine blond hair softly framing his perfect face. His hair doesn't stick out anymore. That was just because he entered the world bottom first.

"He looks like Emerson," Bob says when we get home from the hospital. Emerson is Bob's nephew.

"No, he doesn't," I say calmly. I am high on prolactin and life and I don't want our Casey to be compared to Bob's side of the family yet. Not that there is anything wrong with Bob's family, other than the fact that the males have these foreheads that jut out above the eyebrows, so much so that they sunburn there.

"I think he's far better looking than anyone in either of our families," I say. We are all on the couch together and I'm nursing Casey. At this point I'm able to do this only by taking my shirt off completely so I can stare at my breasts to make sure Casey is latched on the right way. Bob's job is to give me whatever pillows and blankets I need to keep my arms propped up enough to stay in a position that works. This activity, along with all other activities associated with the baby, requires a team effort.

Fortunately, Bob has taken off three months from work. He is an attorney with a progressive company that gives its employees, mothers and fathers alike, extended maternity and paternity leave.

With both of us at home, we are able to fumble our way through the various baby activities. We hover over the changing table arguing about how to fold a giant cotton diaper that's supposed to fit into the tiny diaper wrap, how to use the baby wipes, and when to put Casey in warmer clothes.

"Too bad your mother couldn't have stayed longer than two days," Bob says.

"She had to go back to work. This is her last year of teaching, including summer school, and she wants to be sure she gets the right retirement package. She'll be back as soon as she can."

We don't have Bob's mother either, but we have Stephanie, the caregiver Bob's parents arranged to come for a few hours a week.

"Shouldn't we call her?" I say after Casey has fallen asleep before I could burp him.

"She's coming tonight," Bob says, exasperated.

Stephanie is in her twenties with a five-year-old at home. She came a couple of days after I was home and confirmed that it was indeed normal for my breasts to be almost three times their size and with enough milk for triplets. She cooks meals for us and answers the pressing questions we have such as: When will Casey's belly button not be black and repulsive looking? And when will we know if it will be an outie or an innie?

We are not watching television, as agreed upon, and Stephanie is disappointed. *"All My Children* is on in a few minutes," she tells us on the third day that she's here.

"That's okay. We're not interested," I tell her. I want to add that I'm especially not interested in soaps.

On the fourth day, she brings a tiny set.

"It's for the kitchen," she says.

"I'd rather it not be in the house," I say, as if she's brought a mangy dog inside with her.

She clutches the set in her freckled arms, standing in the doorway, hoping I'll change my mind.

"Most people with new babies have it on all the time."

"I'm sorry," I say.

She thinks I'm weird. Obviously, everyone with a new baby watches television.

Luckily she's not around most of the time and it's just the three of us. We curl up in bed together and the crib remains undisturbed in the other room collecting dust.

Bob starts reading a book that the doctor gave us. I'm lying next to him and Casey is sleeping beside me. He is one month old. I ask Bob about his book.

"It's called *The Continuum Concept,*" he says. "You would like it. It's written by a fanatic."

"I'm not a fanatic," I say. He smiles.

"She ties every problem that adults in our society have to the detached way we raise our children, putting them in separate rooms, separate spaces, disconnected from the adults they need."

"Does she have kids?"

"I know she had a monkey once. She slept with a little monkey."

Bob reads me the part about the monkey.

"Well, monkeys aren't that different from babies." We laugh.

It's fun to be with Bob and Casey. Everything is new, and though it's stressful, we have each other, so everything is manageable. We don't need television. Last week Bob and I watched *Star Trek IV: The Voyage Home,* but that's all. Instead we've taken lots of videos of Casey. This is one of the redeeming values of television, I remind myself, to prove that I'm not rigid.

"I can't imagine anyone I'd rather see on television than our baby," I say.

"How many of these do you want?" Bob asks after he has started a third video. "I mean do you really think you're going to want to watch six hours of him sleeping and nursing?"

"I'll watch them all when I'm very old and he has long since moved away from us."

"Well, I won't be watching them with you."

"Of course not. I'm sure you'll be dead by then."

"Probably from exhaustion from having to make so many videotapes."

We laugh together again because that's what we do now. We are so happy, the three of us. It will be so easy to keep my commitment of two hours of television a week.

UNFORTUNATELY, BY THE time Bob goes back to work, Casey becomes a little less than happy. Then he becomes downright fussy throughout much of the day, and the fussiness can't be predicted.

We take him to the doctor. He fusses in her office so much that she's able to examine him only when he finally latches on to my breast. His ears are fine. His weight gain is perfect. "He could be teething," she says. "He's three months old."

She gives us some natural teething tablets, because she's a naturo-pathic physician who believes that little white tablets containing the microscopic essence of chamomile will make my child better.

"You could also try eliminating certain foods from your diet," she tells me. She hands me a list of the most common ones that can affect breast milk.

"But these are the main foods I eat," I say.

When we get home, Casey takes a nap while Bob looks for recipes that will conform to the horrendous new diet. I walk into the bonus room and stare at the blank television, but I don't turn it on. Without cable, I consider watching *Perry Mason,* forever in syndication on channel 12, always at the same time, year after year, and I still have the schedule memorized. It will be on in ten minutes. Maybe I'll watch it when Bob goes back to work. He only came along for the doctor's appointment. Without him and now without Mexican food, I deserve to watch television, I tell myself. But in the end, I don't.

The next few weeks I refrain from eating all dairy products, broccoli, cabbage, onions, garlic, wheat, eggs, soybeans, citrus fruits, corn, strawberries, peanuts, and anything spicy, which ba-sically means that Thai, Indian, Cajun, and Chinese food are out of the question, too. But Casey doesn't seem transformed by this new diet. He still screws up his little face off and on throughout the day, as if he's furious. I tell him I understand and that spelt burritos without salsa and cheese don't do much for me either.

"What else could it be?" I ask Bob when he comes home from work. I'm dancing around with Casey, trying to get him to settle down.

Bob shrugs. I give him the baby and call my mother in Texas.

"Was I a fussy baby?" I ask her.

"Very fussy."

"What did you do?"

"I gave you phenobarbital," she says.

"I don't think that's recommended now."

"Well, then a try a little Dramamine or drink a beer," she says, and I picture her drinking a Budweiser. "Drink it before you nurse. Give him a sip, too, along with the phenobarbital."

I now remember why I don't ask my mother for advice.

"That's okay," I tell her. "We've been to the doctor and she's not much into alcohol and barbiturates, particularly in combination. She doesn't even believe in using Tylenol, except sparingly."

"Well, the phenobarbital worked," says my mother.

I HANG UP and ask Bob to call his mother. She also suggests some sort of narcotic.

"But did she say what kind of baby you were?" I ask him impatiently over Casey's cries.

"She said I was an easy, quiet baby, never a problem at all."

"Well, we can't prove that," I say as I stalk out of the room holding Casey against my chest. I think about the baby pictures of Bob and the home movie of Bob that his parents sent us. Little baby Bobby happily drinking from his bottle, Bobby in a bath in the kitchen sink peaceably tolerating what amounts to roughhousing. As much as I don't want to admit it, it's most likely true that Bob was an easy baby. He's easy now.

I, on the other hand, am like Meg Ryan in the movie *When Harry Met Sally*. Billy Crystal told her that she was high maintenance. I guess that even as a baby I was difficult. But I'd always assumed that was because my mother smoked, drank, and took a lot of prescription drugs.

The moment I started trying to conceive, I not only stopped drinking alcohol, but I stopped drinking all forms of caffeinated beverages. I gave birth without an epidural, without an episiotomy, without so much as an IV. We didn't circumcise our baby lest we add trauma to his life, and he's getting the finest milk my body can provide on a diet a monk would have trouble maintaining. So what could the problem be?

Bob follows me into the bedroom. "I've got to go back to work."

I'll be abandoned again. I grab him by the sleeve.

"We carry him around like a monkey," I say, "and he sleeps with us every night. I don't understand why he's so sensitive!"

Bob puts his arms around me, which is difficult since Casey is pressed against me trying to nurse. Bob is too kind to state the obvious about the apple not falling that far from the tree.

"Nick said his kids had colic for nine months."

"Well, I didn't think our baby would," I say.

It's true. In spite of the fact that I had fretted over the many decisions in regard to how we would raise our child, when he finally came, I thought that at least in the beginning it would be a relatively easy task. I imagined strangers would see him nestled in my arms at busy shopping centers and be compelled to express their admiration. "My, what an enchantingly beautiful and happy little angel you have."

But he isn't a little angel. He is more like a time bomb, ready to go off at any second. Yesterday I was in the grocery store and he was perfectly peaceful in a sling. The next minute, something disturbed him, a noise, a slight shift in position. It could have been anything. I let go of the shopping cart and tried to comfort him by waltzing around with him in my arms. To no avail. Soon he was screaming at the top of his infant lungs. A middle-aged woman a few feet away from me turned to stare. "What's wrong with your baby?" she asked.

I wanted to say, *It's you. He doesn't like the way you look. I think it's your hair. It's all wrong for you,* but instead I abandoned my groceries in the aisle and left as quickly as possible. Driving home didn't help. I've heard of those babies who are calmed by the motion of the car, but this baby isn't one of them.

I SAY GOOD-BYE to Bob and look at the clock. It's two-thirty p.m. He'll be back at six. I count the hours in my head while I nurse, subtracting Casey's nap time, which could last two hours.

"Let's take a bath," I say to Casey. He has finished nursing and is looking up at me. He seems to understand what I have just said, which provides some comfort. He may be cranky, but at least he isn't stupid. A bath will keep him content for an hour, until around three-thirty. I shift him to my other hip and walk into the bathroom with him, speaking softly. He rests his head against my neck and plays with my hair. Fortunately no one is coming over to disturb us.

Last week I hired a college student to weed our yard and I had to go outside to show him around. Casey was squirming in my arms and I knew I had to keep the conversation short.

"I want the weeds pulled up in this part of the yard," I said, pointing toward the fence, "but please don't pull up these daisies." I spoke quickly and quietly, swaying back and forth, but I wasn't able to finish before Casey started crying.

Later that day when I realized that a good portion of my flowers had been pulled out by the roots, I didn't even care. I had only hired someone to weed in the first place because Bob said he was about to do it himself and then he wouldn't have been available to take care of us. Without Bob around, I can't even talk on the phone for more than a minute. People hear Casey's cries of protest and they ask me if they should call back at a better time.

"What better time?" I shout. "There *is* no better time, unless he falls asleep, and please don't call me then," I say before hanging up or dropping the phone.

I fill up the bath now and get in with Casey still in my arms. "Look at this," I say, holding up a blue dolphin. He grasps it in his tiny fist and we both relax.

BOB COMES HOME with groceries, not a minute late. "I'll do the shopping from now on," he says. He sets the bags on the counter. "And we'll have Stephanie come twice a week to help with cleaning and laundry. I called her today."

He doesn't bother mentioning having Stephanie take care of Casey so we can go out on a date, because he knows I won't let anyone take care of him until he becomes easier. Once we managed to go out to a restaurant with Casey. It was one of those rare moments in which he had fallen asleep in his car seat. We brought him into the restaurant, actually ordered food, and started a conversation. An elderly couple was seated next to us. The grandfatherly man leaned over and pointed at our baby. "What a little cutie!" he said. I turned and gave him a murderous stare. "You wake him, you die," I quietly threatened.

That was the last time Bob suggested we all go out to dinner.

STEPHANIE ARRIVES at lunchtime the next day.

"Are you sure you don't want me to bring over my portable TV?" She is sensing weakness, hoping I'll break down.

"That's okay," I say. "If you could just bring me a glass of water and that book on the coffee table, I would appreciate it." I'm nursing Casey and he's about to fall asleep. I don't dare move until he's sleeping soundly.

I really don't want Stephanie here that much, even though Bob's parents have already paid her. She probably doesn't want to be here either in this TV-free zone. I think about her little portable and what might be on right now. I look at the clock. Reruns of *The Streets of San Francisco* on channel 12. I pick up *The Baby Book* and read the chapter on colic.

I wonder how much longer I can make it without watching television.

WHEN BOB COMES HOME that evening, I have my tennis shoes on before he opens the door.

"I'm going for a walk," I say.

I'm only a few blocks from our house when I run into Deanna, a teacher at the middle school in our neighborhood. I was a substitute teacher there once, too, and Deanna remembers me.

"How's the baby?" she asks. "Your neighbor Peggy told me he's a little fussy."

"A little," I say, and I feel my face turning red.

Everyone in the neighborhood must know that I have a difficult baby. They've seen me run home with him when he starts wailing. Some have offered to help, but I've shooed them away.

"Just give me a chance to calm him down!" my neighbor Lori pleaded with me once. "Let me hold him."

But I refused. She thinks that Casey is fussy because I'm tense. But I wouldn't be as tense if everyone didn't gather around me whenever Casey cries.

"I'm teaching health and sex ed this year," Deanna says. "Would you like to talk to my class about what it's like to have a new baby?"

"Well, that would be during the school day. I'll get Bob to come home to watch Casey."

"Oh, no! Bring him!"

"But, he's fussy, as Peggy told you," I say, and I wonder exactly what Peggy said.

"Yes, I know," she says smiling. "We love fussy."

I arrive at the classroom a few minutes early. I've nursed Casey, changed his diaper, and thankfully he has fallen asleep in the carrier.

Deanna introduces me to her students. They are sitting at tables, looking mildly interested. "This is Ellen. She lives in the neighborhood and she's here to talk about what it's like to be a new mother. Do you mind if I ask how old you are?"

I smile stiffly, because I do mind. These are thirteen-year-olds and I don't want to seem as old as their parents, or worse, older than their parents.

"I'm thirty-seven," I say reluctantly. "My husband and I waited a while to have kids."

"How terrific!" Deanna exclaims. She is smiling broadly at me. "I suppose that gave you time to travel. Have you been to Europe?"

"Well, yes, I have," I say, with little of Deanna's enthusiasm, but she's undeterred.

"How many countries?"

"Eighteen or so," I say, and Deanna looks overjoyed.

"You see, class. She and her husband have traveled everywhere together."

I don't tell her that actually I went to all of those places my junior year of college. Bob and I haven't been on any exciting vacations at all. I'm suddenly struck by how dull my married life has been. Why haven't we been anywhere fun? Because I've been in a television stupor. Maybe I should tell them about my struggle with television.

"You see, everyone," Deanna says, "because she waited to have children, she was able to travel and have an exciting life. That's why it's good she waited."

"Well, of course, you don't want to wait too long," I interject, much to her consternation. "My neighbor and one of my friends who are my age had trouble getting pregnant, because they weren't as fertile as younger women are."

Deanna stops smiling. "Of course, class, these friends of hers might have had STDs that kept them from getting pregnant. Remember what you learned about chlamydia and gonorrhea and how these diseases can destroy your reproductive organs."

I think of Olivia and Tylene and am glad they aren't here to hear these insults. I should speak up for them, tell the class that they did eventually get pregnant. But at this point Casey has begun to stir. I take him out of the carrier, wondering if just this once he will smile sweetly at the kids around him and coo in my arms.

I know I'm only dreaming, though, because a grimace is already forming on his face. I will have to nurse him. I look at all of the twelve- and thirteen-year-old boys and girls, as I discreetly lift the flap of my nursing shirt and latch my baby on. A boy in the first row blushes.

Nursing will buy me time while Deanna asks me more leading questions.

"Notice, class, how demanding babies are. They have to be fed and changed constantly. Hasn't your life completely changed?"

"Well, yes, but . . ."

"Class, life as she knew it before is *over*," she tells them.

She is looking at me as if I have some sort of incurable skin condition.

I want to tell the kids that there are good moments, too, when you have a baby. The first time they smile and laugh, the way they feel when they're snuggled up next to you, the powerful love you have for them. But I can't say anything. Casey has abruptly finished nursing and I have to stand up now and move around with him if I'm going to keep him from screaming. I sway back and forth.

"Notice how exhausting it is for her," Deanna continues. "And sometimes they're like this in the middle of the night."

Casey is starting to cry. I skip around the room and raise my voice over his cries.

"Most babies aren't like this!" I shout.

Deanna is quick to respond.

"That's right, class. You could get a baby even fussier than this. You just never know what you'll get."

As if Casey senses that he's been insulted, he moves into his full-blown crying phase at last. I shout in the direction of the teacher, "I'll need to be going now!" She picks up the carrier for me and I grab it with my left hand, my screaming bundle flailing around in my right arm.

Deanna thanks me and tries to look sympathetic, but I can see a triumphant glow in her face. I imagine her telling the class later, "Well, now you can see why it's a good idea to be careful." Then she'll probably pull out a picture of herpes and pass it around, maybe referring to my friends again.

I put Casey in the car, thankful we'll be home in less than five minutes.

As soon as we're back, I try to relax, but I'm still frazzled. Casey, on the other hand, is immediately happy. I collapse on the couch and he looks into my eyes, delighted to see that we're back home.

"I guess we didn't really like that place much, did we?" I say to him. He smiles, makes a little gurgly sound, and reaches out to touch my lips.

Why didn't the teacher just go to the hospital to bring a crack baby and its mother to class, or one of those babies who's scheduled to have twenty painful surgeries before he can learn to walk? Why use us as an example? I pick up a cloth book and show Casey a picture of a boat. He points to it and smiles.

A few days later the teacher sends me a note thanking me for coming to the class. "I've talked with other teachers and we would like for you speak to health classes at other schools," she writes. I wad the note up in my hand and turn to Casey. "We will not be humiliated. We are better than this," I say. He grabs the wad of paper in my hand and drops it on the carpet. We don't even bother to recycle it.

I vow that these school visits will not be my path to public speaking and certainly aren't the kind of exposure I want for my baby. I had sometimes fantasized that my child would be so cute that people might want to put him in commercials, but this torturous display will not be our claim to fame.

I collapse on the bed next to Casey, holding his tiny hand in mine. At least a lack of love has never been the problem. I have seen enough made-for-TV specials about mothers who abuse their children, mothers who are angry and out of control. I feel no inclination to harm my child, only the adults around me. But what I feel for my child is disturbing nonetheless. It is a fear so deep and so terrifying that I am unable to share it with anyone. I isolate myself more and more, and in my isolation, the fear deepens. It is the fear that, in spite of what the doctor says, maybe there is something very wrong with this beautiful baby of mine, and it's that unspeakable fear that I have to escape, and there is only one way to escape.

THE KEY TO EFFECTIVE backsliding is denial and rationalization. I tell myself that, even though I'm no longer able to resist television, the important thing is to keep Casey TV-free.

This requires hard work and careful planning. Watching commercial television when I'm alone with Casey would never work. If he were to wake up from a nap and need me, I can't be watching a sitcom or drama unless I've taped it ahead of time, and that would require me to actually learn how to record programs.

Having a stack of videos ready and waiting for the right moment is the key. Yesterday I bought half a dozen of them, all movies that I had already seen before, some as many as five times. At first I had tried renting videos, but I was always returning them late. "Can't you see that I've had a baby?" I said to the guy behind the counter, as if that was reason enough to exempt me from late charges forever.

Naturally, I can't watch just any video. *Indiana Jones and the Temple of Doom* and *Alien* would be poor choices. If Casey were to catch a glimpse of the screen, he might see terrifying creatures trying to destroy the human race. Today I'm watching *Hannah and Her Sisters,* one of my favorite movies. I'm like all of the characters, the sisters, the husbands, and the Woody Allen character, who imagines he has a brain tumor.

Casey has done a good job so far. I started the movie as soon as he began nursing, and when he fell asleep, I paused it long enough to put him down in the bedroom. Then I watched some more until he woke up, at which point, I brought him in here to nurse again. I restarted the movie when he was safely latched on, and he fell asleep in my arms once again.

I will probably get to watch this movie in its entirety and he will not have seen the screen. Even if he wakes up, I have strategically placed a chair in his line of vision, so I can see the television but he can't. Beside me is a basket of toys, which can distract him for at least fifteen minutes. If that stops working, I will resort to dancing around with him in my arms, softly singing a song I know by heart, making sure that his face is never turned toward the screen. It's actually possible for me to do this and still follow the video perfectly. Of course, this is where it comes in handy that I've already seen all of these movies many times.

Thankfully, Casey is still sleeping when the sister, who Woody Allen loves, tells him that she is pregnant. I smile victoriously: I have watched the whole movie and Casey never saw a thing. I click it off with the remote before the credits are done.

"You're such a love," I whisper softly to him. Then I look at the clock. Bob will be home in thirty minutes. It's never a moment too soon.

"How's our baby?" he asks when he walks in.

I hand him our bundle.

"We've learned a new trick," I say. "Casey, show Daddy where your nose is." Casey giggles and puts his hand on his nose.

"We read some new books, too." I show Bob the stack of books with *Good Night, Gorilla* and *Goodnight Moon* on top. I don't mention the movie. "I'm going on my walk," I say.

I put on a ski jacket. It's icy cold outside but I don't mind. I don't have to worry about anyone getting cold but me. I'm free. I walk easily to the top of Fairmount and take in the spectacular view. As I gaze at the trees in the distance, I suddenly feel optimistic again. Maybe I'll even spend the evening with Bob and Casey, perhaps help with dinner. But by the time I round the block back to our house, I've changed my mind. I sneak back in and head upstairs to watch *Wheel of Fortune*. A contestant from Texas is trying to come up with the phrase "over the top." It's a piece of cake for me.

"Dinner is ready," Bob calls up to me. He has heated up a casserole he made over the weekend. I fill up my plate.

"I'll just eat upstairs," I tell him.

He shrugs. Casey is trying to eat the buttons on Bob's shirt.

A few minutes later, Bob knocks on the door. I'm watching *Seinfeld*.

"Sarah is on the phone," he says, peeking in. I quickly flick off the set so Casey can't see the television.

"I'll call her back."

He shuts the door, probably wondering what's wrong with me. Sarah is my best friend. I've known her for years, and if she didn't live on the exact opposite part of town, I might see her more often. She isn't addicted to television and she loves me in spite of my shortcomings. She probably would understand why I have no interest in talking to her now, much less getting together with her. I don't want to reach out and cry on someone's shoulder. I want to be with Jerry Seinfeld and his weird friends instead.

Later, after I have nursed Casey to sleep, Bob joins me in the bonus room. *Murphy Brown* is about to come on.

"You're okay, aren't you?"

"I'm fine," I say quickly. "I'm sure it won't always be this way. It will get easier as he gets older."

"I'm sure it will." He leans against me, but it doesn't feel comforting because I sense an attack coming. "Don't you think you're getting away from your television goal?"

"What do you mean?" I ask innocently, knowing exactly what he means.

"Aren't you supposed to be watching two hours a week?" He turns to look at me. "How many hours are you watching?"

I don't want to answer him. I don't know the answer. Maybe twenty hours a week, probably more. This must be what it's like at one of those drug interventions before you have to check into rehab. Everyone wants you to face your problem.

"As far as Casey is concerned, I'm not watching any. That's the important thing," I say.

Bob rolls his eyes, and I want to explain to him about the way I've set everything up so Casey isn't actually exposed to television. But I know I will sound like Bill Clinton when he said he smoked pot but didn't inhale. *I* knew what Clinton meant but he just wasn't understood, and Bob won't understand my explanation either.

"I thought you said it was important to watch less."

"It's fine," I say, grabbing the remote so I can turn on the TV again when Bob finally leaves me alone.

"It's just that, at some point, Casey will realize what you're doing up here."

"I know, but I still have time. When he's a little less sensitive, and that can't be that much longer."

IT DOES GO ON longer though. I refine my television technique with Casey to an art. I manage to see at least one movie a day, sometimes two, and Casey still hasn't seen a thing. I keep telling Bob this, but he doesn't seem impressed.

I resign myself to the fact that Casey is what child expert Dr. William Sears calls a "high-need baby," a better phrase than "fussy baby" or "difficult baby" or "impossible-to-live-with baby." Having a high-need baby explains why I eat my breakfast with my baby in my arms and why I go to the bathroom with him in my lap.

It's why I manage a shower by putting him in a holder and leaving the shower door cracked open so I can keep an eye on him. It drives Bob crazy.

"The bathroom floor is going to rot if you keep doing this," he complains. I look at the floor and see what he means, but it seems like an okay price to pay to keep Casey happy.

I walk around the house, pointing to things and talking about them, letting Casey touch them if they are safe. "This is a light switch," I tell him. He listens to everything I say.

I sing made-up songs, more like mantras. "You're my Casey, my baby, the one I adore."

Car rides are also managed by singing, too, "Aloette" mostly, and by telling endless stories about monkeys and bears. I make them up as I go, never pausing for more than a second, lest the crying begin again.

He may require more work than other babies, but my love for him remains fierce, and I find within me the strength to rise to the occasion. I think about my brother, who served three and a half years in prison, not knowing exactly when he would be released but never losing hope, never giving up.

"If he can do that, then I can certainly do my time with this touchy baby," I say to myself. But even my brother had cell mates, and I realize that except for the grown-ups I see on television—and I see a lot of them there—I'm serving my time in solitary confinement.

4

Cell Mates

"I'm thinking about trying to get to know the neighbors, especially the ones with kids," I tell Bob.

"But you hate knowing neighbors," he says. "Isn't that why you haven't gone to the block parties yet and why we have a big hedge in our backyard?" We are in the kitchen and he glances out the window, probably looking at the hedge.

"Well, yes, but now we need a community for Casey."

Bob nods absently. It's as if I just said that Casey needs some new sweaters for the winter. Next thing on the list is a community, although getting sweaters sounds simpler.

It's true that I don't relish knowing my neighbors. I prefer my friends to be outside of my neighborhood, and even then, I prefer to keep them separate from each other. If I knew my neighbors too well, I couldn't run around the living room in a night shirt or blow my nose on dirty laundry I leave lying on the floor outside of the laundry room. But that won't work now that I have Casey.

As fate might have it, Olivia, the neighbor next door, invites me to a baby shower on Saturday for Lori, the woman who lives three doors down from me.

"It's her second child," Olivia says. "Jenny is two, but no one gave her a shower then, since they'd just moved here. It'll be at my house and I've invited a few of the other moms in the neighborhood. You can bring Casey."

I decide to leave Casey with Bob in case he gets fussy. Since Casey won't be getting to know the kids on *The Brady Bunch*, he might actually become friends with his neighbors, unless of course *they* spend most of their time watching *The Brady Bunch*. This if one of the things I want to discover at the shower.

Olivia offers me a muffin when I arrive. "It's blueberry," she says. Only five feet tall with dark brown hair cut just above her shoulders, she is wearing black pants.

"Thanks," I say. I set it on my plate, knowing full well I won't be eating it, as it is not allowed on my cruel diet. I break it into pieces, in hopes of making it appear as though I have tried it. Unfortunately, it now looks as though a small child has picked through it hoping to avoid what could be nuts.

I quickly grab some carrots and find a place to sit in the living room. It's a spacious room with a spectacular view of the hills, a better view than we have.

"How's that baby doing?" Olivia asks me. "Sleeping okay?"

"He sleeps fine," I say, which is true. I just don't bother to mention that it's because he sleeps next to me with one of my nipples in his mouth. Olivia would pity me if I told her. I remember what she said to me a few days after Casey was born. "You've got to move the bassinet out of the bedroom and into the bathroom or the hall," she told me when she had stopped by with a meal for us. "That's what I did with Luke, and soon he was sleeping through the night and so was I."

She said this in a straightforward manner and she was coming from a caring place. It might even be refreshing to be with someone who is so straightforward, if I were capable of being equally direct with her. But I'm not, any more than I was with my older sister. I wonder if Olivia is an older sister, too.

"How many children are there in your family," I ask her after she joins Lori and me on the couch.

"I'm the oldest of six," she says.

"I'm the oldest of five," Lori announces, all smiles. Lori is fair skinned and almost as short as Olivia. She looks very pregnant, although that could be because she is so short.

I turn to Peggy, who lives across the street. "What about you?"

"I have three younger brothers."

That settles that, I think to myself. I'm surrounded by them. Strong, outspoken older sisters who have probably spent more time telling others what to do than trying to ascertain what others are feeling and thinking. Or at least this is what I think older sisters are like, based mostly on my own experience with Sapphire. But these women are part of Casey's community and I want to get along with them.

Fortunately, they are all friendly and great at getting things done, something I have trouble with most of the time.

"This is the updated list of everyone in the neighborhood," Janice says. "We've added your family to the list." Janice lives next door to Olivia and has a two-year-old boy named Perry.

"She loves entertaining," Olivia says. Janice smiles.

"We have a summer barbecue, a winter holiday party, and a spring get-together," Janice explains. She reminds me of a boss I had once who was always throwing parties and trying to encourage employee camaraderie. She even assigned us secret pals and we left bags of sweets on each other's desks.

I look at the list. This is the world that awaits our family right here in this neighborhood. It feels strange to think about living like this. When I was a kid, getting to know the neighbors meant they would discover how weird we were. It was too risky.

Olivia brings the presents from the other room. I offer to write down who gave which gifts, as I don't have Casey attached to me. I'm starting to enjoy myself and I've forgotten about the television issue, but the first gift Lori opens reminds me of it again.

"My sister recommended them," Peggy says, as Lori pulls out two videos from a shiny yellow bag. "I use them with Ethan. I put the 'Good Morning' one on first thing after he wakes up and he is completely mesmerized. They make babies smarter. Then the 'Good Night' video puts him right to sleep at bedtime."

I glance over at Ethan, who is sleeping in his car seat right now. He is only five months old with tiny ringlets and rosy cheeks. He's unmistakably cute, but I doubt that the videos have made him any smarter.

I write down the titles of the videos next to Peggy's name. I want to add beside the titles three words: *Warning—Gateway Drug.* But I don't. The baby on the cover of the videos looks so friendly and innocent. I pass them to Lori.

She doesn't look that impressed with them either, which appears to be a good sign to me, although, as the videos are passed around to the rest of the group, the ensuing discussion doesn't exactly reassure me.

"I couldn't get Perry to watch anything until he was one, but it was such a relief when he finally did," Janice says. "I'd put on *Sesame Street* and I could finally shower."

"*Blues Clues* did the trick for Luke," Olivia adds.

I don't mention the rotting tiles of our bathroom floor and my method of taking a shower. I remind myself that these are my neighbors and I shouldn't expect them to be my soul mates, joining with me to praise a TV-free life.

I record the rest of the presents, mostly baby clothes and books, except for one more video, a Curious George one. George is featured on the front, smiling in his little red shirt. I want to smile, too, but his face just makes me feel lonely. I am on a difficult journey, and I wanted fellow passengers.

WHEN I GET HOME Bob is bouncing Casey up and down and I can tell that the baby's been fussing. Bob hands Casey to me and sits down on the couch, looking relieved.

I plop down in the rocking chair to nurse before I start cross-examining Bob.

"Why didn't you come get me as soon as he started to fuss?"

"He just started two minutes before you came in, and I looked outside and saw people leaving."

"That's fine," I say.

I remember being told by the midwife that dads need to discover their own ways to calm the baby, and I'm trying to give Bob a chance.

"Was it fun?" Bob asks.

"It was okay," I say. "Did you know that every woman in this neighborhood except April is the oldest child in her family?"

"That's what you talked about?"

"Don't they all seem like they are the oldest in their families?" I add instead of answering him.

"What do you mean?"

"I mean they all act as if they know exactly the right way to do everything."

"I guess you'll fit right in then."

I sneer at him.

"Their kids all watch television," I say, as I switch Casey to the other breast. I've only been gone for two hours but it's as if I've been gone all afternoon because Casey seems famished. "They like those stupid videos for babies, too."

"Are those really that bad?"

"Of course they are! The American Academy of Pediatrics recommends no television for children under two. And for every hour of television one- to three-year-olds watch each day, their chances of developing ADHD at age seven are increased by 10 percent."

"Wow, I wonder how many people know that."

"Not many. Also, babies learn to talk by interacting with real people, not muppets," I say, and I'm thinking that it sounds like a good slogan: Real people, not muppets. "I just wish I wasn't the only one doing this."

"You could tell other people what you're doing, and they might try it, too."

"I'm not interested in waving a banner," I say matter-of-factly. Casey has fallen asleep in my arms. "Do you want to watch *Enchanted April* with me?"

"Ever hear the phrase 'Practice what you preach'?"

"He's asleep," I say. "And last night I didn't watch *Mad About You*. Did you notice?"

He stares at me. "I noticed you took the sign off the bulletin board. You're supposed to be watching two hours a week."

"It will happen," I say.

I set Casey down for a nap and put in the video while Bob goes for a bike ride. I don't really need him anyway. I just need to see a bunch of women find love and happiness in Italy. Besides, I'm worn out from being neighborly. Maybe if I get really comfortable at these social events, I won't need to watch television anymore.

A couple of days later Olivia returns the pie pan I had brought to the shower. Casey is in my arms, content for the moment, but I don't want to risk inviting her inside in case he changes. She would tell me to set him down and let him learn how to soothe himself.

I'M LOOKING THROUGH the packet of papers that I brought home from the hospital, hoping to find a support group for TV-free mothers like me. But there doesn't seem to be a group like that. There's no fussy-baby group either. Of course there isn't. How would they meet? No one would be able to hear anyone talk. What would be the point? To see whose kid screams the loudest?

Halfway through the pile, I find a folder that was distributed in my birthing class. It's filled with resources for new parents, mostly organizations I've never heard of, but La Leche League jumps out at me. "They help breastfeeding women, no matter how long they want to nurse," my midwife had said. I assume that if I go, I'll meet moms who are still nursing preschoolers and children ready for grade school.

I decide to go anyway. At least I'll be around women who won't say, "I can hardly wait to be done nursing my two-month-old." Maybe they won't be as excited about *Blues Clues,* either.

I show Bob the address.

"It's close by and it meets at ten a.m.," he says. "Maybe you'll discover at-home moms who live around here."

"I'm not exactly an at-home mom," I say indignantly.

"Oh, I thought you were."

"Not in the way most people mean."

I feel like someone who's been fired from her job and tells everyone that she's taking a sabbatical or doing consulting work, even though she's actually just catching up on daytime television.

"What do you mean?" he asks.

"I don't spend the day clipping coupons or relining the shelves with contact paper the way real at-home moms probably do."

Bob sighs, most likely dreaming about how nice it would be to have that kind of wife. "No, you certainly don't."

"I don't want to be with women who think mothers should stay at home," I say. "Besides, what's so great about being at home if the kids are put in front of the television all day?"

"I don't know," he says. "But you're still not planning to go back to work?"

"That's right."

He shakes his head and walks away.

It's okay. I'm used to it.

I PUT CASEY in his car seat, and fortunately he falls asleep on the way to the La Leche League meeting so I'm able to look like a normal mother when I carry him inside. I quickly scan the room for women with babies who are Casey's age. My plan is to tell them that I am starting a group for new moms with babies between three and six months. I see several moms milling around with their toddlers, but I also see lots of women with younger babies.

I sit next to one of them, a twentyish brunette named Sonia with an Asian-looking baby who is contentedly playing with one of her sleeves. Next to her is a woman with a blond-haired baby the same size as Casey.

The woman with the blond infant is named Kendra. She's my age, a local actress, part of a theater group, she tells me. She is wearing glasses and her hair is straight with bangs.

"When are you planning to work again?" I ask her.

"Not yet, but then acting isn't exactly predictable work anyway."

"I guess you're right," I say. "Would you be interested in a mother-baby group for first-time moms," I tell her.

"Do they all have to be first-time moms?" she asks.

"I think it's best that way." The truth is I don't want to be around a mom with older children. She'll already know what to do. I want to be around confused and ignorant moms, feeling their way through the dark like me.

Kendra and I quickly find four more such moms, and we pull our chairs together for a few minutes to exchange phone numbers and addresses. Everyone seems excited to get together to talk.

"Do you sleep with your baby?" a woman with wavy auburn hair asks in a businesslike way. Her name is Rebecca, and her son, Camden, is six months old.

"I do, but I sit up to nurse him in the night," Sheri says, pointing to her round-faced baby. "I can't figure out how to lie down and do it."

"I can show you," offers Kendra, and I picture all of us lying around together at my house learning how to nurse our babies while we sleep.

I scan the addresses. Kendra and Rebecca both live a few blocks away from me in opposite directions.

"How long are you planning to nurse?" I ask them.

"I have no idea," Kendra says. "A few years, I hope."

A few years. She wants to nurse longer than my doctor did, certainly longer than anyone on television ever nurses.

"What about television?" I ask everyone. "Are you planning to let your children watch much television?"

Kendra looks taken aback, as if I'd asked her if she was planning to have the baby wear clothes.

"Well, I'm sure she'll watch *Sesame Street* and Disney videos," she answers.

"I hear that *Blues Clues* is good, too," Rebecca pipes in.

I nod, trying not to let my disappointment show. I'm an alien for even asking the question. Of course they're all planning to put their babies in front of the television. Just because they breastfeed doesn't mean they will object to the countless commercials that promote Similac formula and use women's breasts to sell beer. I want to say something, but I am not a zealot! I am not my mother, who spoke out for masturbators everywhere. I am building a community, and this is good enough.

As it turns out, I'm unable to say anything else anyway because Casey has woken up and started fussing. I try to settle him, but after five minutes of his screaming, I get up and walk to the back of the large room. I know he's still disturbing the rest of the group, though, because after another minute or two, the leader joins me with book in hand. As I bop around, I glance at the title, *The Fussy Baby*. I've been given them all now: *The Spirited Child, The High-Need Baby, The Difficult Child*. I tuck the book under my arm, grab my things, and amid Casey's cries, I wave good-bye to my new friends.

At home, when Casey is asleep, I watch *Law and Order*. But I am happier. In fact I'm watching television because I'm excited and I need calming down. Maybe after I get used to my new friends, I'll stop watching shows like this.

THIS MORNING WILL BE the second time the playgroup has met at my house. We've been rotating between each other's houses each week for two months now. I have a real social life with real live people in it again, instead of sitcom characters. Last night, when Bob came home, I took my walk as usual, but I actually skipped watching *Frasier* and *Jeopardy!* to get the house ready for today's group.

For the past hour Bob and I have been cleaning the family room. Actually, I am walking around with Casey in my arms asking Bob to clean.

The average television addict doesn't do a lot of entertaining and I am no exception. But I've watched enough television to know what houses are supposed to be like.

"We need fresh flowers!"

I open the sliding glass door and the window near the front door. A chilling wind blows through the living room.

"What are you doing?" Bob yells from the family room.

"Just airing the house out," I say. "It won't take long."

At times like these, I think of the endless commercials I have seen and how I live in fear of people turning their noses up in the air and making comments such as "Fried fish last night?" or "Oh dear, these glasses have spots!"

I wrap a blanket around Casey and Bob grabs his keys.

"I'll go to the store for your flowers," he says.

I smile appreciatively. It works like a charm.

"Watch the timer," he calls back to me before he's out the door. "The banana bread will be done in ten minutes."

"We get to watch the timer," I tell Casey excitedly. We look through the glass on the oven door. I'm glad I'll be serving something homemade. That's what Kendra did at the last meeting. No muffins from Costco.

I put in an Enya CD that Bob bought, peaceful background music for peaceful babies. At least I hope so. No one noticed last time that there is no television in sight, and I'm less self-conscious about it now. I'm more comfortable with everyone, especially Kendra.

Kendra understands me. When Casey cries, she doesn't say anything stupid such as, "I wouldn't go anywhere with a baby like that." That's what Rebecca said at the first meeting. We were at Sheri's house and I'd moved into the bedroom to try to calm Casey down because he'd become overstimulated. I had been talking too much or too loudly and he began to lose it.

Last week I tried to talk less and change the tone of my voice to make it sound sweet and melodic, sort of a Julie Andrews without the English accent. It wasn't easy to do, and I suppose that if Casey ever stops fussing I'll go back to my usual self, much to everyone's disappointment, I'm sure.

In the meantime, at least I've provided an important service for others. Casey and I make other parents feel better. Sheri told me that the last time Kenny got fussy, she said to husband, "Well, at least he's not as fussy as Casey." Then they both breathed a sigh of relief and took turns calming their baby down.

I feel like Tiny Tim in *A Christmas Carol*. He hoped that when people saw him they would remember that Jesus made lame men walk. I'm not crazy about this new role of mine, but I'm trying to accept it with grace.

Kendra is good about working around Casey's temperament when we are making plans. "What time of day would be the best to go to the water park? Will the car ride there be too long for him?" Last week we went to the zoo together, the children's museum, the park, the indoor playground, and to and from each other's houses. I've gotten together with the other moms, too, but Kendra is my favorite. Casey likes Kendra's baby, Hannah, too. During the group, he doesn't pay that much attention to the other babies, but when Hannah arrives, they sit on the floor together, pulling plastic Tupperware lids out of the cabinet, and also stainless steel pots and pans.

I take the banana bread out of the oven and throw some napkins and plates on the table beside it. Bob bought some apples and bananas. I arrange them in a purple bowl beside a tray of glasses and cups, the way they might look on *Designing Women*.

Sonia and Sheri arrive first and sprawl out with their babies on the carpet where the coffee table used to be. McGregor is sitting up now and happily reaches for the blocks in a basket beside him.

"He loves coming here," Sonia says. Sonia is the youngest mother in the group, at twenty-five. She may be the smartest, too, with a degree in biophysics from Harvard.

"Something different from home," Sheri says.

Even though it's a stretch for me, I enjoy having a group of women in my house. We need each other and our babies need to explore new spaces. It's a desire that TV users eventually lose. With a remote in hand, it's so easy to bring the world into our homes with all of its neon color and rapidly changing scenes. But it's a world that can't be touched. It can't be held. Hannah and Casey can't put the TV world into their mouths or feel its textures against their skin.

I am cutting the banana bread just as Kendra arrives. I consider pretending that I made it, but I realize that I will probably score just as many points by telling the truth about Bob. Rebecca arrives a few minutes later. Everyone starts talking.

We run the gamut: ear infections, teething, our husbands. But mostly we talk about breastfeeding. A group of teenage boys couldn't talk about breasts as much as we do!

"Did you know that not only are we less likely to have breast cancer because we breastfeed, but our breastfed daughters are less likely to get it, too," Sonia says.

"I didn't know that," I tell her.

"You know, in my last group, the one through the hospital," Kendra says, "even the women who breastfed came to the group with bottles, because they didn't want to breastfeed in front of each other. It was really weird."

"My sister hides in the bathroom at restaurants when my nephew needs to nurse," Rebecca says. "How strange is that? It's no wonder she's thinking of weaning and he's only three months old! Who wants to spend your life in a bathroom?"

"Not us!" we all agree.

I'm reminded of living in a dorm my freshman year at college. We were bonded together by our vulnerability, all of us living away from home for the first time. My roommate and I would go out for coffee until three a.m. and talk about everything: politics, psychology, our best sexual experiences. I think of how it would feel to be supported by a group of parents who are raising their kids without television. We'd be able to pat each other on the back and spout off statistics. It would be the way it is for my sister and her vegan group: "I will no longer accept casein in my soy cheese," a member would say, "even if it is organic."

I bring out fruit and crackers for anyone who's still hungry, as the lunch hour looms ahead. Usually everyone leaves before that to be home in time for naps, but I'm hoping Kendra will stick around.

I walk Rebecca to the door.

"Thanks again," she says, giving me a hug, her baby on her hip. She calls out to Kendra, "See you tomorrow."

I turn quickly back to Kendra to see if I've heard wrong. Surely I'm mistaken. Kendra and Rebecca, I say to myself. They are getting together tomorrow without me. Of course, I can see why Rebecca likes Kendra, but why does Kendra like Rebecca? Kendra is nurturing and sweet and full of passion. Rebecca never gets excited about anything, particularly anything good that happens to anyone else. Not to mention the fact that Rebecca gives her baby a pacifier at night, something Kendra would never do. They're completely different from each other. Why would Kendra want to be her friend when she has me?

I paste a smile on my face as everyone else readies to leave. Kendra is the only one left.

"I can give you the banana bread recipe, if you like," I say, as she starts to gather her things.

"That'd be great."

I fumble around the kitchen looking for it, nervous about what I'm about to say.

I hand her the cookbook and a pen and paper, and she sits down on the carpet with our babies.

"You know, Kendra," I say, "I think that those of us in the group should include everyone else in the group when we're getting together with others from the group."

She looks perplexed, as if she's having trouble deciphering my words. "What do you mean?"

I take a deep breath. I realize that what I'm about to say is completely ridiculous, but unfortunately I say it anyway. "If you're getting together with Rebecca, then I think I should be invited, too."

"You can't really be serious."

"No," I lie. "I guess not." I am holding Hannah and Casey on my lap together, and they are playing with each other's hands. I feel embarrassed and quickly try to change the subject. What was I thinking?

"Bob uses honey instead of sugar in this recipe," I tell her. She nods.

"Casey wasn't fussy at all," she says, looking pleased to be onto another topic. "Maybe he's getting less colicky."

"Maybe," I say awkwardly.

After Kendra leaves, I nurse Casey and put him down for his nap, but as exhausted as I am, I'm too upset to fall asleep with him. Kendra is *my* friend, not Rebecca's.

I put in *Back to the Future* and watch it the whole way through, and thankfully Casey stays asleep. A problem doesn't go away by watching television. It just gets put off. But I'm used to putting things off.

When the movie is over, I decide to call Georgette. She was my massage therapist until several years ago when she turned into a real therapist, well, not exactly a real therapist in terms of having the typical credentials. She didn't become a psychologist or psychiatrist. She went to a school in California and came back with a master's degree in some sort of enlightened spiritual discipline. I've never asked her exactly what she studied there. I only know that she's now better at offering counseling than at giving massages, and her unorthodox style suits me.

I arrange to see her as soon as Bob comes home from work. It's been eight months since my last appointment, because I'm not the type to commit to anything on a regular basis, besides television.

We meet at her house, which is surrounded by large fir trees and where I always feel as if I'm out in the country, even though she's five minutes from downtown. As I wind my way up her cobblestone walkway, I hear the tiny fountain on her porch and begin to relax.

She opens the door and gives me a hug. Her curly blond hair is in a French braid and she is wearing a long green and yellow rayon dress. It's the kind of dress that would look too loose and sloppy on me but on her looks magical and elegant. She glides across the room and hands me a cup of lavender tea as I sink into a cushiony chair to tell my story. I don't leave out any necessary details or try to sugarcoat the situation to make myself look better. She's seen me through my most infantile emotional crises, and since I come only once in a while, I don't want to waste time.

"I just don't understand why Kendra likes her," I say. "Rebecca listens to country music and Kendra still goes to rock concerts!"

"People who are different from each other can still be good friends."

"But she's really not that nice!"

"You know, Ellen," she says kindly, "I give a workshop for twelve- and thirteen-year-old girls, and this is the sort of issue they have."

"Are you suggesting I take a workshop with a bunch of twelve-year-olds?"

"No, of course not. I'm just saying that I think there was some work you didn't get to do at that age." She leans forward a little in her chair. "But the good news is that you get to do it now."

I THINK ABOUT what she said as I'm driving home. I feel a little insulted. It's not as if I haven't had *any* friends. I have Sarah and Lisa. They're my closest friends, though I only see them separately. And I had a few friends in college, too. Then there are all of the friends I've made at the various places where I've worked. Unfortunately, the workplace is also where I've ended up having dysfunctional relationships with male colleagues and higher-ups. In fact, that is where most of my focus at work has been.

"You're still searching for the father you lost," Georgette would say to me when I was on the verge of sleeping with yet another one of my employers.

I wonder which is easier, having dysfunctional relationships with men or women. Maybe Georgette is right. Maybe I missed out on an important developmental phase. I should have been spending my early teens fighting bitterly with girlfriends, feeling jealous and angry at them and shedding countless tears when friendships ended. Instead I spent my time watching imaginary friendships on television: Lucy and Ethel and the *Three's Company* trio. And it wasn't just after school. Since my mother left early for work, by the time I was in the seventh grade, I found it wasn't really necessary for me to go to school on a regular basis.

Without school I had time to watch the game shows I used to enjoy only in the summer. *The Price Is Right* followed by *Password*, a show I loved in spite of the fact that I didn't know many of the answers. By one p.m., I was ready for the *Dialing for Dollars* movie. My grades went down, of course, but I managed to get by on the days that I was there by quickly throwing together my assignments in between classes.

My mother wasn't the type to discuss my situation with school officials. The only time I remember her setting foot in the building was when I had worn something to school that was considered inappropriate and I was sent home to change.

"It's time to change this archaic dress code," she bellowed to the principal.

By the time I arrived in high school, I had expanded my daytime viewing into late night viewing. This was made possible by a boy I met in my social studies class. He had somehow acquired a television and needed to store it someplace for a while until the insurance company made payments. I readily agreed, as if being part of illegal schemes was just one of many things I typically did for people I knew. I asked for nothing in return. Watching TV late into the night in the privacy of my own room was all the compensation I needed. In Texas, Johnny Carson came on at ten-thirty p.m., followed by Tom Snyder at midnight. That meant I was up until one a.m.

My mother asked me about the set after I'd had it for a couple of weeks.

"It's a gift from a friend," I said. "He doesn't have room for it."

She looked the set up and down once, but there was no further discussion about it. She had one in her room, after all, an old, twelve-inch RCA. Even when I stopped bothering to pretend to get out of bed to go to school, the television stayed without further questioning.

My sister didn't need television as much. She had found her escape in hallucinogenic drugs when she was in high school.

"Cats are inherently brutal," she told me. "I was tripping last week, and I stared into Chocolate's eyes, and I was able to see his carnivorous cravings, his deep desire not only to kill but to torture. I can give you some of this acid and you can see for yourself." I told her not to bother and continued to watch *Dallas*.

WHEN I COME HOME from Georgette's, I quietly sneak in, hoping Bob and Casey won't notice I've arrived. I head upstairs and decide to call my niece, Trillium. Trillium is the name my niece now goes by from among the seven names she was originally given. I figure she is the right one to call, because if I'm really acting like a twelve-year-old, then I need some sound advice from an experienced thirteen-year-old. Besides, what if she really is the next Buddha? She does exude wisdom at times, although her belly isn't very Buddha-esque. She is in fact still exceptionally thin, despite the fact that she has been living on more than air and eating far more than fruits and nuts for some time now. I remember my sister saying at some point before she starved, "We just found that after a while we had to start feeding her more."

I explain my situation to Trillium and tell her the course of action I'm considering.

"I want to kick Rebecca out of the group," I say.

"But that wouldn't be nice," she says. "Everyone would think that you're mean."

"Well, then if Kendra is going to be friends with Rebecca, I don't want to be friends with Kendra anymore."

"But then you wouldn't get to be with Kendra at all, and you like her, remember?"

We chat a little more and then I hang up the phone. Trillium must think I'm nuts, over the top on this one. Having a group of girlfriends is complicated. I want to go watch *Ellen,* but it's late and I can't take any more time away from Bob and Casey.

By the next morning, though, I know Trillium's advice is sound. I can't kick Rebecca out of the group. Trillium may be young, but she's better at advising me than Bob. When I try to talk to him about Rebecca and Kendra, he quickly tires of hearing about it.

"Why don't you see more of your old friends, Lisa and Sarah."

"Lisa doesn't have kids. I don't see her anymore."

"What about inviting Sarah to your playgroup?" Bob asks me. "She has Courtney."

"Courtney is two years old."

"But Sarah's pregnant with twins."

In the end, I decide to invite Sarah to the next group. She's my oldest friend in Oregon. Bob and I met her in Eugene because we were all working at the same restaurant. She appreciated Bob's cooking as much as I did, although she already knew how to cook. Hence, it was more important that I marry him. If she comes to the group, I can find out what she thinks of Rebecca.

"Maybe you can figure out what Kendra sees in her," I tell Sarah. I have described all of the moms to her and am sure she is looking forward to giving me her opinion.

By the time Passover arrives, followed by Easter, Casey and most of the babies in the playgroup are crawling proficiently. Casey has just gotten his second front tooth, and after much drooling and fussing, he is happy, at least temporarily, and is busy exploring the new tunnel and playhouse his grandparents sent him.

Sarah has been welcomed into the group, although she won't commit to coming very often, because she lives so far away. At least no one cares that Courtney is two. Sonia saw it as her chance to invite Mariana, an artist from Equador who has two children, ages one and three.

"I'm close to reaching my two-hour-a-week goal," I tell Bob. "Last week, I watched only one movie and a couple of sitcoms on Tuesday and Wednesday night."

He nods, barely looking up from his newspaper. He's reading the sports section, probably wondering who he'll pick for the NCAA tournament he won't be seeing. Unlike me he hasn't wavered from our TV agreement. I suppose he could watch sporting events for two hours a week, but he says it wouldn't be worth it.

5

Bag Lady

I'm lying in bed next to my baby, who has thrown up all over me. I'm wishing I had not only a television in my room but a special futuristic set I could turn on with a simple voice command. *Television on,* I would say. I'm thinking that this would be especially useful right at this moment because Bob has gone out of town on business and I'm unable to move away from my baby's side. Casey and I have been sick for more than twenty-four hours, so maybe this is the forty-eight-hour bug. I only know I can't do this alone for much longer.

What good is having a community now? I've worked hard to structure my days so that I would not be alone with my child and thus tempted to put him in front of the television set. But if I'm not going to use television, then I need something more than a group of friends and neighbors who leave me groceries at the door. I need someone who doesn't care how sick we are, who won't hesitate to get in bed with us if necessary and hold wet cloths on our heads until our fevers are gone.

I need my mother, the one I left in Texas fourteen years ago, sure that to start my own life I had to live as far away as possible from her.

I carefully scoot over to the clean side of the bed with my little baby still Velcroed to me, the responsibility for this small being pressing down on me. I try to sleep, but thoughts of my mother keep returning. An hour passes before I'm finally able to detach myself from my offspring. I grab the phone and punch in the numbers. It's one a.m. in Texas and Mama answers on the third ring.

"I need you to come up here," I tell her, and then I burst into tears, the first tears I have cried since Casey was born, and those were happy tears. I let them flow freely now, because they are so long overdue.

"It's just so hard," I say in between sobs. She tells me that she understands, but I keep crying.

"I'll look for a good flight," she reassures me, her voice low and gravelly from having her sleep interrupted.

"Hurry!" I say, remembering that the last time she looked for a so-called good flight, she went to the classified ads and got a ticket under the name of Gene Rostrom because it was a good deal. "Remember the name Rostrom, in case the plane goes down," she warned me before she left.

I hang up the phone, feeling hopeful. I snuggle up next to Casey and fall asleep at last.

By the time she actually arrives, the bug has swept through our house. No one has been spared. I'm changing the sheets one final time when Bob pulls into the driveway with my mother. It's summer and the sky is clear, a blessing for June in Oregon. I grab Casey and run out to meet her.

"Hi, Casey!" she says as soon as she sees him. "You've grown so, and don't you look happy!"

"He is right now," I say. They beam at each other.

Bob grabs her suitcases.

"Take Casey instead," I say, stopping him. He gives me a knowing look and goes inside with Casey.

"I don't want those in the house just yet," I tell her, pointing to her oversized purse and mildewed suitcases.

"Whatever you like," she says, throwing her hands up the air, feigning helplessness. I empty her suitcases on the back deck, put her clothes in plastic bags, and leave the suitcases to air out before storing them in the garage. I throw her clothes in the washer. Most people would think I'm going to extreme measures, but that's because they've never seen my mother's house. My sister wasn't so careful the last time Mama stayed with her and was left with a roach infestation by the time her visit was done.

"When do you have to go back to teaching?" I ask. We're standing in the laundry room. She's leaning against the wall, looking exhausted.

"I've finally retired," she says. "The dean gave me a package I couldn't refuse. They wanted me out of there. After all, I am sixty-nine. Such an obscene age, isn't it?"

I nod, but try not to encourage her in this line of humor. She came to it late in life, along with her use of four-letter words, and she has never moved on. My sister and I have only ourselves to blame. When we were teenagers, we took up the word *fuck* as the great all-purpose adjective, noun, and verb that it is and used it frequently. "You tell that fuckhead to fuck off or I'll fucking kill him." After a few days of hearing us speak this way, Mama chose to adopt the word, too, rather than attempt to limit its usage by her children. But she never quite got it right. "When will you parasites take your fucked plates to the kitchen?" she would yell.

"It's fucking plates," we would yell back, in hopes of correcting her. But it was pointless.

As I finish rinsing out the inside of her purse at the laundry room sink I wonder if she will try to restrain herself in front of Casey. We are so proud of the words he has learned so far. Nice words like *baby, dada,* and *mama. Fucking* just isn't high on the list.

I walk with Mama up the stairs. She's even slower than I remember, and I try to be patient, which isn't natural for me. I open the door to the guest room. It's the quietest room of the house, filled with some Hummel figurines I don't like but can't give away because Bob's aunt gave them to us.

"You have your own radio," I say, "and there's a stack of fresh towels for you in the bathroom right outside your room."

She looks around quickly. "Why isn't a television in here?"

"We just have one now, and it's in the bonus room next door."

"Do you still have C-SPAN?"

"We don't have cable at all," I say annoyed. "We've got channel 10 and you've got public radio, too." I point to the radio again.

This is like telling someone who likes chocolate cake that they can have a carob-flavored muffin instead.

"Don't you want cable for Casey?"

I open her closet so it will be ready for her when her suitcase and clothes have been debugged and sterilized.

"Casey won't be watching television," I tell her.

"Not even *Sesame Street*?"

I cringe at the words.

"We're skipping *Sesame Street*," I say.

I lead her into the bonus room, show her the television, and explain how I've managed to keep Casey away from it.

"I think he'll be more creative and able to entertain himself better without it. That's why I don't want you to watch it if he's in this room."

She nods in agreement, but I can see by her expression that she's already feeling put out. I take consolation in knowing that she feels even more put out when she's staying with my sister, whose rules have always been even stricter: "No meat will ever enter this house, no fish, no chicken, no carcass of any kind. Meat must not be cooked here, eaten here, or even stored here. You step into my house, and you step into a meat-free zone."

My mother complied with my sister, frequently sneaking out to buy roast beef and sliced turkey at the deli, which she stored in a cooler in the backyard shed. I assume that she will comply with the television rule, too. Maybe she'll get a tiny TV and hide it in the back of my garage.

The truth is that she of all people should understand my rules about television. Born in 1927, she is of a generation who grew up without it. She read a lot on those cold nights in Iowa when she was a young girl. And when I was young, she would often refer to characters from books she had read in her childhood and assume that I knew what she was talking about. "I was like Jo in *Little Women*," she would say. "Never heard of him," I would answer. When did she think I took the time to read these so-called classics? When the commercials were on?

"I was hoping that we wouldn't be watching much television on this visit," I say as we head back to the guest room. She nods, probably wondering what sort of drugs I have been taking. So much of our time together has been spent in front of the television, often with both of us intoxicated. That's how we've been most comfortable together. But I'm not drinking at all because I'm nursing, and Mama has just been told that she has cirrhosis.

"I should be all right," she told me over the phone a few months ago, after she came back from the doctor, "aside from not being able to drink for the rest of my life."

"Do you still get to smoke?" I asked her, hoping that the doctor told her she has to quit smoking, too.

"It's one of the only pleasures I have left," she said.

"Your doctor should have told you to quit."

"Well, she's from Texas, and we don't antagonize smokers as much here."

I'm reminded of when she was visiting and I was pregnant and sensitive to the slightest hint of cigarette smoke on anyone's breath, even if the person hadn't smoked in over an hour. Mama would stand out on the deck to smoke, but it was never far enough away for me.

"Your smoke is drifting in through the upstairs window," I would shout down at her from the second story.

Finally I banished her to the back of the yard.

I pull down the shade in my mother's room, because the sun is beginning to make the room too hot. I decide not to remind her of the smoking rules just yet. I don't want to hear about how smokers are a poor, oppressed group made to huddle on street corners in the middle of winter.

"Let's go downstairs," I say.

Mama sits on the couch in front of Casey, who is on the carpet playing with his DUPLOs.

"My, this baby must have everything!" she exclaims as she surveys the room filled with colorful sets of blocks and stuffed koalas.

"Bob's parents have been really generous," I say, and immediately feel bad for saying it. "But Casey loves the book you gave him, *A Hole Is to Dig*," I quickly add.

It had been one of my favorites Mama read to me as a child.

She mailed it to us a few months ago and it arrived musty and mildewy. After putting it in the freezer for a few days to kill anything living in it, I flipped through its pages, glad to see that they were all there. On the inside cover, I saw my childish scrawl, my first attempts to write my name.

I step around all of the shiny new toys and grab the book.

As I sit reading it with Casey in my lap, I feel myself relaxing. With my mother and husband here, I think to myself, I can handle this baby just fine.

And even better, Bob can handle my mother. They've always been nice to each other, mostly because my mother adores him. I still remember her toast at our wedding. She looked at Bob and then out to the group of eighty or so guests and said, "I wish I were thirty years younger, so I could marry him!"

The toast didn't go over too well, made worse by the fact that my mother rambled on and on in a drunken state for twenty-five more minutes, until my sister's mother-in-law forced her back into her seat. But Bob has always remained kind to my mother, probably in an attempt to compensate for my continual criticism of her. He is cooking her favorite Oregon dinner, salmon and baked potatoes, while I finish reading to Casey.

"Would you like some nonalcoholic wine, Ginny?" he asks her, holding up a bottle from the fridge.

She looks at the pale, pink liquid with interest.

"How thoughtful of you. I'd love some of the Zinfandel," she says smiling.

I suppose I could feel bad that she doesn't tell me how thoughtful I am, too. But I'm not all that thoughtful, and I can live with that. The important thing is that we can all coexist together, and after the first week, we settle into a routine that works well for all of us.

I take care of Casey in the mornings while Bob is at work. Mama remains close by, bringing me snacks and books if Casey falls asleep in my arms and I'm afraid to move. If I have what I need, she walks around the house with duct tape defacing cracked plastic hampers and trash containers in her attempt to "fix things." Unlike other mothers, she wouldn't think to put fresh shelf paper in the kitchen cabinets or cedar sachets in the chests of drawers. Mama would rather look for cracks in the ceiling, and she'll be the first to spackle whatever she finds. But what I really like is that she's willing to come with me on errands.

"Sit in the car right next to Casey," I tell her in front of the Mail Boxes, Etc. "I'll only be a minute. If he gets upset, sing 'Alouette,'" I tell her.

I run in to mail a package to my nephew. I glance back at them. It's a clear day and I can easily see them both through the window. She's in the backseat and he looks happy beside her. I can do anything now.

Maybe next time I'll even leave her at home with Casey, but I doubt it. Her hearing is bad and she's slow to respond. I consider sending her to do my errands while I stay at home with Casey, but that would be difficult for her, too.

"What sort of acidophilus powder am I supposed to get?" she would ask me over and over.

Going out together, the three of us, works best. If Casey loses it, her presence keeps me from spiraling downward, and she is good company, even if the relationship is a bit lopsided.

"I'm her slave," she tells Bob after shadowing me all week. But she says it in good humor and I don't feel guilty. Instead I feel as if a longstanding karmic debt is getting repaid. For all of the time that she wasn't around when I was a child, she's at my beck and call now. And Bob feeds her fabulous dinners. He has just made his famous Florentine lasagna. He pours my mother a glass of nonalcoholic wine.

"It's almost as good as the real thing," she says to Bob, thankful that she has found a substitute for her worst vice.

I'm cutting back on television, too, no longer feeling a desperate need to barricade myself in the bonus room when Casey is napping. With Mama here, I'm not carrying the heavy weight of being the sole caregiver during the day.

Even better than not watching as much television, though, is that I have a perfect excuse to watch it when I do want to escape.

"I think I should keep Mama company," I tell Bob after dinner, hoping that he will think that I'm just a dutiful daughter trying to make her mother feel at home. "Do you mind watching Casey?" Bob nods, maybe impressed that I'm actually thinking of my mother for a change.

We watch *Mad About You* together, one of my mother's favorites. She wants to watch *The NewsHour with Jim Lehrer* at seven p.m., but I try to talk her out of it. It's the same with the other programs she likes on Oregon Public Broadcasting.

"There's a show on later about the solar system," she tells me, TV guide in hand. "It's about new moons on Jupiter."

"How about *Seinfeld*?" I say. "It's about silly, self-centered people living in New York."

By the end of the week I've watched an average of an hour a night, but because I haven't watched much of anything during the day, I'm closing in on my original goal. I'm even becoming productive during Casey's nap, ready to enlist my mother's help in various projects.

"Let's get these baby clothes boxed up," I tell her as soon as he's fallen asleep.

We've been accomplishing so much together that I haven't felt the need to see friends as often, but when Kendra calls and asks for the third time if she can meet my mother, I agree. If I don't, she might spend more time with Rebecca.

"TOMORROW YOU'RE GOING to meet one of my friends and her daughter, Hannah," I tell my mother.

"Wonderful!" she says, all excited. Most of my life I've tried to keep my friends and boyfriends away from her.

"Let's have a look at what you might wear," I suggest.

I open the closet and pull out the first outfit, a sleeveless knit top and pair of white stretch pants. I pick out a second one, a summer knit dress.

"What shoes would you wear with this one?"

"The sandals," she says.

I inspect the sandals next to the bed. They haven't yet needed repair with duct tape.

"These are nice," I tell her. "And it's not just because I cleaned them."

"Yes, well, I know you don't like my bag lady look."

I feel embarrassed. A bag lady is what she started calling herself a few years ago. I guess she decided it was time to acknowledge the truth about her appearance. Even though she was a college professor, if she hung out in certain parts of town, she could definitely be mistaken for someone homeless.

Or maybe she called herself a bag lady because of her handbag itself. It was the size of a large watermelon, made of brown vinyl, visibly torn in places where the duct tape had come off, and it was always bulging with medicine bottles, old Kleenex, a Thermos bottle, and cigarettes. She would sling the bag across her stooping shoulder and walk around in a pair of pants covered with dog hair and a polyester blouse stained with coffee.

But what really made her look like a bag lady was what she always carried with her. In her right hand she clutched a warped plastic cup filled with coffee or scotch, depending on what time of day it was, and in her left hand she held a cigarette. The heavy bag alone slowed her down, but with the plastic cup and cigarette, she walked at a snail's pace.

Whenever she came to visit, I wanted to go on walks with her but I hated moving so slowly. Once I tried walking in circles around her and then back and forth, but I stopped because I didn't want anyone to think I was mentally ill. I suppose I should have thought of my mother as disabled back then and been more sympathetic, but mostly I was disgusted and, deep down, afraid. I always felt that if I went a few steps in the wrong direction, I could end up just like her, a prescription drug addict and alcoholic. It was only my anger and disgust with her that kept me on a different path.

I would complain to Bob about her. "She's walking around wearing one blue sock and one brown one. People probably think she has dementia."

"When we lived in Eugene, you used to walk across the street to the store in your nightshirt and nothing else," he reminded me.

"That was in Eugene," I said, as if that should explain everything. "Besides, I just looked youthful and reckless. She looks senile."

I look at my mother now, and the change is remarkable. Even her bag, although still large, isn't as hideous. Maybe it's because she's stopped drinking. Whatever the reason, her clothes are presentable. Saying this, even to myself, makes me feel like my grandmother.

HANNAH AND KENDRA arrive a little late. "Thank God you've got air-conditioning!" Kendra exclaims.

Hannah is wearing a T-shirt and diaper. Kendra sets her down in the family room and within minutes she is trying to scale the gate I have erected. Kendra pays no attention, probably seizing on the possibility that my mother might take care of her instead.

"When did she start walking?" my mother asks after being introduced.

"At nine months," Kendra says.

"My, you're a fast one," my mother says to Hannah. She bends down to pick her up, looking thrilled to get to finally hold a baby without someone hovering over her, scrutinizing her every move as I do. And Kendra has no reason to think of my mother as anything but perfectly competent.

Hannah is playing with my mother's hair, pulling it out of her makeshift bun.

"Kendra is an actress," I tell my mother, hoping to impress her.

"Have you been on television?"

"I'm in a theater company and I'm about to start rehearsing a play." She sits down and I bring her a cup of tea.

"I didn't know that," I say.

"Well, I just found out."

My mother puts Hannah down next to Casey and I dump out a basket full of toy animals for them to explore. I decide I will tell everyone in our group about Kendra's play so we can all go see it together, if Kendra hasn't already mentioned it to them. I'll even tell Rebecca, because that's what a mature friend would do. I'm pretending to be mature.

"I can show you the script," Kendra says suddenly, and she heads out to her car.

Mama tests her on her lines before we all have lunch. Kendra will play the part of a supposedly happily married woman who is actually in love with her sister-in-law. She doesn't want to tell her husband, although if she did, she would discover that he's actually in love with his brother-in-law. It's as entertaining as television.

"THANKS FOR HELPING with Hannah," I tell Mama after Kendra has gone.

"I didn't embarrass you?"

"No, of course not," I say, and I note to myself that I am actually telling the truth. I'm getting better at letting my mother be herself. My list of forbidden topics for discussion is getting smaller, too. I had only one request before Kendra came over.

"Please don't make a big deal out of Casey not watching television."

"I won't say a word," she said, and that's all she said. That was a big change, too. In the past she would have been annoyed by my need for privacy.

"So many secrets," she said to me once after announcing to the pharmacist that she needed something to get rid of pubic lice. "My teenage daughter has been complaining about itching," she said in a voice loud enough to fill the store. "God knows, a lot of people sleep at our house!"

When I told her to keep her voice down, she yelled back.

"I'm sorry." She turned back to the pharmacist. "She is so self-conscious. I can't understand it. My life is an open book."

I flinched, recalling all the times I wished she would have closed it.

• • •

I GUESS IT'S NOT that easy to get a baby to watch television at first. Babies are programmed to be in close contact with those around them, affectionate people who laugh and smile with them. It's what they require. But television producers work hard to woo babies to their shows, and so do parents.

"I'm just trying to get Hannah to like *Sesame Street*," Kendra says. We are on the phone together, and I have just pulled out a drawer filled with cloth napkins and napkin rings. Casey likes to play with them. As close as I'm becoming to Kendra, I still don't feel comfortable telling her what I think about television.

"Let me call you back as soon as I put a video in," Kendra says in an exasperated tone. "Then hopefully I'll be able to have a simple phone conversation."

By the time she calls me back, Casey has begun to tire of the napkin rings and I'm having trouble focusing on the conversation. I'll have to find something else for him to play with tomorrow. Last week in desperation, I dumped out a box of condoms and let Casey fiddle with the shiny gold packages inside. Kendra probably thinks I'm nuts for not trying *Sesame Street* instead. I imagine her talking to Rebecca.

I don't know how or why she chooses to keep him away from television.

It's a bit extreme.

They probably pat each other on the back for putting the limits they do on television, and they're certainly better than most. They aren't like the woman who lives down the street from Rebecca who lets her toddler watch *Beavis and Butt-Head* until he falls asleep. I heard them talking about it at the last group.

I guess it's all a matter of degree, but as Casey's first birthday rolls around, more and more of my friends are using television. Soon their babies will expect it the same way they expect to nurse and play with stuffed animals, except after they're weaned and have outgrown their teddy bears, some of them may be stuck with a television habit, if they're anything like me. On the other hand, Casey, as he gets older, might have an inexplicable attraction to condoms.

SAPPHIRE'S BEST FRIEND told me that a child is supposed to have as many friends at his birthday party as his age. "It should be a quiet, peaceful celebration," she said. I have invited fourteen children along with their twenty-eight parents to Casey's birthday party.

"You've gone crazy!" Bob complains when he finds out. Compared to any parties we've had in the past—and I can recall only one—this one is giant.

"Well, we don't know if everyone can come," I say. I'm madly cleaning the kitchen and throwing hampers full of dirty clothes into closets, out of sight. Unlike Bob, Mama is excited about the prospect of meeting more of my friends now that I'm comfortable with her in social situations. My fear now is that no one will show up if I don't invite a lot of people. I eternally imagine myself as the unpopular child that I was.

But everyone does come and they are a varied group, which makes things especially complicated. In addition to inviting everyone from the playgroup, I have daringly invited several of the neighborhood families. I worry that, with everyone here, people might compare notes and all of the separate parts of my life will be exposed. Bob says the world doesn't actually revolve around me and I shouldn't worry.

Olivia arrives first with Mindy and Luke. Lori brings Jenny and her new baby Belinda. Thankfully it is a pleasant August day, and people spill out into our backyard. Bob watches Casey while I attend to the guests and try to catch tidbits of conversation. I move in closer when I see Olivia talking to Kendra.

"Well, actually she's always been active," Kendra says.

"Has she tried to climb out of her crib?" Olivia asks.

"Well, she sleeps with us."

"Does she?" she says. "How do you get any sleep?"

"I sleep right through her nursing, so it really isn't a problem."

"You're still nursing her?" Olivia asks.

I move away from them, not wanting to join the conversation. I don't want Olivia to know that I'm like Kendra, a nursing freak. I suppose if I were as open as Kendra I would even tell people, *We're not really interested in having Casey watch television. I think he'll be a lot better off without it.* But I'm nothing like that.

I suppose I could take lessons from Kendra, but I'm not sure I'd succeed. Maybe it would be the way it is with cooking. I wanted to do it well, but I've resigned myself to simply admiring Bob.

I head back downstairs but Lori grabs my arm on the way. She looks agitated. "Where's your television? Jenny needs a video."

"The television's up in the bonus room, but I don't have a video for her."

"You don't?" She is shocked, but quickly recovers. "That's okay. I have one."

She reaches into her diaper bag, pulls out *Clifford the Big Red Dog,* picks up Jenny, and heads up the stairs.

Back in the kitchen I run around chatting and bringing out trays of lox and bagels and guacamole and chips. I am in top form. I might actually pull this whole thing off, bringing together old and new friends, neighbors, my mother, and so many babies to celebrate my child's first birthday.

After everyone has left and Mama and Casey have gone to

sleep, I try to explain to Bob how momentous this occasion has been.

"But you've been completely stressed out and hyper all day. It's a miracle Casey didn't pick up on it and lose it."

"But it's a new kind of stress," I exclaim happily.

I ALWAYS ASSUMED that family communication would be drastically improved by the absence of television. I imagined that the members of a TV-free family would eat dinner together, share the best moments of each other's day, and blissfully get to know each other on ever-deepening levels throughout their lives.

What I can say is that my mother and I have been talking with each other more than ever, but it hasn't always been cheery, probably because I now feel compelled to discuss things that I thought I would never discuss with her. I call it my list of grievances, although I haven't actually written the list down. It's in my head, and I remember it whenever my mother does something that irritates me.

Bob doesn't think I should ever share the list with her. "Whatever your mother did in the past, whatever way you think that she failed you, is not worth mentioning now. Let her enjoy her old age in peace."

"But if I don't say anything, then I'll stay angry with her, and then we can't have a good relationship."

He shakes his head and walks away, and in the end I disregard his advice. What does he know? His idea of a close moment with his mother is talking about real estate.

My mother and I are having breakfast in the kitchen when I decide to talk with her about the first item on the list. She's pouring herself a cup of coffee. I'm drinking a new herbal tea that's supposed to taste like coffee, except that it doesn't.

"Why didn't you do something when I started skipping school in seventh grade?" I blurt out suddenly.

She settles herself in her seat at the kitchen table before she answers.

"Well, you didn't want to go! And who could blame you? I knew how repressive the school system was in Texas. I figured you needed the break."

"But by the time I was high school, I was only going to school one third of the year! I'm surprised I graduated at all!"

"Really?" she exclaims.

"Yes!"

She pauses for a minute and takes a bite of a banana muffin Bob made.

"Well, I'm sorry." She sets her muffin down and looks into my eyes. "I made mistakes. I wasn't always good for you."

I stare back at her, temporarily speechless, a rare event. I move my uncoffeelike tea away from me. She has said exactly what I needed to hear. I feel like the Grinch at the end of the story *How the Grinch Stole Christmas,* when his heart grows three sizes bigger. Maybe I won't need to finish the list.

"It's okay, Mama." I get out of my chair and put my arms around her. "I'm sure I was no picnic either."

Later that night, I tell Bob what happened.

"Good," he says. "Now maybe you can be nicer to her."

"I think so," I say, snuggling up next to him. As I drift off to sleep, I think about her words again. *I'm sorry. I made mistakes.*

The next day I *am* a little nicer to her. I take her to her favorite Goodwill store. I watch *The NewsHour with Jim Lehrer* with her the day after that. In fact, I'm nice to her for a whole week, but then before I know it, the anger creeps in again, and I'm pulling out another item on my list of grievances. Most of my complaints aren't really fair. She couldn't help it if she wasn't like the mothers I saw on television.

"I don't understand why you needed to run for the board of education when you were already so busy. You were a tenured professor with three children to raise. Why wasn't that enough?" We are sitting in the family room folding clothes.

I hear myself say these words, knowing that what I really mean is why wasn't being a mother more important than anything else. I wonder if John Kennedy's daughter asked her dad why he ran for president.

"I ran for office to prove myself to the bastards I had to work with every day," she says. She throws a pair of Casey's clean socks into a basket. "I was lucky to be teaching at the university, lucky to be able to support you kids at all. But good teaching and raising the consciousness of countless young women were never enough. Even after tenure, those bastards there expected me to publish articles and books year after year. Well, I never wrote enough for them, but by God, at least I was on the Texas State Board of Education!"

"Yes, indeed you were," I say. I remember when she was running for office, a letter circulated around town, an anonymous hate letter that said my mother shouldn't be elected because she couldn't discipline her own kids.

I thought about all of the school I'd missed, all of the hours spent at home watching *Three's Company*. I knew the letter was about me and my delinquent brother.

"You never seemed to notice that anything was wrong with me," I say.

"But you kept so much to yourself!"

I fold Casey's blue cotton shirt and think about what she's saying. I did work hard to pretend that nothing was wrong, laughing when I should have been crying, lying when I should have been telling the truth.

"I think family counseling would have helped," I tell her.

She stacks the towels in a pile.

"No psychologist at that time would have understood a feminist raising three children by herself," she says at last. I am sitting across from her and trying to convey understanding, trying to act the way a therapist who understood a feminist raising three children by herself might act.

"I always had you in mind," she says emphatically now. "I was making the world a better place for you and for generations of women to come. You didn't need a world where women were treated like second-class citizens. You didn't need to be paid less than men. I got on the board to make a difference, so you wouldn't have to read sexist and racist textbooks."

"It's okay. I didn't read them anyway," I say. "I was too busy watching *I Dream of Jeannie.*"

"Well, I wish you had watched the *NewsHour* with me. Then you would have learned that all the work I did was to make the world a better place for you. Every candidate I helped put into office, every peace march I joined to end the war, and every battle for equal rights was fought for you!" she says. "And I was doing it all alone. Martin Luther King had a wife while he changed the world."

"Why didn't you marry again?" I ask tentatively.

"Another marriage would have meant more work for me. Men of my generation never learned how to cook and or change a diaper." She hands me a pile of clean socks.

I'd always wanted my mother to remarry, and I had fond memories of all her boyfriends. I remember making a Father's Day card for Greg Olson, the man she had dated the longest. I think it might have been this very card that scared him off for good. At the time, Mama gave me other reasons, but I didn't buy them.

When that relationship ended, my mother said she would only marry a widower. This seemed really depressing to me, but then when I thought about *The Brady Bunch,* I figured it could work out well. Surely Mike Brady's first wife must have died and the same must have been true for Carol's husband. There were never any ex-spouses in the picture picking up the kids for weekend visits.

After a while, though, my mother seemed to give up completely on marriage. She said that no one would want to marry someone with three kids, and no one wanted someone who was older than thirty-two. I guess that's why she kept telling people that she was thirty-two, just in case. And if anyone asked her how much she weighed, she would say 120 pounds. The answers were the same no matter how big her body grew or how much she aged, and if we were somewhere where alcohol was forbidden, the drink in her Thermos cup was cough medicine. These were the simple facts that I, a gullible, not-so-curious child, accepted just as a five-year-old accepts Santa Claus and the Tooth Fairy.

My mother stacks Casey's pants. "Bob doesn't expect you to cater to his every need," she says. "You've got a good marriage. You can thank me for that. If I wasn't there for you, it was only because I was just trying to help us all survive, get food on the table."

We continue in this vein for a while, until once again she apologizes, tells me how she knows she could have done better. And once again the anger and resentment recede. I feel so much happier. I'm finally done, I say to myself.

But a week later, we repeat the process yet again, until magically the list of grievances as well as the anger and the resentment that accompanied the list are gone. In its wake, I'm left with a deeper understanding of my mother and myself.

"What was the point of this again?" Bob asks me when I tell him what happened. "Why did you have to put her through all that?"

"Because we're present with each other," I say cheerfully.

I tell Kendra how well this technique works and recommend that she and her mother use it. "It's amazing," I say. "As soon as she apologized, all of the bitterness was gone."

"My mother isn't comfortable apologizing," Kendra says.

"I'm sorry," I say.

"It's just not a good subject for me," she says, not bothering to pretend that everything is fine.

I notice the tension in her face, and it occurs to me that for an actress, she doesn't do much acting in real life. And for someone who has never been paid to be on stage, I sure do a hell of a lot of acting.

My birthday follows Casey's a month later. By mid-September my little boy is walking. At fourteen months he has gone from uttering single words like *baby* and *mama* to speaking his first two-word phrase. "Daddy's working," he says. "That's right," I say, and I find myself smiling easily much of the day, because a miracle of sorts has happened. Mama, who has been staying with us for five months now, notices it, too. "He's stopped fussing," she says.

It's true. After months of being temperamental and cranky, my baby, my toddler, has become a delightful bundle of joy.

"He just didn't like being helpless, is all," Bob says. "He had things to say and places to go and we didn't understand. How frustrating was that? He must have been thinking to himself, *These guys are so clueless. I need to hurry up and figure out how to talk and walk or I'll never get what I want.*"

"I think he just had a hard time with teething," I say. "Maybe the homeopathic remedy finally worked. Or maybe it was my diet."

"Well, the phenobarbital would have worked better," my mother says. We are eating leftover birthday cake and cranberry bread on the deck. "But it certainly helped that you talked to him so much."

Maybe a little too much, I think to myself, recalling how I endlessly described every facet of life to him. "Now I'm reaching for the toilet paper. See the toilet paper?" I would say.

Everywhere we go people comment on how well he speaks. "He just asked you for an avocado," the cashier at Nature's says. I nod. It's nice for me that Casey is noticed for something besides screaming.

Best of all, Casey and I can talk to each other now. "Mama loves Casey," he says, and in no time at all, he forms the words perfectly, so happy to have them at last.

6

Doing Dishes

Casey's improved disposition has helped me feel rested. Without the time bomb factor, we go places easily, even without my mother, who has gone back to Texas. We spend our mornings with friends out and about, and Casey is delighted wherever we are.

At home I can actually sit on the couch and talk on the phone while Casey sits on the carpet in front of me, fitting shapes through holes or building with his toddler-size LEGOs. As Bob's parents have supplied us with enough puzzles, books, and toys for a lifetime, my child is not deprived of interesting things to explore. I begin to breathe a little easier.

This would be a good time to get serious about really withdrawing from television, maybe at last reaching my two-hour-a-week goal. But as happy as Casey is, now I'm dealing with the tedium that other parents deal with. I'm bored. Admittedly it's an improvement over the anxiety and near despair I felt before, but it still makes me want to watch television.

How many times can I hear Casey say, "Throw the ball," and then hear myself say, "Catch the ball"? I'm weary of watching him try to climb off of the couch without hitting his head on the coffee table.

Worse, because he's so mobile now, it's harder to get away from him when Bob is home and I want to escape. Long gone are the days when I could watch television with Casey in the same room and make sure he didn't see anything. Blockades are out of the question. He would simply knock them down.

Now when Casey wanders into the bonus room, I'm taken by surprise, unsure whether Bob even knows he's up here. My first impulse is to tell him to go away because I'm watching *Friends*. But I remind myself that I'm committed to a different life, a more civilized life, a TV-free life. I greet him enthusiastically when I see him standing in the doorway smiling at me. Then I quickly grab the remote and turn off the television.

"TV, I don't need TV!" I say, as if it were some weird accident that the television was on at all. "I've got Casey!" Then I give him a big hug.

He smiles and we leave the room together before I find out if Rachel and Ross are really back together. Casey doesn't know that I'm thinking about the show. He doesn't even know that I care one way or the other about that flickering box. He doesn't know that I want to find Bob and clobber him for not giving me time for mindless entertainment.

IT'S EARLY IN THE afternoon when Casey goes down for his nap, and I'm still awake and energetic. I consider being productive and organizing the toys on the shelves downstairs; that's the sort of thing I did with my mother here.

"Don't stay away too long," I told her before she left.

"I'll be back in the spring or summer when it stops raining so much."

I didn't dare let her know that it always rains too much.

I walk into the bonus room contemplating watching *Falling in Love,* a movie I've seen only once a long time ago.

I set the video back on the shelf, throw on Bob's raincoat, and decide to do something useful like get the mail. It's a cold and drizzly day, and when I come back inside, I have to turn up the thermostat. I look at the bills, which I have no interest in paying right now, and flip through the pages of the monthly neighborhood newspaper. It's filled with stories about zoning disputes and the proposed library location. I was a city hall reporter once and wrote stories like these. It wasn't my favorite job. I had simply fallen into it after college, the same way I had fallen into majoring in journalism. Junior year rolled around and I had been switching majors the way I had always switched channels. I ended up in a writing class for journalists and developed a crush on the professor. That seemed as good a reason as any to settle on a major.

He was twenty-five years older than me and liked my writing. I agonized over every paper, staying up at all-night cafés drinking coffee and eating cheesecake with my best friend. Of course, this was also because I usually waited until eight p.m. to start papers that were due the following morning. But I worked hard with each one, finishing at the last second, showering, and arriving in class with my hair still damp, windblown and lightened from the Texas sunshine.

Somehow I got the idea that sleeping with this man was the main goal of the class. I didn't want to do it to get a good grade. I just thought it would make the learning easier, as though by taking him into my bed I would also take in the secret to successful writing.

But he never took the initiative. Maybe it was because he was married. Maybe he didn't want to lose his job. Maybe it was because his twenty-year-old son, a student in my Spanish class, kept asking me out.

I turn this local newspaper over in my hands now. I could write for this paper, I say to myself. I could do it right this minute instead of watching *Falling in Love*. I think about what my mother said before she left. "Now that Casey is getting easier, you should work again."

I turn on the computer and type a few lines, but it doesn't feel right. I grab a pen and paper and write a few more lines. But that doesn't feel right either. I head to the kitchen and return with a piece of blackberry pie. I finish eating it in ten minutes and I still haven't written anything. Maybe what I need is just to have the television on in the background while I write. I am halfway upstairs before I turn back around. Even writing simple thank-you notes is a bad idea while watching television.

"You used the word *wonderful* three times in a row," Bob said once, after reading my note to his parents that I wrote while watching *The Cosby Show*.

"You write them then," I shot back impatiently. "They're your parents and I'm trying to find out why Cosby's son is having trouble in school."

I flip through the newspaper and study its various sections. I sit down on the couch, pad of paper in hand. Picking up a pen, I begin to write in earnest.

I manage to complete a very rough first draft before Casey wakes up. I read it over while he nurses, and later in the afternoon I'm still thinking about it, turning over ideas in my head, while Casey counts the dogs in his puzzle.

"Two dalmatians and one golden retriever."

I smile at him sincerely because I'm thinking about my story and am no longer bored living in his simple world.

At dinner I keep a pad of paper close by in case a thought occurs to me that I want to add to the article. My mind is actively engaged again. I'm not preoccupied with the latest episode of *Murphy Brown*.

I make an appointment with the newspaper's editor for the end of the week. This will require me to finish the story by then, and I thrive on deadlines. As I head to his office on Friday, I'm looking forward to working with someone out in the so-called real world again. I'm wearing a green sweater that shows off my breasts, which due to nursing are still larger than what's usual for me. The editor is a serious man in his fifties named Donny. It seems like a silly name for a man with gray hair and bifocals.

I stand across from him. Thankfully, I have no interest in sleeping with him. The stories he writes are thoughtful pieces about our city and its poorly funded schools and libraries in need of expansion. My story is exactly the opposite, a light piece detailing my adventures in the neighborhood with my fussy baby. Nervously I hand him my work. He reads it without smiling, not even when he comes to the part where I knock on the door of a complete stranger and ask if I can come in out of the rain to nurse my baby. I want to yank my story away from him and tell him that I didn't actually write it.

"It's good," he says, his face still expressionless. "I'll put it in the next issue."

"Great," I say.

He hands me a form and gestures toward a chair.

"That's our standard payment," he says.

I smile. I had forgotten that I was actually going to be paid.

"That's fine," I say.

BOB IS WAITING for me with Casey when I return home.

"Maybe you should have asked for more money," he says.

"It's a small newspaper. I don't think he was trying to rip me off," I say. "I'm not concerned about the money."

"Of course you aren't," he says irritably.

When the article comes out, I'm thrilled that everyone in the neighborhood now knows that I'm more than a mother at home with her child. I am employed. Neighbors ask me what else I'm planning to write about. I'm not exactly sure. I have lots of ideas, but the editor calls me the following week.

"I have a story that might be right up your alley," he says. "Can you come in tomorrow morning?"

"Well, I might have to bring my baby."

"That's fine."

Kendra calls to ask if I want to go to the zoo with her and Hannah.

"I have to meet with my editor," I tell her, and I feel so important when I say it.

Casey ends up staying home with Bob since my appointment is early in the morning. I arrive on time and wait in Donny's office while he finishes a call to some school board member. When he hangs up, he hands me a *Wall Street Journal* article. It's about mothers who choose to stay home even though their own mothers had high-power careers.

"I want a local angle on this. Are more mothers like this choosing to stay home with their kids, and if so, why?"

I consider turning the story down. It's too loaded. I don't want to annoy women who work outside the home. On the other hand, this story would help justify my existence. I would be seen as more than an at-home mother by virtue of writing the article about people whose existence needs justifying.

"I'll get right on it," I say in a voice that I imagine Lois Lane might use.

I work hard the next week, mostly when Casey is napping.

I interview women with home-based businesses, women with part-time jobs, and women who stay at home simply to be with their kids. To be balanced, I find a woman who stresses how important it is for moms to be at home only if it feels right for them. "It's not for everyone," she says. To keep from being sexist, I find at-home dads, too, and write a special sideline story about them to go with the main article. Mostly, though, I interview all of my friends.

"Why are you not working outside the home?" I ask Sheri from the playgroup.

"I didn't want to miss all the first things, his first step, his first words."

"How about if you say it this way," I tell her, and I hand over a sheet of paper.

"You've written down what you want me to say?"

"Well, only if you feel comfortable saying it."

"You know, I don't think this is the way reporters are supposed to do it."

I recall now why I had such a hard time as a reporter in the past. I always wanted to improve upon what people actually said. Sometimes I would write up the entire story before interviewing anyone, making up what I wanted them to say, thinking to myself, *Now I just have to find people willing to say these things.*

"You might be right, Sheri," I say. She hands me back the sheet of paper.

MY ARTICLE IS THE lead story of the next issue, and as pleased as I am with it, I'm not sure what kind of writing I want to do next.

"It's too hard to write these articles," I tell Bob.

"Sticking to the truth can be so limiting."

"Exactly," I say.

But working is good for me, calling everyone, using every spare minute to write and rewrite. I sit on the bathroom floor watching Casey pour water from one cup into another while I make necessary revisions. I don't need television anymore. I have watched only five hours this past week.

I show Rebecca my latest story the next time she comes over.

"I'll show Kendra your story when I see her tonight."

I smile. Casey and Camden are playing together and having a great time. I wish I could enjoy Rebecca, too, and I might, if she could just quit mentioning seeing Kendra.

DONNY CALLS ME to offer to give me extra copies of my latest article. I stop by with Casey to pick them up.

"I've got another story for you, if you're interested."

"What's it about?"

"The new community garden."

I nod. Community gardens can't be that controversial. And writing the story can't take up that much time.

I like freelancing work. I have a job and yet I don't have a job. I can think of myself as an at-home mother or as a professional out in the world. I can smoke pot, but not inhale.

I hand Casey one of the newspapers on our way out and he waves it around in his hands.

"Time for the swing," he says, and we head across the street to the park.

• • •

Bob is glad that I'm working.

"I'm still going to write fiction on the side," I tell him.

"Like a romance novel?"

"No."

"But will it have sex in it?" This seems to be a pressing concern of his right now, as we are in bed, but unfortunately for him, it isn't a pressing concern for me.

"It will have sex, but it won't be the romance novel kind," I say.

"What do you mean?"

"In romance novels, the woman is thrown on the bed like in *Gone with the Wind*."

"You read *Gone with the Wind*?"

"I saw the movie," I say. "Anyway, I would write a sex scene to appeal to women like me. The female character might still be thrown on the bed, but she would be almost forty, with five extra pounds, and she would probably be having her period. But the man, who would be perfectly fit, would be so good in bed that she wouldn't feel the slightest bit self-conscious and she would even forget that she's having her period."

"Didn't you try this once before?"

"Having sex with someone who was so good that I forgot I was having my period?"

"No, writing fiction."

"Well, that didn't really count," I say.

It was the summer after my first year of teaching and I made a writing schedule, which consisted of waking up by nine a.m. to watch reruns of *The Golden Girls* and *Kate and Allie,* followed by *Little House on the Prairie* at ten, *Streets of San Francisco* at eleven, and *Perry Mason* at noon. I would eat lunch and straighten up the house while watching *Donahue* and finally begin writing sometime between four and five p.m. until Bob came home, and then, of course, I would watch my prime-time programs after dinner.

I CALL MY MOTHER to tell her my new plan.

"Well, you're going to need a babysitter if you're serious about writing more," she says. "You remember Mrs. Small, don't you? She was retired. She watched you kids while I finished my dissertation."

"How can I forget her? Don't you remember the nightmares I used to have?"

"I don't recall."

"She used to read the Bible to us, Revelation mostly. Did you know that? And she gave sermons to us about hell and damnation all the time."

"Well, she was inexpensive. Retired people don't charge much."

"Good to know," I say, but I have no interest in someone such as Mrs. Small. To be on the safe side, I decide that I won't bother interviewing anyone older than me. I don't want some grandmother coming in and telling my child about the boogeyman, or worse, thinking she knows more than I do when it comes to raising kids just because she's already had them.

"Be glad you don't have to think about where the next nickel and dime is coming from," my mother says. "If you did, then the Mrs. Smalls of the world wouldn't look so bad."

"I'm very glad," I say, "but if I were ever worried about my next nickel and dime, I would work out a trade with Rebecca and Kendra," I tell her.

What I don't tell my mother is that even though Rebecca and Kendra have offered to babysit, they wouldn't like not being able to have the television on when they're with Casey. The last time

Kendra was at my house and we talked about my writing, she asked me if I wanted to borrow one of her videos.

"How do you think I managed to learn all those lines for my last play?" she said.

I smiled graciously and told her I'd manage, and then had to remind myself that I was actually managing, at least some of the time.

I LIKE TO THINK about what a help wanted ad would say for the electronic babysitter parents actually use, complete with prime time commercials and Saturday morning cartoons.

> Wanted: Young, sexy female needed to be with my children. Must not listen to or interact well with kids. Should be good at gyrating hips, flashing breasts, and engaging in other provocative behavior. Violent, hyper personality a plus. Must be willing to promote hundreds of products, especially junk food and Coca-Cola. Drug and alcohol use okay.

I am, of course, looking for exactly the opposite, and Bob thinks my standards are impossibly high.

"You'll never find anyone!" he says. I've just gotten Casey to bed and we're lying on the couch together.

"I've been interviewing people all week," I tell him. "I'm sure I'll find someone soon."

"Does this mean that we might actually get to go out together?" I'm resting my head on his chest and not in the mood for an argument.

"When I find the right person."

It's not that I haven't tried. I even invited over a few of the older girls in the neighborhood to play with Casey, but they were too young to be left in charge. I remember something Rebecca said when Casey was still fussing a lot: "He's the kind of baby that might get abused or neglected if you put him in day care," she said. Rebecca had worked in a day care center once and had seen that happen.

"What was so bad about Dana?" Bob asks me. I had mentioned her to him earlier.

"She thinks it's weird that I don't let Casey watch *Sesame Street*," I say, as I reposition my head on his chest. "And she watches a lot of television."

"Do they have to buy into every part of your parenting philosophy?" he asks.

"No, but you should have heard the stupid way she laughed. That dumb fake way she talked to Casey as if he were a baby."

"Isn't he a baby?" Bob asks.

I'm sitting up now. So much for relaxing.

"He's a one year old, and it's still no reason to laugh the way she did. She sounded like a middle school cheerleader."

Bob sighs.

"What about Leila, the one you interviewed before her?"

"I don't think Casey liked her. She hardly ever smiled. Plus she said she wanted to work here because of what her psychic told her."

"What's so bad about that?" Bob asks.

"Well, what if her psychic tells her to quit? Or worse, what if her psychic tells her to take Casey away to a commune where everyone has to worship a David Koresh type?"

"What is it that you want?" He is sitting up, too, now completely exasperated.

"Mary Poppins," I say. "We will go out on a date when I find Mary Poppins."

I INTERVIEW TEN more people before getting a referral from my friend Sarah. Sarah doesn't actually know the person whose name she is giving me, and so I'm especially skeptical. Her name is Kellie, and I decide to meet her away from my house at a neutral location. It's much easier to turn someone down when she's not sitting on your couch.

I ask her to be at Marco's, my favorite restaurant, at ten. She arrives on time, and although she hasn't floated down from the sky via umbrella, I know within minutes that I have found our Mary Poppins.

"I'm studying to be a midwife," she says. She has light brown hair just past her shoulders and a slight southern twang. She's from Kentucky.

I tell her about Casey's birth, leaving out the part about the endless orgasms. She seems interested and asks me more questions before telling me more about herself.

"I want you to know that I'm not really interested in working in a house where the television is on," she says.

"You're not?" I say, and I know my eyes are wide open.

"No. I just think it's a waste of my time and yours. Plus, I like taking care of kids who don't watch a lot of television. The last kids I babysat wanted to watch television no matter what else I suggested we do."

I think to myself that maybe Bob knew about this meeting and tipped her off so I would hire her. I look up at the ceiling of the restaurant and notice for the first time that there are more than a dozen colorful umbrellas suspended upside down from it. I'm sure it's a sign.

We try Kellie out the following Friday, and Casey doesn't cry when Bob and I leave for the evening. He cries when we return and it's time to say good-bye to her.

"Kellie going!" he says, his face streaked with tears.

I HIRE KELLIE for twelve hours a week, which includes a weekend date for me and Bob. I'm in such a good mood on our date, the first we've had since Casey was born, that I have sex with Bob in the car in the dark parking lot of the movie theater.

The next time Kellie comes over, it's during the day, and I'm completely at peace. It is a state of euphoria I haven't experienced since before Casey was born. Come to think of it, I don't think I experienced it then either. As they head over to the playground together, to the woods, or to the zoo, I know in my heart that my baby is in good hands. I am finally free.

My mother is delighted when I call to tell her about Kellie. I am sitting up in bed with my legs stretched out in front of me with the phone in one hand and a plate of nachos in the other.

"Maybe you'll get to do some serious writing now in addition to your work at the newspaper.

"Perhaps," I say, and think to myself that I will if I can just keep from watching television this time.

I'VE ENROLLED IN a writing class at Meredith College for extra motivation and to keep my teaching certificate current. Maybe this class will help me finally learn how to write with ease.

I'll be able to put my thoughts into a logical sequence, something kids like me raised on TV sometimes have trouble doing.

The class is taught by a thirty-something woman with three children. She is what I imagine a "writer" to be, someone whose life has been plagued with painful experiences. She reads us a short story she wrote based on her own life in which she describes how she lost the ability to see colors when her husband died unexpectedly. It was like living in a black-and-white movie, she writes. She sets down her story, which is in an actual book, thereby proving that she has been published. I assume this is supposed to impress us and it works for me.

"For your first assignment I want you to write about your elders and their influence on you. Think back to when you were a child and what you remember about your grandparents or other older people who shaped you," she says. "Then start writing." I look around the room and see people taking out pads of paper. She means now. Shit! What kind of class is this? I expected to sit back and pretend to take notes if I was tired until the hour was done. I pull out my pen and try to think. Everyone is already writing, even the teacher. She's getting paid to write with us. I look back at my own sheet of paper, completely blank. Who the heck are my elders anyway?

My grandparents were hardly ever around or they were dead. I decide to write about my mother's friend Lydia Fairbanks, a beautiful woman with long dark hair and olive skin who ran political campaigns in Texas. I guess she's my elder. I write about the day she sat with me on the curb outside her house. I was thirteen. Her husband and kids were inside. I had just finished babysitting.

"Yesterday when I saw Dennis," she told me, "I put my hand on his leg." Dennis was a young college student and campaign worker whom Lydia had a crush on. "He didn't move at first," she said, "but then he put his hand over mine. We were sitting together at a wide table at the Democratic headquarters, so no one could see what we were doing."

I put my best work into this essay, considering that I have just thirty minutes. I describe how my eyes were opened to the complicated issues that can arise in a marriage. I figure the teacher might even enjoy reading it, after having dwelled on death and a colorless existence for so long.

"Now we will go around the circle and share our work," she says. I stare at her dumbfounded. I look around the room. No one seems surprised. A girl on my left starts, so at least I'll get to be last if we continue in a clockwise direction. I listen as one student after another reads about baking pies with a grandmother or learning to fish with a granddad. When it is at last my turn, I read as quietly as possible. No one says anything. I set my pad of paper down.

I want to leave immediately, but I don't.

It will get easier, I tell myself on the drive home.

The following week, I loosen up a little and tell an equally embarrassing story. My classmates like my writing, and I keep telling myself, that if all goes well, I won't have to see these people ever again when the course is done.

At home I'm finding that I can actually be entertained by writing and I really like to be entertained. When Kellie arrives or when Casey takes a nap, sometimes I actually hurry to the computer to fix the piece on which I'm working. If the phone rings, I don't always answer it. It's the way I used to feel about telephone interruptions when I was watching television. And last week I watched only six hours.

"Writing can be a television substitute," I tell Bob proudly.

We are in the kitchen and he has just come home to a stack of dirty dishes on the counter.

"That's great, but I was sort of hoping that maybe cleaning the house might be a substitute for television, too." He is aiming for humor because he doesn't want to come across as some sort of pig. He doesn't expect to walk into a clean house and have me fetch his slippers, the way Samantha might have done for Darrin on *Bewitched*. Of course, Samantha had witchcraft to help her get the housework done, at least when she wasn't trying to live the mortal life.

I don't have witchcraft, and unfortunately cleaning doesn't rise to the top of my list of priorities on a day-to-day basis. Part of the problem is the way I was raised to feel about housework.

Cleanliness is next to godliness was not embroidered and displayed in the kitchen I knew as child. When my mother came back from a political convention once, she brought home a poster that she proudly hung up on the wall next to the refrigerator. FUCK HOUSEWORK, it read, and those words became our household slogan. We all detested cleaning, and often found ourselves staring at plates and pans coated with dried-on gravy, week-old pot roast, and pieces of moldy chicken sandwiches.

My mother used to shout, "You're a bunch of parasites, all of you!" I wasn't sure at first what a parasite was, but I could tell it wasn't good.

Even after the roaches came, we didn't change our ways. I remember watching my mother in the kitchen making coffee while I served myself a piece of peach pie. "Cover it up when you're done," she would shout as she hurriedly placed a bowl over the butter dish in front of her before the roaches could get to it. These roaches were bold Texas roaches. They needed only a few seconds to overtake whatever they considered edible. I had a great opportunity to observe their life cycle, the tiny babies that grouped together on the cutting board next the stove, the oversized adult roaches that took off across the dining room table while we were eating dinner.

The rats were worse. After finding a beady-eyed one in the bathroom early in the morning, I stayed home from school and without consulting my mother called a pest control service I found in the yellow pages. The exterminator who came over was a Vietnam vet who had recently returned from the war. He was still in combat mode. After surveying the house, he pulled up a chair and spoke quietly, as though he feared an enemy might be listening.

"You've got about three hundred rats in your attic," he said. He went on to tell me more than I had ever wanted to know about the species, about dominant male rats that sometimes consume their own kind and sewer rats that can swim for miles before they emerge from people's toilets. Then he gave me an article, which had a list of "Rat Facts." Number one was "A rat the size of a small opossum can compress its body to fit through a hole the size of a quarter."

Needless to say, I didn't sleep well after he left. Eventually we brought home cats to get rid of the rats, but each cat brought a treasure trove of fleas. I used to put sheets on the furniture before sitting down, in hopes of not getting bitten before I had watched my morning programs. "What's with all the sheets?" my mother would ask. She never noticed the fleas.

As an adult, I did manage to become a little neater, mostly after I bought a portable television to help me clean. With *M*A*S*H* in the background, I could keep my mind off the menial nature of the work and block out my mother's words, stuck in my head. "Where is the satisfaction in this?" she would say when she actually did clean. "This is the work that women have always had to do while men throughout the ages have been able to create art and share profound ideas!"

Now I not only don't have a portable television, but I also have a toddler and his little friends who aren't exactly neat and tidy.

"Things get messier now," I explain to Bob.

He shoves the stack of dirty dishes aside and starts filling the sink with water. "I thought that with Kellie helping and having Clarissa once a week that maybe you could do a little extra," he says, no longer trying to sound like a sensitive New Age guy. I frown.

Clarissa is the housekeeper who comes once a week. She is a large, good-natured woman with bleached blond hair. She is my age but she already has two grandchildren. I give her toys Casey has outgrown. I do this mostly because I feel bad that she has to scrub our toilets.

I try to explain how I feel to Bob. "When I have free time away from Casey, I don't want to spend it cleaning. I'll feel resentful if I do."

To me, not getting resentful is one of the keys to good parenting.

I don't want to end up like Rebecca. She's constantly getting annoyed with Camden and complaining about her husband, who expects her to have dinner on the table and a clean kitchen every night. That's why she puts Camden in front of the television, to get everything done. Kendra does the same thing, except that she has a television in her kitchen, too, so she can watch CNN while Hannah is in her room watching *Blues Clues*.

Last year Bob and I went to the Street of Dreams, an exhibit in the Portland metroplex of some of the newest and most ostentatious houses available. Each of the houses had multiple televisions:

in the kitchen, the family room, and in each of the bedrooms. Most had big screen theater rooms as well. Is that what Bob wants? I don't think so.

"It will be better when Mama comes back," I tell him.

He looks at me incredulously. He's seen the FUCK HOUSEWORK poster in my mother's kitchen.

"She keeps me company while I clean," I remind him.

At least my perspective on cleanliness has become more realistic. I'm seeing more actual houses rather than just the ones I saw on television growing up. There were no colorful blocks strewn about even if a baby was in the show. Even the single working mom on *The Partridge Family* had a house free of dirty socks and overflowing ashtrays on her coffee table.

I glance over at Casey, who happily views the chaos of our house as one big playground. He is in the middle of the carpet putting pink and purple dinosaurs in the secret passageways of a big volcano. Bob, on the other hand, doesn't look happy at all. I want to put my arms around him and make all kinds of promises to him, but I know I won't keep them. That's what I used to do, until he stopped believing me.

"I'll work on it," I tell him. "But I'm not going to use my time away from Casey to clean, and I'm not going to put Casey in front of the television so I can write."

"I wasn't asking you do that," he says and stalks away. I wonder if the portable television might have to come back after all.

I REMEMBER WHEN I was eight years old climbing into bed with my mother because I couldn't sleep. I had just had a bad dream. Rather than singing a pretty song to me or telling me a cute fairy tale, she picked up the book by her bed and started reading it aloud. It was *The Autobiography of Malcolm X*. It wasn't exactly age appropriate, but it was something she needed to read in order to teach her black history class the next day. I'm sure she reasoned that she might as well kill two birds with one stone, get the kid back to sleep and get ready for her class.

Maybe that's how I should approach the housecleaning problem I have now. Maybe the answer has been sitting right in front of me — or climbing all over me, as the case may be.

Bob has gone to work. He was in a slightly better mood when he left, which is the only reason I feel like trying to be helpful.

I reach out and take Casey's little hand in mine.

"Let's go look for dishes," I say, as if I've suggested that we're going on an Easter egg hunt.

"Dishes," he says as he accompanies me to the living room.

"We're collecting dishes to put in the dishwasher," I say. I grab a cup and saucer and carry them in my left hand.

"Putting the plate in," he says when we are back in the kitchen.

I carefully place the cup and saucer in the dishwasher and he smiles approvingly.

I push a straight-back chair up to the counter and let him help rinse. It isn't as painful as it could be.

"You get to rinse the plastic ones," I say.

"Mama cleans the glass ones," he says as I pick up a coffee mug.

"That's right!"

"Rinsing the blue sippy cup," he says as the water flows over the rim of his cup. "Rinsing the yellow one."

As we stand beside each other, I'm amazed at his enthusiasm. This is not a deadly boring task to him, and as we work together, it no longer feels like total drudgery to me either. In some ways, it's even entertaining. Certainly it can compete with *Highway to Heaven*.

I finish loading the dishes he has rinsed and wipe the counters around us. Casey's shirt is soaked and the floor below him is spotted with puddles.

"Next time you get to wear your painting smock," I say. But I'm not concerned about the mess or the extra time it has taken to do the dishes together. That's hardly the point.

"We'll do this after lunch, too," I say as I change his shirt.

We sit on the couch together later and admire our work. At least I can help Casey have a good attitude about cleaning. Maybe he'll grow up learning that doing dishes is a natural part of a sequence. We cook, we eat, we clean up after ourselves, and in the simplicity of it all we find joy in our work and each other's company. Stranger things have happened.

I call Kendra to tell her about my new strategy. "The point is that by combining two tedious activities, cleaning and caring for a toddler, neither activity feels quite as tedious." I want to tell her what I think is the real accomplishment, which is that I was able to resist using television for both.

"That's nice," she says, and I can tell she thinks I'm absolutely out of touch. Maybe I am. After all, I am doing something that my ancestors did. My mother, who grew up on a farm, said she learned how to drive a tractor when she was ten. When there wasn't the option of plugging the kids in, grown-ups included kids in their work.

I hang up the phone and sit back on the couch with Casey.

"I like cleaning the kitchen with you," I tell him.

"Dishes all done," he says smiling, and he looks truly happy, much happier than all of the people in the commercials who are only pretending to be enthralled with their sparkling pots and pans.

I smile back at him. We are teachers and students, both of us.

"WE CLEANED THE KITCHEN!" Casey tells Dad excitedly as soon as Bob walks in the door.

"I see," Bob says, and he is clearly surprised.

I look away from him, suddenly afraid that he'll expect this to happen every day and I'll be relegated to nothing more than a housekeeper, a housekeeper who gives blow jobs. Maybe I made a mistake.

Bob grabs Casey by the hand. "You can help me do the laundry, too."

"Wow that will be fun!" I say to Casey, and already I'm feeling better about Bob. At least we will all be relegated to housekeepers.

"Throw the laundry down," he tells Casey when they are at the top of the stairs.

Casey gleefully empties the hamper, tossing socks and towels and underwear down into the hallway outside of the laundry room. Then Bob puts the clean pile of clothes from the dryer into a basket along with Casey.

"Going for a ride," Casey says as Bob pushes him across the floor. He sets the basket on the couch.

"Now we get to sort the dirty clothes into piles," Bob tells him. "You can do the reds and pinks and other colors. I'll start a load of whites."

They are both laughing and making a sport of it. I almost join in, but I stop myself in the nick of time. Why should I interfere with their father-son bonding? Besides, it's probably not as fun as it looks.

7

. . . .

Kid Friendly

Mama arrives carrying an extra suitcase of old books she has brought for Casey. They are reference books from Goodwill, and some of them are so dated, I'm sure I'll get rid of them as soon as she leaves. But there is a newer series, too, about continents. I flip through the pages in the South America one and show Casey the golden lion tamarin.

"So he's still not watching any television?" she asks.

"None at all, so far," I say.

She looks disappointed. She's probably returned to her solitary habits in Texas and isn't ready to withdraw from television again, just as I'm cutting back more than ever.

When Casey takes a nap, I follow her upstairs to the bonus room. I move her chair up close to the television and move mine farther back behind hers. She turns around toward me.

"Don't you like sitting next to me?"

"I just want to be able to hear people when I'm sixty."

I take boxes of books out of the storage space and stack them up three feet high around her.

"I feel like I'm in a fort," she says. "Casey would like this."

"Casey is the reason you're in this fort," I explain. "He's pretty mobile now, upstairs and downstairs."

"Why don't we just shut the door then?"

"The cat box is in here now." I point to it. "Fluff needs to come and go as he pleases." I'm sure my mother wishes she could do the same.

It's almost eight o'clock and she settles in behind the fortress. "Do you want to watch *60 Minutes* with me?"

"Sorry," I say, and walk away.

She tries her luck later with Bob, who is downstairs reading to Casey.

"There's a great special on the Civil War that comes on at eight," she suggests.

He looks up at her briefly. "Maybe I'll tape it."

She heads back upstairs. I consider giving in to watch it with her, but it's too brainy of a topic. I decide to take a bath instead.

I sink back into water much hotter than Casey would be able to handle and close my eyes. The luxury of a hot bath is something I will never take for granted again after having shared so many lukewarm ones with my child. Baths are my favorite television replacement.

I'm drying off when I hear Casey upstairs. Bob is on the phone, explaining why he has no interest in supporting Oregon State Public Interest Research Group. "I'm not sure I understand what you're spending your money on." It sounds like something he would like to say to me after opening our Visa bill.

I open the door and notice that Casey is wandering into the bonus room.

"Mama?" he calls.

"Come here," my mother says, from behind her fortress.

I wrap a towel around my body and stand near the doorway, quietly watching them. She picks him up and lifts him over.

"The world," she says in a soft, soothing tone, pointing to a globe turning around on the screen. It is the beginning of one of her public television shows. He turns away to study the fortress, standing in my mother's line of vision.

"Look, it's spinning," she says enthusiastically, and she moves him back so he's facing the set again. I run into the room, not bothering to catch the towel that is falling off of my breasts.

"Hi, Casey," I say excitedly.

He turns and squeezes out of the fortress.

"Hi, Mom," he calls out. The sight of my naked breasts is enough to distract him from the television. Maybe they're enough to distract the next-door neighbor, too, since our curtains aren't drawn.

I pick him up and grab the remote to turn the set off.

"Why not offer him heroin, too," I say to my mother.

"You're so melodramatic," she says.

"That's because I've watched a lot of television," I say.

AFTER CASEY GOES to bed, I manage to move the television into the guest room.

"But it's not that comfortable to watch in there," Bob says when he sees what I've done.

"You can move a chair from the dining room and put it in the corner," I say curtly.

"But the bonus room is so much bigger. We could all watch there."

"We can all get on the bed to watch," I tell him. "It'll be like a slumber party."

Bob rolls his eyes. He isn't exactly on slumber-party terms with my mother.

MAMA IS DELIGHTED with the change. She keeps the schedule and remote next to her bed and would probably fall asleep watching the latest made-for-TV movie, if I didn't complain.

"It's too loud," I tell her the third night that she leaves it on after ten p.m. I storm back into bed after making her turn it off.

Bob looks annoyed with me. He thinks I should be more tolerant. "You could barely hear it from our room," he says.

"I could hear it and I couldn't sleep!"

"Why are you so cranky about it?"

"I just don't care for it."

I don't tell him the truth, which is that I'm jealous. If anyone is going to get to stay up watching television until they pass out, it should be me. And if it can't be me, I sure as heck don't want to be in the same house with someone else who gets to do it. God, I'm getting to be like my former neighbor, Tiffany. We lived in the same apartment complex when Bob was in law school. A recovering alcoholic, she was always telling me exactly how long she'd been clean and sober. "Three years, four months, two days now."

"That's great," I'd say, glad that I hadn't had anything to drink lately, because Tiffany kept track of everyone else's drinking, too. "I can smell wine on her breath," she'd say about the old woman who lived across the street. Sometimes she would casually glance into our recycling bin. "Lots of beer bottles in there," she'd say. Maybe she's part of the reason I haven't wanted to know my neighbors. She was less tolerant of drinkers than anyone I knew, but then, of course, I had known mostly alcoholics.

I lie back on the bed wondering if I'm actually becoming Tiffany, someone unable to be around anyone who has not freed themselves from whatever their dreaded vice is, in my case television. What if I end up like the Baptists I knew in Texas, totally preoccupied with sex because they aren't having it? That is not part of my plan. I'm supposed to be easygoing about the whole thing. I'm supposed to be like Sam on *Cheers,* I remind myself, except that Sam isn't a real person. Maybe there aren't any Sams in real life. I don't know any recovering alcoholics who own bars. I don't know any ex-smokers who like being around smokers. Most of them complain louder than the people who never smoked in the first place.

But I'm not like Tiffany, I tell myself. If I were, I would know exactly how many days I've been without television, or at least how long it's been since I've watched more than two hours a week. Of course, I have yet to reach that goal, but I have kept track of Casey's time without it. He's almost two years old and hasn't watched anything. This is a significant victory. It might not be something I tell my friends about. One by one they are putting their kids in front of a set for longer and longer periods of time.

My mother is reading my latest story. "You make everything sound really exciting," she says.

"When you've seen a lot of commercials, it's easy to put a positive spin on even the most boring event," I tell her. She has just finished reading about a do-it-yourself auto repair class for women.

Unfortunately, I'm working on a story about pet day care. I've been staring at my laptop screen and notes for fifteen minutes. I'm tempted to give it up and watch *First Wives Club.* I look over my notes again, trying to focus. Kellie is with Casey and I'm sure my mother would like to watch a good movie. She's still annoyed that she has to turn the television off at ten each night.

She sets down the newspaper and heads upstairs. I fiddle with the cursor for a few minutes before I go after her. I find her in the guest room looking at the TV guide. I want to grab it away from her, but I take a deep breath instead, the way I would in a yoga class.

"I don't want you to watch television while I'm writing," I say sort of calmly.

"But you're not writing and you won't let me read anything that you have written!"

"I let you read all my articles."

"You don't trust me enough to share your other work," she says at last.

"But I trust you enough *not* to read what I've written," I say. "That's even better."

She shakes her head in wonder, not understanding that I have just given her a compliment. She was never a nosy parent. She never searched my room or made me take a drug test. My brother and sister were the nosy ones in the family. I had to stuff my diaries under my mattress so my sister wouldn't find them, and plug up the holes my brother had bored into the wall dividing our rooms when I discovered that he had been inviting his friends to watch me undress.

I like to think that my sister and brother have improved with time, but my sister still picks up the phone to eavesdrop on conversations and the last time my brother came for a visit he brought a listening device, a scanner of some sort.

"You want to hear your neighbors' phone calls?" he asked.

"No," I said. "I have no interest."

He looked disappointed. Maybe it was his idea of how to enliven a party. I asked him to pack the thing away and not use it until he got home.

"I'll let you read something of mine," I say to my mother, "if you come downstairs." She sets the TV guide down and follows me reluctantly.

"Here, this is from my writing class." We are back in the kitchen and I hand her the piece I wrote the first day of class.

"You wrote about Lydia Fairbanks!" she says after she finishes the first paragraph. She adjusts her glasses and continues reading. "I had no idea she was sharing this sort of personal information with you. You were way too young!"

"I was thirteen."

She is on the second page now. When she gets to the end, she sighs.

"The problem was that Todd never gave her oral sex."

"She never told me that," I say.

"I'm surprised she didn't."

LOTS OF ADDICTIONS are easy to be around. You don't necessarily notice them. In college I simply shrugged my shoulders and said to myself, "To each his own," when my roommate's boyfriend snorted a line of cocaine in our room. But I never let him smoke in front of me because I would have been forced to breathe in the smoke whether I wanted to or not. Television is like smoking. Casey is accosted by it as soon as we step out our door.

Bob, Casey, and I have just arrived at Emma's birthday party, and amid the Disney decorations, a big-screen TV is blaring, right there in the family room, and it's a small room. It fills the entire space with its presence. Emma and her mother, Charlotte, are from the playgroup, although they have attended only once or twice. The last time Charlotte came she was wearing a Borders bookstore T-shirt. I figured that she must be a reader, maybe someone who shuns TV. I should have known better. I once wore a shirt that said, WISCONSIN, THE LAND OF THE MANY LAKES, although I'd never been to Wisconsin and I didn't know anything about its lakes.

I turn to Charlotte's husband, Billy, and try to sound relaxed, jovial even.

"*The Lion King?*" I say.

"Yeah, I just thought it would be good to have it on in the background," he says. "They've probably all seen it."

I nod, all warm and friendly. I remember when I was watching a lot of television and one of my neighbors came over and I left the set on in the background because I wasn't sure what we would have to say to each other. But I wasn't a two-year-old.

I clutch Bob's arm and whisper to him, "What should we do about it?" Obviously, I don't have to tell him what "it" is. My body language is a giveaway. Anyone who didn't know me would think I'd seen a rifle in the room.

"Just ignore it," he says, in what would never pass as a whisper.

"Well, I'll just see what there is to eat," I say, as I quickly escort Casey into the kitchen. I look around for Kendra and Rebecca, but don't see either one of them yet.

I pile up a plate with strawberries and grapes.

"Are they seedless grapes?" Casey asks.

"I think so," I say, sticking one of them into my mouth.

The kitchen is small, and the chairs have all been moved into the living room in front of the television. The only other rooms in the house are bedrooms, and no one is gathering in there. I sit on the carpet with Casey, so his back is facing the screen. We make the most of the food, as there doesn't seem to be another activity planned besides eating and watching *The Lion King.* There is no colorful piñata, no pile of wooden blocks, no books.

In a far corner of the room I spot a basket with a few toys. Bob brings them over to us. I call over Sonia's son, McGregor, a regular since the first playgroup. He stops watching the movie to see the shape toy I have found. Casey is in front of me while I gather the triangles and squares.

Kendra arrives and comes over after she has parked Hannah in front of the movie.

"How long have you been here?" she asks.

"Not long," I say in an unnatural voice. I am too preoccupied with Casey and McGregor to say anything else to her. She heads to the kitchen.

"I can't hear the movie," Miranda complains. Miranda is Emma's older cousin and she's standing eight inches away from the screen. I've seen this movie and even from my distance I recognize the voice of Scar, the evil uncle who kills Simba's father.

Miranda's mom comes in and turns up the volume.

Casey and McGregor look away from me for a second.

I hand them each a triangle. I am working hard to keep my voice down and still keep them engaged, which is difficult because I am also trying to keep Casey from shifting positions, lest he catch a glimpse of the movie. Charlotte comes over.

"Doesn't he want to watch the movie?" she asks me.

"We're having a lot of fun here," I say, holding up a plastic circle and trying to look thrilled about it.

"It's not a scary movie," she assures me.

"We're fine," I say, still feigning cheerfulness and willing her to go away. I don't want Casey to know that I care one way or another about the television, so I'm trying to act casual. I wish I could just nonchalantly ask Charlotte to take her TV outside, the way someone with allergies can ask a guest to take a dog outside.

I look at the clock above the mantle. It's been forty minutes. How long until the cake, I wonder. Surely, they'll turn the television off when the cake is served and it's time to open presents. It's just supposed to be background, after all.

Bob looks frustrated, too, but probably not for the same reason. Toddler parties don't excite him, with or without videos. He wants nothing to do with our little shape game and my valiant attempts to keep Casey from seeing a bunch of animated jungle animals.

I glance about the room. Sheri's boy, Kenny, from the playgroup, is wandering away from the set. I invite him to join us. He toddles over, and now we are three. I smile deviously. I have lured him away from the evil hyena who has Whoopi Goldberg's voice.

"This is a shaker, too," I tell them, and I close the lid over the container holding the geometric shaped pieces. "Listen!" I say, and I vigorously shake it.

Sonia comes out of the kitchen to check on McGregor.

"Maybe we can ask Charlotte to turn the movie off," I whisper quietly to her, so Casey can't hear what I'm saying. "McGregor isn't watching either."

Sonia says she doesn't want to make waves. I'm sure Kendra wouldn't want to either. Everyone thinks I'm some sort of freak. *It's just* The Lion King, they would say. *It's not* Die Hard 2. But to me it's still Pandora's box and I'm not ready to open it yet. I ask Bob what he thinks when he comes over to check on us.

"I'm not asking them to turn it off," he says, "if that's what you're suggesting."

I turn back to Casey and marvel at the shape container, as though it's the most exciting thing I've ever seen.

"WHAT I'M DOING isn't as difficult as talking about what I'm doing with others," I tell Georgette. "It's so hard sometimes."

I'm sitting in Georgette's floral-patterned stuffed chair with a wool blanket wrapped around my legs. Georgette is sitting across from me. Today her hair has two tiny braids falling down against the left side of her face. I've just finished telling her about Emma's party.

"It's hard because you're not being honest," she says.

I consider what I could I have said at Emma's party. "Charlotte, it's fine if you have the television on, but I'm not really interested in having Casey watch it until he's a little older." I wouldn't have to ask her to turn it off. I could keep playing with Casey in the corner, but at least I wouldn't have to expend so much energy keeping my thoughts a secret. On the other hand, it would probably sound rude and judgmental no matter what. That's what happened when Bob and I were at a photography studio with Casey.

The photographer, who wasn't much older than eighteen, kept trying to get Casey to smile by holding up a stupid Elmo puppet. When that didn't work, she tried a *Blues Clues* puppet. Finally, after several more tries with several more TV show puppets, she turned to me and asked in exasperation, "What programs does he watch?" I gave her a sour look and informed her that, believe it or not, my child hasn't watched television. I told her that it was too bad that she wasn't a very creative photographer, but that people who watch a lot television often aren't.

I feel embarrassed to admit to Georgette that this is what I said. "That's what happens when I try to tell the truth."

Georgette nods, her eyes full of understanding. She's good at conveying understanding.

"You just need more practice, that's all," she says. She pauses to take a sip of her tea. "But don't worry. You'll get lots of other opportunities." Her eyes sparkle when she says this.

I smile weakly. "I'm not sure I want more opportunities," I say finally.

She sighs now and speaks slowly, exuding the utmost patience.

"You are a teacher, Ellen. It's time for you to own that." She's leaning forward, the way she always does when she's making these sorts of statements. "There is work to be done, work that you are meant to do."

I'm not really sure where she gets these ideas about me, but she has yet to lead me astray.

WHEN I COME HOME, I find my mother upstairs in the guest room studying the fall lineup. Casey and Bob are in the family room reading picture books together.

I'm thinking about what Georgette said, about all the times I could have spoken up, the times I could have said something, that it might have made a difference, maybe even helped someone. My mother never hesitated to speak out. It's why she can support me now in my television zealotry. She may not agree with it or even understand it, but she understands what it is to be committed to a cause.

"You might like this episode of *Mad About You*," she says, referring to a passage in the TV guide. "It says Helen Hunt is going to breastfeed her baby in public."

"Fine," I say. I'm too weary to care about my television goal for myself anymore. Anyway, the show is about breastfeeding. And just because I decide to watch this show doesn't mean I will end up watching *Seinfeld* and *Frasier* afterwards.

I stretch out on the bed next to my mother to watch. "See, she's nursing!" my mother exclaims a few minutes into the show. Helen Hunt is breastfeeding her tiny baby at her husband's place of employment and later at a restaurant. My mother glances my way hoping that I am pleased. She wants me to jump up and down and tell her how wrong I've been about television. She wants me to tell her how progressive and neat it is, in hopes that everything can be like it was in the old days, when we spent hours and hours watching TV together. She wants me to put Casey on this bed to watch with us, so we won't have to take care of him anymore.

But I am unimpressed. "Helen is breastfeeding an infant," I say. "So what? She's less than two months old. It won't last long." She tells me to wait and see. Of course I'll wait, because I'm watching television and I rarely stop watching before any show ends.

But by the time the show is almost over, I'm more than just unimpressed.

"Look!" I say to my mother. "The baby has ended up with a bottle of formula. They could have had Helen pumping and storing her milk for her husband to use!" I say impatiently.

"You're right," she concedes.

"And did you notice the formula company, right there featured on the show, in case the commercials you see every day aren't enough!"

"I did," she says quietly.

"The formula companies probably pay to have scripts like this."

"Hmmm," my mother says, and then she doesn't say anything else, and I don't either because *Seinfeld* is coming on. It's not a groundbreaking episode, but at least it doesn't annoy me. I'm not looking to be impressed with television anyway, just entertained.

KENDRA DOESN'T MENTION Emma's party, nor does she ask why Casey wasn't watching *The Lion King*. She and Hannah are coming over to trick-or-treat with us because our street is the safest.

"Be here at five-thirty," I tell her over the phone.

"One thing," she says and her voice sounds strained. "Hannah is going to be a Teletubby." She hesitates. "Will Casey be okay with that?"

"I'm sure he will be fine with that," I say. I think, *Why would he care if his friend is dressed up like a deformed baby alien?*

"Well, it's a television program," she says.

"I know, Kendra." She must think I'm an idiot. Every adult who listens to the news or reads the paper has heard of the Teletubbies. Even NPR covered the gay Teletubby controversy. Kendra probably thinks I stand in front of the television set telling Casey how bad shows like *Teletubbies* are and making sure he knows that he is forbidden from ever seeing them. But Casey doesn't know or care about television, much less the Teletubbies.

"I don't have a problem with Casey knowing television characters, Kendra," I say truthfully.

"Oh, well, I didn't know."

I hang up the phone and it dawns on me that Kendra doesn't understand the subtlety of my method with Casey. I feel like one of those artists creating something no one understands. I am Van Gogh without the desire to amputate part of my ear.

Kendra and Hannah arrive a few minutes later.

"Hannah is a Teletubby," I tell Casey. "It's from a television show." I want to ask Kendra if Hannah likes the gay one. I imagine bigoted parents having a heated discussion on the topic: *He can be the blue one or the green one, but he is not going to parade through our neighborhood dressed up like Tinky Winky.*

That their toddler is staring at a screen for hours doesn't concern them as long as all of the TV characters are straight.

Casey looks at Hannah. He doesn't have much to say about her Teletubby costume and neither does Hannah. I help Casey into his.

"He's a monkey," I tell them.

"What kind?" Kendra says.

"I'm a howler monkey," Casey says.

"They live in Costa Rica," I say.

Kendra takes a picture of Casey with me and Bob. When Bob puts his arm around me, I lean in toward him affectionately for the perfect family photo. Then I zip up my raincoat, although thankfully the sky is clear. It's my first time to trick-or-treat since I was a child. Kendra takes Hannah's hand and I grab a hold of Casey's, feeling nostalgic.

"Say 'trick or treat' when we come to the first house," we tell them.

They take turns ringing the doorbell and we help them carry their candy around in plastic orange pumpkins. We make it around the entire loop in an hour and a half. Kendra and Hannah come inside when they're done.

"Let's see what you have," Bob says.

Hannah is eating a package of SweeTARTS. Casey dumps out his pumpkin and starts sorting his candy into piles, the shiny gold ones, the brown, the red, and the green ones.

"Do you want some, Dad?" he asks, holding up a package of peanut butter cups.

"Maybe later," he says.

Casey doesn't want to eat his candy. It's not that he doesn't like sweets. He loves cookies and muffins from the coffee shop near our house, just not candy. I suppose he'll have great teeth, but I worry that he will become so different from Hannah and every other kid. No one will like him, and it will be my fault for not exposing him to thousands of Snickers commericals.

"Do you want some of these?" he asks Hannah. She takes a Kit Kat from him. At least he's happy to share his candy, which could make him a few friends.

"You were a wonderful Teletubby!" I say to Hannah as they're leaving. Kendra smiles and I try to reassure myself with what Georgette said about friends not having to be just alike. Then I wonder if Georgette has any Republican friends with Armani suits. It seems unlikely.

BOB TURNS OUT the lights and blows out the jack-o'-lanterns. I'm hoping we won't be disturbed by any last minute trick-or-treaters. We are lying on the couch just in case.

Without television to distract us, I always imagined we would be having even more sex. But that's what I imagined when I was still pregnant and not yet a parent. Now that Casey's here, even when he's sound asleep, I think about what time he'll wake up in the morning and wonder how much sleep I'll get. I know every hour spent having sex is one less hour I could have spent sleeping.

Bob snuggles against me only too aware of my hierarachy of needs. He reaches for the zipper of my jeans and pulls them off in a couple of seconds.

"Remember just do the stuff I really like, nothing else," I command. He doesn't answer because he's already busy. In the past I would have been happy to let him take his time fumbling around in my pleasure zones, because whatever he was doing would eventually do the trick. But now that time is of the essence, I don't even bother being subtle. "That's not working," I say if I haven't had an orgasm after five minutes. I'd like to say that I'm not fixated on climaxing and that the deep spiritual, tantric connection is what really matters, but it isn't true.

I only know that if Bob is going to be inside me, the preliminary orgasms are a must.

"That's it," I say breathlessly after a few minutes, and he grabs a condom.

"Just do it the way I told you," I say, and he does, and surprisingly, he doesn't seem to mind.

BY THE TIME December rolls around, I'm dreaming about playing in the snow and sledding down hills with Casey. We don't get much snow in Portland, but it's in the forecast for tomorrow.

Casey and I are at Meier & Frank looking for a snowsuit. I'm not used to shopping for his clothes because Bob's parents send loads of stuff to us from Lands' End and Hanna Anderson.

Yesterday I asked Rebecca where I should shop. I didn't mention that Kendra and Hannah had come over to trick-or-treat with us. I figured if Kendra says anything to her, at least Rebecca will see that I'm not trying to flaunt the friendship.

"Go to Gymboree," Rebecca said. "It's really kid friendly. They usually have *Arthur* on and Camden will gladly sit there until I've finished all of my shopping."

"That's nice," I said, but maybe I sounded smug. I've been to Gymboree and having a television on is not exactly my idea of being kid friendly.

"Oh, that's right. You wouldn't like that."

"No, that's fine," I lied. I didn't want her to think I would be a total pain in the ass to shop with. I pictured her shopping with Kendra. They would leisurely peruse the racks while their children watched *The Little Mermaid*. Later, when they had finished shopping, they might get together at one of their houses and have tea while their kids watched *The Berenstain Bears*. I would just be in the way.

I hold Casey's hand as we go up the escalator to the second floor of Meier & Frank. When I see the sign for the children's department, I'm struck by how open it is all around. Gymboree, in spite of its television, feels safer because it has only one entrance and exit, one and the same. I hold Casey's hand a little tighter as we make our way over to the kids' clothing. Then I see it, right in front of us, a giant screen showing a video with the characters Casey knows and loves from his favorite Winnie the Pooh books. I carefully maneuver him to my other side and look for a salesperson. There isn't anyone in sight.

"Look at this great big Kanga," I say, quickly moving to the pile of stuffed animals opposite the big screen. I hand Casey Kanga and he hugs her against his chest.

"She has a little Roo," he says, pointing to Kanga's pouch. I am positioning my body in front of the screen, acting cheerful and casual in a manic sort of way. I can hear Kendra's voice in my head, *It's just a Pooh video, for God's sake!* She's has a point, except that I want the books to remain special in Casey's imagination. I want Piglet to remain a she for a while longer. "There just aren't enough female characters," I explained to Casey when we started reading the books, and he agreed.

Casey is trying to take the Roo out of Kanga's pouch. I edge my way closer to the imposing screen, glancing around cautiously. I press the power button and make the screen go blank, then I smile gleefully. I'm like Julia Butterfly Hill, the woman who lived in a giant Redwood to save it from the forestry company. I am brave and defiant. Some might say intense and extreme, but I'm sure they said it about Julia Butterfly Hill, too.

I glance around me. There are still no other children or salespeople in sight. I am victorious. I suddenly wish I could do this all over town, sneaking around turning off televisions everywhere: doctors' offices, restaurants, day care centers. That would be so much more satisfying than learning to express my feelings in a healthy way.

We walk over to the racks of coats and I pick one out as quickly as I can. A red one with a hood. Casey likes red. On our way out, a mother with a three-year-old in tow looks up at the blank screen and tells her daughter, "I don't know where Pooh has gone." I want to point to the table opposite the blank screen where at least ten Poohs are waiting to be noticed, soft, cuddly baby ones and large, squeezable, toddler-size Poohs next to all of the Piglets and Eeyores. Casey puts the Kanga and Roo back in the pile, just as a sales clerk approaches.

"Well, I don't know how that happened," she says exasperated, as she fiddles with the VCR button. I don't say anything as we hurry out.

"WHY DON'T YOU just tell Casey not to look at the television in those places?" Bob asks me the next morning. He is calling from work.

"Then I would have to explain why, and I don't want to do that."

"Why not?"

"I don't want to draw attention to it. It's better for him to remain happily oblivious. That's why he hasn't asked to watch it."

"Sounds exhausting for you," he says. "I mean, would it really hurt if he watched occasionally somewhere else?"

"Yes, it would," I say as firmly as I can sound, as much to convince myself as Bob.

He doesn't argue. He knows that I have a stubborn streak, and I can't deny it. When I was nine, I told my mother that I wasn't going to eat mayonnaise anymore, not anywhere, not on anything. I stuck with my promise until I moved away from home. I suppose that I could agree with Bob that in certain situations, a little TV would be okay for Casey, but television is now the way mayonnaise was for me then. I'm steadfastly commited to keeping Casey away from it.

I hang up the phone. At least things are easier at home, I tell myself. I grab the newspaper. Without television the newspaper has taken on a heightened importance for me, not because of the actual news in it. The front page generally doesn't merit more than a glance. Casey and I have better things to read than stories about Bosnia. We sit on the couch together, snuggled under blankets every morning. I hand him the weather page because it's colorful and interesting with its maps and graphs.

Casey points to the northern region of the United States. "That says?"

"Cold," I tell him. "It's cold in the northern states." He points to the Midwest.

"Windy," I say. He studies the rest of the page while I read the comics. The comics are necessary now, an essential sitcom substitute.

Today I'm starting with *Doonesbury,* followed by *For Better or Worse* and *Stone Soup.* When Casey was one, those were the only comic strips I read. Now I read all of them except *Family Circus.* Casey likes *Family Circus* though, which I think must be the only reason it exists, to serve the toddler market.

Casey has finished looking at the U.S. map and has moved on to the world map, followed by the pollen chart. My goal is for him to stay occupied long enough for me to get through all of the comics and then have time to read the advice columns. I have just finished reading *FoxTrot* when Mama comes downstairs. She is wearing one of my bathrobes, but it's too long for her.

"How's my grandson?" she asks.

"I'm fine," he answers, barely looking up at her.

"And what's the weather like in Texas?"

He looks at the map.

"Steaming," he says. She leans over him and looks at the page. "That's right!" she says.

Casey climbs off the couch and goes over to the CD player. I get up to find my mother some coffee. We stand at the sink together.

"I'm telling you that he's gifted," she says to me.

"Everyone thinks they have a gifted kid," I say.

"He's the smartest two-year-old I've ever seen. You've done an amazing thing, teaching him to read."

"I wasn't trying to teach him to read," I say. She doesn't understand that I haven't been trying to do anything except get some time to myself, the same thing Kendra wants when she puts Hannah in front of *Snow White and the Seven Dwarfs*.

"He reads because he's gifted." She gets out her favorite mug, which has a picture of Casey on it taken at the beach.

"I'm just glad he's happy," I say. I'm filling up a coffee filter with French roast for her. Whenever she says the word *gifted*, I know she wants me to do what she did with my sister. She had her tested at age four and, based on the results, put her into first grade that same year. My sister was a head shorter than her classmates and was frequently teased. By the time I was old enough to be tested, my mother had lost her enthusiasm for the idea, or more than likely, I didn't inspire her sufficiently. My sister was using linear perspective at age four. At the same age, I was still scribbling. But Mama seems to be getting her zeal back with Casey.

I sit back down on the couch and move on to *Dear Abby*, followed by the People section. Charlie Sheen just got married. I like knowing about these people even if I'm not following their TV programs or films. I don't want to be out of the loop when I'm at a party and everyone is talking about how Robert Downey Jr. just went into rehab again.

I'm about to read about Meg Ryan and her husband when Casey calls out to me. "I'm putting in another CD," he says smiling. He speaks with a sweet baby voice but he has the vocabulary of someone working at Microsoft. "I'm programming it now."

"Thanks," I say. We have been listening to George Winston since we woke up this morning at seven a.m. and it was still dark outside. I lit a candle and placed it on the coffee table in front of us.

We like George Winston in the morning because it is peaceful and soothing and I can read the paper without the distraction of lyrics. I suppose I could be watching *AM Northwest* right now on a new big screen and Casey could be watching *Barney* upstairs. Our life reminds me of being at a meditation center.

"I'm replaying song number seven, eight, and nine," Casey says.

He pushes the buttons thoughtfully. If he is gifted, it's in a way I find totally boring, although admittedly useful. He could finally teach me how to program the VCR if I were so inclined.

"I'm pressing the repeat button."

I don't understand exactly what he has done, but I do know that his using the repeat button will mean that after about an hour these songs will be embedded in my brain. At least he isn't playing "Here We Go Round the Mulberry Bush" sung by a group of six-year-olds from the CD Bob gave him the other day. Then I would have to leave.

Bob has purchased nearly every CD we own, because I've never learned how to shop for music. When I was a teenager, I didn't have a group of friends to sit in my room with, playing album after album full blast, backward and forward, looking for hidden meanings. I had a full schedule of TV shows instead, and watching MTV never interested me either. I need dialogue, and even the thinnest dialogue will suffice. "Gilligan, you've got to get the Professor!"

Casey, satisfied with his selections, sits down next to me again.

"Song number nine is my favorite," he says. I nod, even though I have no idea which song it is.

OLIVIA DROPS BY and asks me if I want to send Casey over to play later.

We are listening to the soundtrack of *The Sound of Music* when she steps inside. Because I have seen the movie several times, it's easy for me to picture Julie Andrews and all of the von Trapp children singing and laughing and scheming. It's almost as good as watching the movie, better in some ways, even though the song "Sixteen Going on Seventeen" is sexist. With or without a CD, I can sing all day to Casey and he loves it.

"Mindy likes that video," Olivia says cheerfully.

"Casey really likes the songs," I say, not mentioning that he's never seen the movie.

"Do you want to send Casey over to play then?" she asks again.

"That would be nice, but we're already going somewhere."

Olivia looks rejected. I've had Mindy over plenty of times, but I've never sent Casey over. She probably wants to tell me that she doesn't live in a crack house.

I can hear Georgette with her gentle wisdom prodding me:

Just tell her you're not comfortable with the television being on when Casey is there.

But I'm not ready to do that. Worse, I'm not always sure that what I'm doing is right.

I CALL MY YOUNGER niece, Amber, who is nine and a half. She is Trillium's younger sister and not ever considered to be the next Buddha. She was well fed from the start.

"Do you wish you had watched more TV?" I ask her. Both of my nieces have watched very little television at home.

"We watched a lot with you," she says. "All of those Disney movies we saw at your house."

"But that was just when you were up visiting. What about when you were at school and all the kids were playing some game from a TV program you hadn't seen?"

"Well, sometimes they would be playing Power Rangers, but they would just tell me about the show and what character they wanted me to be. It was pretty easy to do."

"So you didn't mind that you hadn't actually seen the show?"

"No, not really."

I think of Casey and imagine him trying to play *Superman* with another kid. Maybe he could figure out what to do. How hard would it be to pretend you can stop a speeding bullet?

My sister, who has been listening on the extension, pipes in, "So what if Casey is different? The world is unevolved. It's better to be different."

"I thought I was talking to your daughter," I say.

"When is Mama going home?" she asks without apologizing for eavesdropping.

"Next week," I tell her, but I'm not doing anything to get her there quickly. She is mine. She has her own television in her own room, which means she has everything. And I get so much done when she is here.

Now that I have a child, I can see how poorly I used my time before when I had no responsibilities. I could have written volumes and finished multiple degrees if I hadn't been so hooked on television.

8

Sex Fiends and Shooters

Mama has finally gone back to Texas, and without her here to tempt me to watch *Mad About You*, I'm not that interested. I switch over to the nightly news, but it doesn't excite me either. Of course, it never has. I try my favorite rerun channel. *Matlock, Murder, She Wrote,* and *The Cosby Show*. These shows seem so contrived to me now. All of Matlock's cases end the same way. I guess when I was watching a lot of TV, any show was an improvement over living inside my own head.

By the time spring arrives, I've managed to get down to no more than seven hours a week on a consistent basis. Maybe soon I'll get down to two hours a week as originally planned. I'm feeling pretty proud of myself.

Casey and I are having lunch together. We're eating broccoli, which he calls little trees, when Kendra calls.

"There's been a shooting at a high school," she says. "I think it's around where your sister lives."

I hang up and call Sapphire immediately. "It's in Springfield, the next town over, full of rednecks," she says. "We're all fine."

I was working at a large newspaper in Texas when both Reagan and John Lennon were shot. There was a kind of voyeuristic excitement in air as the reporters all rushed around digging up the latest tidbits of news. "Hinckley lived in Texas for a while," someone said. "I'm on it."

The Thurston High School shootings have that sort of energy around them. As soon as Casey takes a nap, I put a heavy blanket up against the door and keep the monitor beside me so I can hear him when he wakes up. In fact, in a perverse way, I am welcoming this horrible excuse to watch television. When Bob comes home from work, I ask him to take care of Casey.

"I need to see this. It's in Springfield," I say importantly.

He eyes me skeptically but doesn't voice any objections. I crawl under the covers in the guest room and watch the high school students breaking into uncontrollable sobs as the camera operators and journalists who have arrived on the scene eagerly record the victims' pain for the television viewers. After having seen so many thrillers with Harrison Ford and Bruce Willis, I have to remind myself that this is real.

I shift the pillows around on the bed so I can watch more comfortably. I'm sad for these families and I'm sure if I knew them, I would be devastated. Instead I can't help but think about the TV movie that will be made about this. Leonardo DiCaprio would be good in the role of the shooter. And his parents could be Meryl Streep and Dustin Hoffman. But I doubt actors of their caliber would make a made-for-TV movie.

When I finally go to bed, I try to answer the questions the reporters posed. Over and over they kept asking, "Why?" and "How could this have happened?"

"He was hurt and alone," I tell Bob as I pull the covers over my

shoulder. "That's what we have to prevent. We need to stay connected to all the children we know, not just Casey."

I have no idea how I will do this, but watching six hours of
television news doesn't seem like a good place to start.

IT'S BEEN TWO DAYS since the school shootings have
occurred, and I've mostly forgotten about them as well as my goal
of staying connected to children everywhere. That's the way it's
supposed to be if you watch television. You aren't supposed to actually remember the event of the day or week. You're supposed to
move on to the next big news. For example, what is Julia Roberts
doing after her divorce?

"LET'S START A GARDEN," I say to Casey with as much
enthusiasm as I can muster. I'm hoping the garden will help somehow. I'll get in touch with the earth and commune with the nature spirits. Then I'll forget all about television again. It's been
three weeks since Thurston.

"Can we have zucchini?" Casey asks. We are in the backyard
sitting in the grass. He's just woken from his nap, which has been
happening later and later in the day.

"Of course we can," I say.

We walk to Nature's and look at packets of seeds that we
can plant in June. I've never had a garden before, so it's a big experiment.

"Carrots might be good," I tell him. "They're a root vegetable."

"I like green beans," he says, pointing to the picture of the bean
stocks on the seed package.

We pick up a few bags of mushroom compost, some tomato starts, and four packages of seeds: green beans, carrots, butternut squash, and basil.

"We'll have to water our garden every day," I say when we're back home. I pull the hose over to our garden space and Casey makes sure he is drenched in a matter of minutes. He loves playing outside and knows every nook and cranny of our wooded backyard.

I'm not sure we'll be able to keep up with a real garden, but every day Casey runs outside to see if anything has sprouted through the ground.

"Are those the carrots?" he asks.

"I don't know," I say. "This is my first garden, too."

Within a few weeks everything appears to have come up, and in another month and a half, we are ready to harvest our first crop. I wonder if it's just beginner's luck or if I have a real talent. I suggest the latter to Bob, hoping he'll be impressed.

"We live in the Willamette Valley," he says. "Everything grows well here. That's why I'm always hacking things back."

Casey hands me a carrot covered in dirt. The dirt surprises me for a second. "You have to wash it off," he tells me.

I run it under water, scrubbing it lightly. Then I take a bite. It really is better than any carrot I have tasted before. I can imagine a good commercial for this carrot. *Available in your own backyard,* it would say. I take another bite. It's a good carrot.

"Do you want the rest?" I ask Casey. He happily takes it as if I've offered him a chocolate chip cookie.

I smile at him, amazed at the way he lives his life in the moment. I, on the other hand, am still so often just going through the motions, living this new life I've chosen because it's what I want for him. But the strange thing is that every so often when I'm going through the motions, I lose myself in the process.

OLIVIA AND I are standing in the street talking. I have just given her some green beans from Casey's garden.

"Casey has given up his nap," I say.

I tell her what a painful adjustment it is for me to see the nap go. I am, in fact, grief stricken. His nap has been free child care, free time for me to do whatever I wanted—write, sleep, and watch television.

She nods her head knowingly. "Mindy gave her nap up three months ago, and I made that a video time," she says. "I did that with Luke, too."

"That's certainly an option," I say, an option that is looking more and more appealing to me. The average three-year-old watches thirty hours of television a week, more than any other age group. I'm sure now that it's because so many three-year-olds give up their naps.

"Does Mindy sleep longer at night at least, since she doesn't nap?"

Olivia shakes her head. "Not really, but you get used to it. It gets easier."

But after another month of no naps, I'm still not used to it. It's Tuesday and Casey isn't with Kellie today and Mama is still in Texas. Rebecca and Camden came over in the morning and we went to the park. I asked them over afterward, but Rebecca said they had stuff to do at home.

"And I've got a video for Camden," she added.

I sit down on the couch looking at the clock. It's two p.m. and the thought of the rest of the day without a moment to myself is depressing. It's not that I want to watch television. I just don't like *not* having the option to watch it. I want the option to sleep, too. Casey's nap always meant that a nap was possible for me, if I needed it. Maybe if we moved to Mexico, Casey would nap. I think everyone still naps there.

Casey has just eaten a bowl of corn flakes with blueberries and he is happily putting together a dinosaur puzzle on the coffee table, but it doesn't matter. He will talk to me any minute. He will show me the T. rex when it is complete. I will smile and answer his questions and then go back to doing whatever it is I am doing, which is nothing, because I don't want to do anything because I know I will be interrupted. That's why parents turn to television. They want uninterrupted time, even if it's just to rest in perfect silence.

"See the T. rex head," Casey says.

"I see it," I say, with false enthusiasm.

I take a deep breath and finally face the reality of the situation. After that, it's never that hard to think of a solution. That's what I've found anyway.

I sit down beside Casey on the carpet and wait until he finishes his puzzle.

"I want to show you something," I say. I walk over to the timer on the stove. "Has Dad shown you how to work it yourself?"

"I set it when we make enchiladas," he says proudly.

"That's great, because you're going to get to set it every day!" I make it sound as if he's just won the lottery.

"How many minutes?" he asks.

"Twenty. It will be my turn for twenty minutes," I say. "That means that you can't say anything to me or wander around the house or interrupt me at all for twenty minutes."

"What if I bump my head?"

"You can interrupt me if you bump it hard," I say. Then I remember the film *Harold and Maude* and the kid who was always trying to get his mother's attention by faking suicide attempts. I hope I'm not creating a similar scenario down the road.

"Should I set it now?" he asks. Casey thinks this is a blast.

"You can," I say. "I'll be on the couch right over there resting."

"Then it will be my turn," he says cheerfully.

I nod and go lie down on the couch, thinking that after he sets the timer, he'll probably go back to his puzzle or play with his LEGOs for the twenty minutes. I close my eyes, but I'm sure I won't fall asleep, especially because in the next minute I hear the sound of a chair being dragged across the kitchen floor.

I look up and see the chair directly in front of the stove timer. Casey is sitting there, barely moving, watching the seconds go by. I assume he'll get tired of this activity pretty soon. How interesting can it be for a three-year-old to watch some numbers when he could be building a tower for his little monkeys?

But he doesn't move. He just stares at the timer. After ten minutes, I drift in and out of sleep, looking up occasionally, only to discover that he's still in the same place.

"Maybe it's his way of zoning out, since he doesn't watch television," Bob says later that evening, after Casey has gone to bed.

"It's as if he's aware of every moment we're apart, every second that I'm not available to him," I say. "It's as if time is on hold for him."

"Does he seem sad about it?"

I consider this. "No. Actually, he seems perfectly content."

After a few weeks of staring at the timer, Casey gets more creative at entertaining himself. He ventures back into the family room to put together a puzzle, glancing up every now and then to see how many minutes are left. I start to relax more. Sometimes I fall completely asleep and am abruptly awakened by Casey's gleeful voice.

"Time's up!"

"Great job!" I say. "I feel so much better." I say this even if my body and mind are still crying out for more rest, because I want him to feel good about this new system. I wonder if I'll ever be completely straightforward with him.

Gradually I begin to increase the time to thirty minutes, then forty. My goal is to reach an hour, almost as long as it takes the average three-year-old to watch *Sleeping Beauty*.

I'm hoping for a long-term payoff, having a child who can amuse himself without watching *The Jungle Book*. And I want the same for myself, which is why I refrain from slipping upstairs to watch *Oprah*.

When Mama comes back, I explain to her how Casey has quiet time each day and that she and I can write together and work on projects.

"Well, that would be harder if you had more than one child," she says as she empties her book bag. "If you had three kids who fought the way you all did, you would never know peace and quiet. That's what's behind all this television watching."

"I can imagine," I say. "But actually only children watch a lot more television than kids with siblings."

"Well, I suppose when you weren't pulling each other's hair, you did play together."

She takes out a thick green book with a shiny new cover. She has started writing book reviews for a political science journal.

"I can read a book to Casey during his quiet time," she offers.

She's moving more slowly than usual. We just walked up the stairs, but she sounds as if she's just run a marathon.

"Don't you want him to watch television instead?" I say. "That's what most kids do instead of napping, as you said."

"I think it's marvelous the way he doesn't watch television."

I put my arms around her. I hadn't realized that I've needed to hear this from her.

We sit on the guest bed together and she shows me the book she is reviewing, a textbook designed for a Women in Politics course. I show her Casey's recent drawings. This is, in my opinion, the best part of having my mother visit. To whom can you really brag about your kid, if not to your mother?

"See how well he draws with these markers!" I say.

"He's a wonder!" she says.

"This is a monkey climbing in a banana tree," I tell her.

She takes the picture from me and I notice that she sways a little as if her balance is off when she stands up. I steady her with my arm. I feel sure that she hasn't been drinking again. Her mind is the same, but something is off, and being a hypochondriac, I imagine the worst.

"I like those dresses," Casey says. "Will you wear this dress on the vacation?"

"I sure will," I say.

Casey is in my room where I have spread out an assortment of summer clothes. Yesterday I went to Just Right for Me, a store in our neighborhood filled with clothing from Indonesia and India, which usually isn't just right for me at all, except that we are going to Hawaii. I bought three colorful silk dresses and a couple of sarongs.

Casey loves when I wear bright colors, something I'm not generally inclined to do. I like showing him my purchases. Unlike Bob, Casey has no interest in how much anything costs.

I pull a floral-patterned bikini out of another shopping bag.

"That's pretty, too," Casey says.

I lay it on the bed. Casey will think I'm pretty in it. He won't even begin to think of me as anything but beautiful even though I'm almost ten pounds heavier than I was before I had him. The size twos in my closet look foreign to me. Was I really that tiny? I think of my housekeeper Clarissa's three-year-old grandchild telling her that she's too fat. "It really surprised me that he felt that way," she said. I nodded sympathetically. What was she thinking? Her grandson has seen countless Disney and TV characters with miniature waists and exaggerated curves. Of course Clarissa is unacceptable.

But Casey has been programmed by me and Bob, and our programming seems to have taken so far.

"Aren't you glad you have a big, soft mom?" I say to Casey each day when we cuddle on the couch. "What if you had a hard, bony mom?" I say, emphasizing the words *hard* and *bony,* and he cringes as I say them.

"That wouldn't feel good," he says.

"No, it wouldn't," I say. "Moms' bodies are supposed to be soft," I continue, my voice soothing, almost hypnotic. I'm hoping, with this subtle brainwashing, that he'll grow up to appreciate women of all sizes, never harassing his girlfriend if she puts on a few pounds. Maybe he'll even like Rubens paintings and pictures of Marilyn Monroe. But I hope he won't be prejudiced against skinny girls.

Later, when Casey is downstairs with Mama, I model my bikini for Bob. I'm thinking that I look pretty good in it now in spite of the few extra pounds. Maybe Casey isn't the only one who has benefited from not being bombarded with *Baywatch* bodies.

"Is that new?" he asks. He's sitting on the bed a few feet away from me.

"It's from Goodwill!" I answer sarcastically. At least I can count on him to be predictable. "Do I look okay in it or what?"

"You look great, but I don't see why you needed a new swimsuit."

I roll my eyes. Bob doesn't care that I'm not skinny anymore. What matters to him, what's most pressing to him right now, is seeing the price tag dangling under my left armpit. I turn around so that the tag is farther away from him. I stand up as straight as I can in front of the full-length mirror to make myself look taller. I am five-four. At least that hasn't changed. I wonder what age I'll be when I start shrinking.

Bob gets up from the bed. "Was it over fifty dollars?" He's walking toward me, trying desperately now to see the price tag. "Did you buy a lot of other things for the trip?"

I scoot away from him and then turn to glare at him. "You know, a lot of men would have already ripped this suit off of me by now and it wouldn't be because they wanted to see how much it cost!"

"I'm sorry," he says suddenly. "What was I thinking?" He moves toward me now and tries to look amorous, or maybe he really is feeling that way.

He attempts to put his arms around me but I push him away. "It's too late! You'll have to try again later after the price tags are buried in the bottom of the recycling container."

He stalks out of the room. Good riddance as far as I'm concerned. I slip the top off, and not bothering to find scissors, I yank the tags off. Maybe when I'm in Hawaii I'll find a man who won't ask how much my swimsuit costs. I could meet him on the beach and he could take me to one of those gazebos away from everyone. He might be a native Hawaiian and I would apologize for the way Americans have destroyed his ancestors' way of life by turning his homeland into a tourist attraction.

I slip the bottom off, remove the tag, and tuck the bikini into my suitcase. My mother wouldn't approve of the gazebo idea, and she is coming with us. But at least she would approve of my taking the bikini. If I told her that watching television had made me think I had to be skinny forever, she would quickly point out Oprah.

Oprah is God. She doesn't count, and she's lost weight besides, I would say.

My mother has always made a big deal about how great it is to have role models of women playing professionals on TV. "Look at Susan Dey on *LA Law,*" she would say. But seeing her mostly taught me that women had to look perfect or they would never be successful in the corporate world.

I remember when Bob became an attorney at one of the big law firms in town, I was amazed at the attorneys I met there, particularly the women. They were far from perfect looking. One had dull brown hair, bad skin, and not much makeup. Another wore dowdy-looking dresses. Why weren't they wearing designer suits like the woman on *Matlock*? Where were their straight white teeth, size-four figures, and perfectly shaped legs revealed by stylish skirts cut above the knee? How could they have become so successful while looking so plain and unpretentious? On television, plain women are only featured if they're about to get makeovers as part of the storyline.

Real life, especially the life I saw growing up, was a far cry from what's shown on television. I always assumed that the only reason my mother survived professionally was because she was in academia. Her panty hose not only ran; they were smoke damaged. And my sister had something you never see on a woman in *Law and Order*. She had a beard.

It wasn't a heavy beard, but it spread two to three inches across her chin, and it was at least three inches long and curly. I used to cringe with embarrassment when we went places together, but eventually I got over it and began to get a kick out of watching other people pretending not to be shocked. I wonder if her beard would seem so bizarre to me if I hadn't seen so many CoverGirl commercials. Maybe. Maybe not.

I close my suitcase and decide to forget the gazebo fantasy and wait for Bob to make amends.

"Do you have a Game Boy for the trip?"

I am across the street at Peggy's borrowing snorkeling equipment.

"No. I think he's a little young for that."

"Well, do you have a television in your car?"

"No, but we're flying," I tell her. I remind her that with Hawaii, there's that problem of the ocean between us.

"We had a video player in the car when we drove to Yellowstone and it made the trip so much easier," she explains.

"I bet," I say. I'm thinking that my mother probably would have appreciated it. I remember giving my brother flying-angel rides in the backseat as we sped along the highway on long trips. We thought it was funny when drivers would see him floating in the air happily waving. It was great not having to bother with seat belts. And videos in cars were nonexistent.

I wonder if Peggy's kids or anyone else's bother to look out the window occasionally on these long trips. Do they miss seeing the Rocky Mountains because they're watching *The Parent Trap*?

"You can get a Game Boy at Fred's," Peggy says. "They're on sale until Friday."

I nod again, carefully holding onto the masks looped around my arm.

"Thanks for lending us your snorkeling stuff."

This is our second vacation with my mother since Casey was born. Last year, when Casey was two, we all went to San Diego. Mama enjoyed it as much as Casey and it made me feel like a good daughter, which Bob felt was a long time in coming. And he didn't mind having her along either.

When we get on the plane, Casey decides to sit between Mama and Bob and do connect-the-dots books. I, on the other hand, have the aisle seat across from them. I have a little screen in front of my seat, my own personal screen, well out of Casey's sight. The flight attendant offers me headphones and I beam at her.

"It's *Erin Brockovich,*" she says.

I give her some money and wait for what seems like a delicious, decadent dessert.

AT THE BEACH, I don't miss television in the slightest. The ocean provides such a full sensory experience that I'm almost surprised anyone who lives on the beach watches television at all.

The beach near our condo isn't long, like the beaches in Oregon, but it doesn't matter. In Oregon you can't run around half naked on the shore. Most of the time, you layer your body with fleece sweatshirts and rain gear. Here in Kauai, we are covered mostly in sunscreen. Every day we swim, snorkel, and explore the island. We eat fabulous feasts of fresh fruit, grilled fish, and broccolini. I wish we had planned a longer trip.

"I'm going for a swim," I tell Bob the day before it's time to go home.

"Be back in time for dinner," he says.

I weave along a path surrounded by tropical flowers until I get to the ocean. I slip off my sandals and stare out at the waves, looking for whales, looking for absolutely nothing. I'm never lonely near the ocean. I want to call Georgette and tell her that I'm finally relaxed and in touch with my true self. I am one with God. I am complete. I jump over the first small wave and smile. I could stay out here forever.

I dive into the surf and ride the next wave in. I look up and find that Bob is waiting for me, looking worried.

"Your mom isn't feeling well," he says.

"What's wrong?"

"She's in the bathroom throwing up. She says she's dizzy."

THE NEXT MORNING we are packing up and getting ready to check out. Mama says she's feeling better and wants to go for one last swim.

"Are you sure you're okay?" I ask her. She's still looks unsteady on her feet.

"I'm fine," she says.

But she doesn't look fine at all. "I'll go with you."

We walk down the path with me in the lead. I didn't think it was possible for her to be even slower than she usually is.

"Are you sure you want to swim?" I ask her when we finally reach the beach.

"I'll be all right," she says, and wades into the water. I watch her bellyflop into the first wave she sees. She tries to ride it in. I see her head go under and I wait for her to break the surface, to come up again to take a breath. I count the seconds.

It's too much like watching Casey, watching and worrying. It's not supposed to be this way with her. I'm only supposed to have to worry about her doing something embarrassing, like telling the lifeguard what a nice young stud he is.

I toss off my sandals, my eyes still fixed on the water. I wasn't planning to swim. I was out here shortly after breakfast and I've already showered. I stare at the place where my mother went under. I fling off my sun hat as I run into the waves. I feel the cool water break against my knees. I get to her just as she rises to the top. A second wave washes her in and she lies there sprawled out flat on the shore.

She is panting and spitting up sand and saltwater. I pull her into a sitting position and try to move her up further in case another wave comes.

"I'm all right," she says, but she's still breathing hard.

"I'm not letting you swim alone anymore," I tell her.

9

Passion Is Everything

"You promise you'll see a doctor when you get back to Texas?"

We are back home now and Mama seems much more like her usual self, which has never been exactly what one would call healthy, come to think of it.

"I have a checkup already scheduled for next week when I get back."

We've been talking all morning about preschool for Casey, now that he's three. It's a big step. I've kept him in a safe little world, never leaving him alone with anyone I didn't trust.

"I hate that he'll be exposed to so many mainstream values," I say to my mother. "He'll be around kids with guns who watch *Batman* and *Star Wars* and eat gumdrops and lollypops."

I hear myself and know that I sound like a fundamentalist Christian who is worried about Satan and sin. But my mother has her own take on the situation.

"He needs to be with gifted children," she says. "He already reads, for God's sake!"

"He reads the weather page," I say.

"He reads every sign he sees," she says.

"I don't care about that," I tell her. But my mother is fixated on this gifted thing. She wants me to find a preschool where the kids are learning Einstein's theory of relativity and advanced mathematics. She wants him to be a Nobel Prize winner by the time he's ten, but I'm thinking that being off television will make him different enough.

I talk to Kendra about the places she knows about, including the one where Hannah goes. Kendra says it's a preschool, but it seems more like a day care to me. Hannah is there for six hours a day and the kids watch television in the afternoon. "They're just Disney movies," she tells me. "*Sleeping Beauty.* Nothing inappropriate."

I picture Hannah learning to look beautiful while she waits for her handsome prince to arrive. Seems inappropriate to me.

"I was sort of hoping for a place without television," I say hesitantly. We are at my house eating biscuits with orange marmalade.

She gives me a look of pity, as if she is explaining something to a misinformed child. "Anytime kids are somewhere for more than three hours a day, there's going to be television. You can't expect anyone to be with little kids for longer than that without it."

"But I don't want him to go all day," I say.

Hannah has been at this school since September and Kendra says it's been the best thing for both of them. It's already November but I wasn't ready to think about preschool before now. Casey is potty trained but he's still deathly afraid of loud toilets.

"You'll be lucky if you can get in anywhere at all," Kendra says. "You better start calling around."

I GET OUT THE school directory that came with the local parenting magazine.

"Ask about what they do for gifted children," my mother yells when I pick up the phone to call. She's about to return to Texas and wants to put in her two cents one last time.

I ask about the toilets instead.

"Are they the modern kind like the ones at Nordstrom? They don't flush by themselves, do they? He hates those."

Fortunately, the toilets are fine, kid-sized with old-fashioned flushers. As far as the television issue, Kendra was right about the all-day programs.

No one seemed all that apologetic about it, either.

"We show educational videos, too" is the best some can say.

I check out the shorter programs, where Casey would only go for two and a half hours per day, two or three days a week. There are lots of these to choose from, although many are full. I visit the first one on the list.

"Ours is phonics-based," the teacher says. She shows me the charts she uses.

I look at the charts and don't bother to mention that Casey has already mastered phonics. What he needs, particularly as an only child, is time to be with other kids.

"What you want is a cooperative that is play-based," the next teacher tells me. She hands me a list of these.

I think about the last cooperatively owned business I was a part of, a natural foods restaurant in Eugene. We had weekly meetings where we all sat around discussing whether we should switch to Nicaraguan coffee to help support the Sandinistas even though the coffee wasn't organic.

"How are women treated by the company?" one of our partners would ask.

"Are they homophobic?" the woman beside me would shout.

No one ever asked, *Does their coffee taste good?*

Since we were supposed to reach consensus and there were twelve of us, the meetings would drag on for hours.

I CHECK OUT the first name on the list, Friends School. "Would I have to put in a lot of time?" I ask.

"Once a month you help out in the classroom."

Casey and I visit two more schools like this before finding the most progressive one. I assume it will also be the best.

Casey sits in a circle on the carpet with the rest of the children while I stand on the sidelines talking to a young mom who has a girl Casey's age.

"We make a point of bringing in as many families of color as we can," she says. "And we also have a family with two mothers," she says.

"That's great," I say, hoping that these families also don't watch much television.

I watch Casey sing songs with the other children and snack on apples and whole-grain crackers. No Gummy Bears here. Everything would be perfect except that the teacher is not Kellie. In fact, she isn't warm at all. She frowns at the kids a lot. I picture everyone at the meeting when they hired her, so glad that she likes tofu that they forgot to notice that she isn't nurturing.

"I'll stay with you on your first day of school if you like it here," I tell Casey on our way out. "Did you like the teacher?"

"I like the one at Pine Ridge better."

"I guess you can go to Pine Ridge." I smile and try to seem enthusiastic.

Pine Ridge was my last choice. It's a cooperative, too, but the teacher is conservative and probably not inclined to acknowledge that two-mother families exist. Her name is Mrs. Sanderson and that's what the kids must call her. No first names, and Fruit Roll-Ups and cupcakes are the snacks of choice.

Mrs. Sanderson is not exactly what I had in mind for Casey's first teacher, but she is nurturing and he likes her. She tells me that I can stay at school with Casey for as long as he needs until he feels comfortable separating. Knowing this, he easily says good-bye to me the first day with a big smile on his face and goes off to experiment with the Play-Doh next to three other children.

I leave quickly with little tears in my eyes that I don't want Casey to see.

A couple of the moms outside notice me crying. They've had their kids here since September.

"Is everything okay?"

"Fine," I say. "It just feels like such a big step." I'm acting as if I'm in one of those commercials for Kodak.

They look at me strangely. Maybe they haven't seen the Kodak commercials lately.

I wipe my tears with my handkerchief and make a point of talking to one of the moms who has a boy Casey's age.

"What does your son like to do?" I ask.

"He likes playing Batman."

"Oh," I say, and I smile in a way that I hope looks friendly. I want to ask what Batman is like these days. Do they still flash the words *Pow!* and *Oof!* across the screen during the fight scenes?

I head home, which is only five minutes away, and stare at the empty kitchen. It's 12:35 p.m. and I've finished my latest article. I have two hours and twenty minutes to myself. I give some thought to what I could do right now for fun—reading, walking, seeing friends. I head upstairs to the guestroom, not bothering to shut the door behind me. I look through the videos. *When Harry Met Sally* is 96 minutes long. *Far and Away* is 140 minutes. I will be able to watch almost anything but *Titanic*.

I'm sure it's normal to be nervous and that I'm just adjusting to the change. My baby is in preschool and I want to be sure he's happy there. I say this to myself as I put in *When Harry Met Sally*.

I ARRIVE TO PICK up Casey five minutes early, giving him a big hug when I see him.

"How was it?"

"It was fun." The teacher waves to us and I wave back. I take his hand and walk with him to the car.

"What did you do?"

"I played with the Play-Doh shape maker and made a house with the blue sticks."

I try to remember what the blue sticks are. Maybe they're from Discovery Toys.

THE NEXT WEEK, I come a few minutes early. The kids are outside on the playground. That's where they go the last ten minutes of the day, weather permitting. A group of girls is on the deck and a couple of boys are chasing after each other with pretend guns. "Gotcha. You're dead!" Casey is sitting alone under the play structure digging in the dirt.

He's happy to see me and I act happy, too, but in my typical alarmist fashion, I assume the worst. How can he be happy if he isn't playing with anyone? Where is his pretend gun? Does he want a pretend gun? Surely, he'll be telling me soon that he doesn't want to go to this place where he feels so alone and different.

But he doesn't.

"I got to feed the rat," he says.

"That's nice." I don't tell him how much I hate rats.

"Maybe he needs to watch *Batman,*" I tell Bob after the first few weeks of school have passed.

"Why?"

"Because whenever I pick him up, he's by himself. If he watched *Batman,* he might have friends there."

"I watched *Batman,*" he tells me, "but I still didn't have very many friends."

"That's because you were shy."

"Maybe he's just shy, too."

My sister gives a different perspective when I call her.

"You're obsessed with this friend issue!" she yells at me over the phone. "Be glad he isn't some hyper, brainwashed idiot running around and pretending to shoot at everyone!"

"I am glad," I say, but I don't feel very glad. I wish my mother were here, but she's been staying with one of her sisters in Iowa who has been ill. It could be months before I see Mama again.

I stock up on more videos, the lighter the better. *Romancing the Stone, Risky Business,* and *Animal House.* Each time I drop Casey off at school, I head home as quickly as I can and rush into the guest room to watch.

The hours that Casey is at school begin to take on the power to determine whether or not he will succeed in life, become a happy member of the human race, as opposed to a pathological loner. Before I had been concerned about aggressive, television-addicted kids being a bad influence, but how can he be influenced by kids with whom he barely interacts?

After a month of listening to me fret, Bob can't take it anymore. I'm back to watching my nightly sitcoms, too. He is in the
guest room counting the new videos I've purchased while I watch
Mad About You.

"It's just preschool!" he says. "He'll be fine."

I grab the stack of videos Bob has been counting and hold them
protectively against my chest.

"I just want it to work out for him," I say.

"I'm not worried about it," he says.

Of course he isn't worried about it. School always worked out
for Bob. He certainly wasn't popular, but he was brainy and he
channeled his energy into healthy extracurricular activities. I've
seen the numerous debate trophies, scholastic awards, and rib-
bons that his mother sent in a big box after we were married. Bob
liked school.

I, on the other hand, saw school as a prison, and junior high
was the worst sort of prison, in part because of girls like Kay and
boys like Henry. Kay stole my purse and ripped other girls' earrings right out of their ears. Henry shoved his hand down my
blouse once when I was unfortunate enough to be alone in the
hall with him. Learning anything was beside the point there, and
since I didn't have the right clothes to wear, what reason was there
to go in the first place?

"Why don't you just pull him out," Bob says, "if you're going
to be so uptight about it?"

"That won't look good when we apply to other schools," I say.
"He has to get a good recommendation now if we want him to get
into the best schools."

"He's three, for God's sake!"

I don't try to explain how it works to Bob. I'm afraid I'll end up sounding like the uptight East Coast parents Diane Keaton met in *Baby Boom*.

I call Georgette.

"Remember that this is *his* life," she says. "Casey is supposed to figure some things out for himself, have his own challenges."

This reminds me of my mother telling me how women who live their lives through their children have no life of their own. But that isn't my plan. I just want him to have a good start, so I can hurry up and do more of what I want again. Besides, the way I see it, it's the parents who expect their children to raise themselves who will have their work cut out for them later on.

"He doesn't see that he has any challenges," I tell Georgette.

"This isn't just about Casey and his childhood. It's about you and your childhood."

"I see," I say, and pretend as though she is sharing something profound. Of course this is about my childhood. So what?

"If you want to get a clearer perspective about how he is doing, I suggest you have a talk with his teacher."

AFTER BEING ANNOYED with Georgette I decide she might have a point.

I tell Casey to wait in the classroom while I talk with the teacher outside. She reassures me that all is well, that lots of kids tend to play by themselves more than with others at this age. "It's a small class and Casey is one of only three boys, but he interacts well with the other children. He shares and take turns."

I thank her and start to walk back into the classroom, but she stops me.

"He's really smart, you know. How did he get that way?"

"I don't know," I say truthfully.

"You must really work with him." She probably pictures me sitting down with flash cards, testing him on his addition facts.

"Not really," I say. I shrug my shoulders and go to retrieve my little genius, my sweet son who has no interest in playing Batman.

THE NEXT WEEK all the moms at the school meet for a clean-up-the-classroom day. The dads were told to stay at home to watch the kids. I wish I were so lucky. The fumes from the Windex, bleach, and Comet make me long to open a few windows, but no one else seemed to notice.

"I sterilize all of my children's toys weekly," Lenny's mom says, a bottle of bleach solution in hand. I don't tell her that it's something I've never done. Lenny is the oldest of the three boys in the class, including Casey, and Casey mentioned him once.

"Would you like to bring Lenny over to play tomorrow?" I'm hoping it will help Casey join in more at school.

Before she comes over, I scrub the toilet but can't bear to spend my time sterilizing the toys. I wipe a few of them off with a fresh towel. They arrive on time. Lenny's mom looks around and must decide that my house is clean enough, because she leaves to run some errands.

"I'll be back in an hour," she says. "He likes playing Batman."

"Do we get to watch *Batman*?" Lenny asks after his mother has left.

"Not today," I say. "But you can play with Casey's train set."

Lenny and Casey manage to pass the time. They put together the tracks and make the trains go around, but it's not a match made in heaven. The chemistry is missing. Maybe this is why arranged marriages aren't very popular anymore. Or maybe I just need to get Casey a Batman toy.

I decide to ask one of the girls Casey likes to come over next. But her mom says her daughter doesn't play with boys. I'm betting she doesn't play Batman either.

GEORGETTE WANTS ME to practice living in the present and not keep imagining future catastrophes. Casey has been in preschool for three months now and I'm convinced that if he doesn't make any friends there, he'll become a lonely, misguided adult, even though he says he's perfectly happy. I'm watching *Good Will Hunting* for the fifth time.

Matt Damon and his friends are beating the hell out of a group of guys, one of whom Matt knew from kindergarten. I close my eyes for that part but otherwise I manage to remain spellbound, staring at the screen, hypnotized, the pain in my life buried beneath the constant images of someone else's life. I watch the Matt Damon character transform in Hollywood fashion, becoming a self-actualized person, complete with the girl of his dreams. I am fully present during this movie, although I don't think this is what Georgette had in mind.

I buy videos, five at a time now, and keep them out of Bob's sight, like an alcoholic hiding her liquor. I don't want him to know that I watch television during this so-called precious time I have to myself, a time when other mothers are probably shopping for groceries or consulting with a client regarding the state of his portfolio.

The time when Kellie is here is the only time I'm able to work. I study for my class and write quickly and efficiently because I'm not worried about Casey when he's with Kellie. They're on the way to the park. Just as I'm about to start working, Kendra calls me.

"I had a fight with Quinn last night and he spent the night at George's house," she says, and then she starts crying.

"I'll be right over." I run out the door and make it to her house in less than five minutes. I should have walked. It would have given me more time to think of what to say.

"Hannah heard us fighting last night," she says, as soon as she lets me in.

I put my arms around her. Tears are streaming down her face. "Before she went to school today I apologized to her and explained that it was an argument between her daddy and me, and that it had nothing to do with her."

"I'm sure that helped." We sit down on the couch together.

"I'm so depressed. I'm going to try to get on antidepressants," she says. "Quinn wants me to be nicer."

Quinn expects her to do too much is what I think. "You're doing the best you can."

"I don't want Hannah to see us fight again."

"I know," I say.

She wipes her face and looks at me. "Do you ever feel this way about Bob?"

"I'm too busy being neurotic about Casey. It's a full-time job, believe me."

She laughs and I tell her about how hard preschool has been for me. She looks at me, puzzled.

"But Casey has friends outside of school, especially Camden. So what if he doesn't have any there?"

She's right. Camden loves coming over. He and Casey are still best friends and Rebecca and I have bonded because of their friendship. When I finally told her that I didn't like hearing about Kendra, she got really defensive. "You're such a drama queen," she said. But since then she's stopped mentioning her.

"You're right about Camden," I tell Kendra. But Casey's a little different," I say, and she smiles. Like Bob, she's probably thinking about the apple not falling far from the tree.

"Do you want to go for a walk?"

"I want to watch a movie," I say. "It's what I do now."

I tell her about my growing video collection.

"Well, now I know where to go when I need one," she says, and we both laugh.

Kellie says she can take care of Casey for a couple of hours longer. I rummage through Kendra's refrigerator.

"I'll make nachos," I tell her. It's one of the few dishes I can make well. It's a Texas tradition.

"This is a real indulgence," she says as she props up pillows on the bed. Hannah might stretch out in front of the television a lot, but unlike me, Kendra usually doesn't stop moving long enough to watch a movie. Even when the television is on, she's still working, cooking, cleaning, getting things done. She has to be productive. And the more she feels she has to do, the more she needs Hannah to remain sedentary, out of the way, content in front of the set hour after hour.

We're watching *Ever After*. It's one of Hannah's movies but Kendra has never seen it.

"You'll love it," I tell her.

"You've seen it?"

I smile. "I've seen everything."

IT IS FUNNY HOW sometimes it takes something awful happening to make me see that the way I had it really wasn't bad at all. I was watching *City Slickers* for the third time this month, because I hadn't gotten around to getting to the video store. The phone rang and I only answered it in case it was the school calling to report an injury. That's never happened, and not having caller ID, I answered without fear.

"Hello, Ellen. This is Mrs. Sanderson."

I gasp for breath. "Is Casey okay?"

"You need to come get him," she says, and I note that she doesn't sound laid back and her words aren't cushioned with the usual niceties.

"Is he sick?"

"No, he's dumped out all of the puzzles and I'm afraid he'll do it again," she says. "I can't watch him that closely."

I throw on shoes and look around for my bra. I've never liked wearing one and often I hurl it on the stairs when I walk through the door.

I immediately take Casey home after quickly saying good-bye to the teacher.

I am calm, and I wait until we're in the house before I ask him exactly why he dumped out the puzzles.

"I wanted to see what they would look like all mixed together on the floor."

"Well, that's not okay to do at school," I say. He follows me into the living room.

"This is my work time," I lie. "See this photo project." I show him the job the school had given me to do, putting the photos in envelopes for each parent and labeling them.

"Can't we play a game?"

"No, you'll have to play by yourself while I finish this," I tell him. "You're supposed to be at school and I count on this time for doing important projects." I think about the movie I've put on pause upstairs. I spread out the work I have been putting off for weeks and try to concentrate on it.

"Mom, I have a question," Casey says after a while.

"Not now," I say. "I will talk to you in an hour when the time I counted on for my work is done." I try to focus on the photo list in front of me but I'm faking it, too sick with fear to be productive. Here I was worried about Casey being a loner, when what I really should have seen was his potential to be a hoodlum, a troublemaker, a child completely lacking in self-discipline. But I will meet the situation head on, remembering most of all to do the exact opposite of what my mother would do in this situation. I will not give in. I say nothing to him, and after a while Casey seems to get the message because he says nothing, too. The minutes tick by.

On *The Brady Bunch* the parents were always meting out consequences for their kids' actions. Marsha Brady would be grounded for lying to her parents and so on. In my mother's house, there were no real consequences, just threats that we knew she would never carry out. "I'm not going to put up with this!" meant "I'm going to bitch a lot about this." Nothing more.

We ruled ourselves. When my sister turned sixteen, she moved her eighteen-year-old boyfriend, Mitch, into her bedroom. It took my mother a while to figure this out, although my sister and her boyfriend made no attempt to hide it. When my sister was eight, she had secretly moved a cat into her closet, and my mother didn't discover it until the litter box my sister had never changed filled the house with noxious fumes. In the end we kept the cat. I assumed my sister would be able to keep Mitch, too. On the fifth morning, when he emerged from the bathroom with a towel around his waist, a light went on in my mother's tired brain. She was walking down the hall with a cup of coffee. But she didn't say anything until later in the day, and she spoke to me first.

"Is Mitch living here?" she asked.

For a moment I felt a little sorry for her, she was so out of touch.

When I explained that yes indeed he was in fact living here, her yelling drowned out the sound of the television I was trying to watch. She was so upset I didn't have the heart to tell her that he was also dealing pot out of my sister's bedroom. She ranted and raved for several minutes but in the end she wasn't upset about what I expected her to be upset about. She wasn't concerned that my sister might contract a sexually transmittable disease, get pregnant, or be in line for a broken heart.

When she confronted my sister that evening she said, "How do you think it makes me feel, having Mitch here for you when I have no one!" I couldn't picture Shirley Jones having this conversation with her eldest daughter on *The Partridge Family.*

Mitch stayed until summer, and then my sister, with my mother's Chevron credit card in hand, headed to the West Coast, boyfriend in tow. They found that they could buy not only gas but groceries at lots of the Chevron stations.

Each time my mother opened the bills that summer, her anger would fill the house. "What does she think she's doing? Why is a gas station attendant letting a sixteen-year-old buy gas and groceries? I should cancel those cards." But I knew she wouldn't. I was bitter about the car, too. They were driving the oversized Bonneville my grandparents had given my sister and me for Christmas. It was an old car, but my grandparents had taken good care of it. Maybe they had forgotten that fourteen-year-olds like me can't drive.

By August, my sister and her boyfriend had wrecked it. I never got to drive the car, but I did learn a valuable lesson from my sister, and true to form, my mother did not. I went on a spending spree with my mother's MasterCard instead. None of this Chevron grocery store stuff. I was headed to Neiman Marcus. Like my sister, I felt entitled.

Unfortunately, my brother took things a few steps further. He not only used my mother's credit cards but hocked her jewelry as well. Coming home was always a surprise. What would be missing next? Our grandmother Polly's silver?

My mother did her usual yelling, but my brother wasn't the type to listen passively, preferring to break the windows in our living room instead. Mama would spend the weekend filling putty in around the new glass she had purchased. Eventually she abandoned the idea of glass at all and taped old remnants of Plexiglas into the window frames. My brother never paid for any of it.

"He just gets really angry," she would say apologetically. I would shake my head in disgust.

When he started manufacturing methamphetamine on her property, she didn't ask him to move out. "He might kill himself," she told me. This was probably one of few things I can honestly say that my brother wouldn't dare to do. Admittedly, he was down at times, but rarely for more than fifteen minutes.

When he finally went to prison, she was sure he would be destroyed there. She consulted with lawyers and wrote the judges. She would call me up to read what she had written to them.

"'It has come to my attention that the chemical my son purchased is also used to manufacture deodorant,'" she began, and I would interrupt her.

"Are you trying to convince the judge that your son was going to make Mitchum or Soft & Dri?"

"I'm just trying to help your brother," she said angrily, "so his life won't be over!"

In the end my brother thrived in prison as he had never thrived on the outside. It helped that he was in one of the finest federal prisons in the country, not one of those dangerous, overcrowded state penitentiaries. It was what some people call a country-club prison; it gave my brother all of the services he needed: a Narcotics Anonymous group, ministers, a workout room, a part-time job, and best of all, college courses. He even learned Spanish from a Colombian inmate. "He speaks excellent Spanish," my brother bragged, "because he's well educated. Lots of the guys here are smart. My cell mate has a Ph.D. They're not what you'd expect!"

When I went to visit him, I had to agree. It was a minimum-security facility. The prisoners were able to move about and some were allowed to work off the grounds. My brother took me out to the main living space surrounded by a lovely courtyard. He introduced me to some of his fellow inmates and their families. I had expected to meet sex-starved maniacs, but no one even bothered to whistle at me. Junior high was a much more threatening place than this was. In fact, this crowd was considerably better than the crowd my brother had hung out with at my mother's house, where he had always lived.

He completed his bachelor's degree and got a nice, white-collar job as soon as he got out of prison. He had served only three and a half years, less than the five-year sentence he'd been given. After prison he no longer wanted to live at home. "That place is filthy," he said of my mother's house. Prison had made him into Felix Unger. He married someone without an arrest record and they bought a brand-new home in the suburbs. My mother cosigned the loan. Some things never change.

CASEY DID NOT act up again. He remains well behaved and cooperative. But I'm still on edge, wondering if the teacher will call again. So for the rest of the school year, I keep the phone next to me and jump when it rings, pausing the movie I'm watching in case it's Mrs. Sanderson. By June, I have purchased and watched twenty videos. Mrs. Sanderson still hasn't called.

As the school year comes to a close, it seems a happy medium has been reached. Casey hasn't made any friends at school, but he hasn't dumped out any toys there either, or at home for that matter. He's not the class president, but he's not Jack the Ripper.

He's growing up. By the time summer starts he is completely weaned. I'm not advertising this fact to everyone, as the world probably assumes I weaned him ages ago. For the past several months he had been nursing only once a day in the morning, so he was more than ready to be done.

"Does this mean you'll let me touch your breasts again?" Bob asks when I give him the news.

"Not yet," I say. "But someday, I'm sure."

I wonder if I'll miss the prolactin. Rebecca said nursing always made her feel more relaxed. According to Georgette, I'll relax only when I stop perceiving things as rougher than they actually are.

At least everything is easier when my mother is here, and she's coming to stay all summer again, maybe longer. She calls a week before she's scheduled to arrive. It's two in the afternoon and her speech is slurred. She could be drunk, but she doesn't sound the way she used to sound when she was drunk.

"I've called your brother and he's driving from Lake Dallas to take me to the hospital. I've lost sensation in my left arm."

"Lake Dallas is over an hour away from you. Call an ambulance, now!"

I call my brother and tell him to meet her at the hospital.

"She's having a stroke," I shout at him.

"I don't think it's anything like that," he says. But he isn't a hypochondriac like me. He hasn't studied the danger signs for every malady.

I call my mother back to make sure the ambulance is coming.

• • •

BY THE TIME I've caught a flight to Texas, it's the next day. My mother has been moved out of intensive care into a room where they put people whose strokes have worsened. I've arranged for Kellie to come with Casey.

"Just leave him here with me," Bob reasons.

"No, it will stress me out more if I have to be away from him for so long, and you have to work."

I hang up the phone and get back in bed with my mother. The hospital bed is barely big enough for the both of us, but I don't care. We're watching a rerun of *Mad About You* together and Helen Hunt is having a turkey fiasco on Thanksgiving. Mama isn't laughing the way she usually does and I don't laugh either.

"Mama, everything's going to be all right," I say, stroking her head, fiddling with the loose hairs that have come out of her makeshift bun. "Do you want me to change the station?"

"That would be all right." She speaks in a monotone and doesn't elaborate. She reminds me of my old Texas boyfriends, unemotional, their voice range limited, their expressions the same. It's something I tolerated in them but can't bear in my mother, who was always so passionate.

I switch to C-SPAN, hoping for more of a response from her. She looks mildly interested in the congressional hearing, but she doesn't say much about it.

"At least she has her speech," my uncle tells me when I call to give him the news. "If the stroke had been on the other side, she wouldn't have been able to talk."

But she would be able to do both if she had gotten to the hospital sooner. I blame my brother for that, for not insisting she go immediately. I blame the doctors for not giving her the magical injection she needed. I blame myself for not talking long distance to the doctors in the hospital. I blame a whole host of people, past and present. My sister just blames my mother most of all. "She didn't take very good care of herself." But she was doing better; she had stopped drinking and she only smoked in secret when she was with me, and it couldn't have been that much.

When I'm not busy blaming everyone for this misfortune, I'm feeling sorry for myself. I've been cheated. I finally got to have my mother all to myself. She was really here for me at last. She was my slave. It had finally been my turn. I got to drag her around with me and I could accomplish anything. She had finally retired but I only got to have her for three short years.

"The first eighteen months can show the most improvement," the doctor says. "After that, don't expect much." We are standing over my mother. He has just finished examining her.

"What exactly can we expect?"

"She's lost a lot of affect," he says, "and she'll probably never walk again. She'll always need full-time care."

I quickly look back at my mother, hoping she hasn't heard this grim prognosis. It's not exactly the positive affirmation she needs to heal. But she's staring at the television watching Senator Biden speak about health care reform.

"I need to get her out of Texas."

THE GOOD THING about having siblings is that there are enough roles for everyone to play when there's a crisis. My brother offers to pack up my mother's things. Although he has been leading the life of an upstanding citizen as far as we know, my sister and I are still afraid he will sell or confiscate anything of value for himself before he ships off the rest to her here, but that's a chance we'll have to take. To his credit, he moves quickly and efficiently, responsibly gathering her things. He calls me when he's done.

"I'll look after the house until she gets better," he says. We don't talk about when that might be, but for a minute, we are strikingly real with each other, raw and exposed together in our fear.

"I love you," he says, and in spite of everything, I know I still love him, too.

I assume the role of liaison. I communicate with the doctors, nurses, and social workers. My sister with her beard is not well equipped to function in mainstream society. Her role is to look for a new house that they can all live in, within a tight budget.

Sapphire has never had much money. "I'm an artist ahead of my time," she says, and it's probably true. A lack of talent has never been the issue. Her husband, Simon, makes little more at the natural food store he manages. I donate a good portion of our savings to help with my mother's care.

I am mostly relieved that I will not be the one to bear the burden of living with my mother. Casey is almost four and I would resent having to take care of him and my mother at the same time. Besides, unlike my sister, I'm short on optimism, maybe because I've been the one listening to the doctors and their grim prognoses.

After a week, my mother is moved into the occupational therapy unit. I try to jar her memory.

"These are pictures of us in Hawaii," I tell her, but she doesn't remember our vacation. I show her the photos of the sand castles she built with Casey, but she stares blankly at them. She doesn't even remember the helicopter ride over the island down into the deep valley next to a giant waterfall.

I try to explain the situation to my sister, but she remains full of hope.

"I've brought in a powerful Reiki master," she tells me. "She saved her own daughter from a suicide attempt. She brought her back to life simply by laying her hands on her."

I want to ask her, *If she is such a great Reiki master, then why did her daughter try to kill herself in the first place?* But I welcome the master with open arms. I even write her an extra large check. I hire an acupuncturist as well, and I ask Kendra's Episcopal church to remember my mother in prayer. We cover all the bases.

I talk to my mother the same way I talk to Casey. Some of her needs are as basic. "Do you need a new shirt? Did you spill on that one?"

"Yes," she says, but she doesn't elaborate.

After a month in rehab, she is moved into a spacious new house with my sister and her family. "We helped her sell her property in Texas so we could afford this place," my sister says. She shows me the kitchen, which overlooks the five-acre lot.

"Nice," I say.

"Finally, we will be able to control her diet," my sister says, opening the fresh-produce door on her new refrigerator. She has done her best to keep my mother off the hospital food. "I'm going to put her on a raw foods detox diet as soon as she's strong enough to handle it."

I nod and think that once again my sister has someone too help-less to object to her diet. But I remind myself that at least she's gotten over the breatharian goal, and Mama's diet of daily cinnamon rolls and too much coffee could use some improvement. I don't voice any objections about the caregiver my sister hires either.

"This is Elliot," she tells me when I come down to help. "He's agreed to take care of Mama forty hours a week in exchange for free rent and meals. He's wants to be a vegan chef."

I nod and reach out to shake his hand. Elliot is almost thirty-five but reminds me of a teenager, with a constant need to impress everyone around him. "My IQ is so high, I was given the oppor-tunity to skip high school," he tells me. My sister is impressed mostly because he worked at a rainbow gathering, a huge hippie campout my sister tries to attend each year.

"Elliot played music there and he embraces the rainbow way of life," she says.

Elliot, it turns out, is also a true TV addict and this fits well with his caring for Mama. He makes sure Mama gets unlimited cable and begins amassing an enormous video collection, one that could easily rival mine.

MAMA'S MIND STILL WORKS, but without the emotional expression, she is gone for me and I am devastated.

My sister, on the other hand, schooled on Timothy Leary, seems fascinated by the changes in my mother. "Notice how she is only able to understand where her pants are on one side of her body, but not the other. That's why she doesn't understand that she hasn't pulled them up all the way. That part of her brain was damaged by the stroke, and yet her ability to write or read the newspaper is completely intact."

Some of the changes are profound. My mother was always a cheapskate. Her love for warehouses filled with smoke-damaged goods and her desire to eat anything, even if it's rotten, were wiped out by the stroke. Under Elliot's influence and the constant imprinting of more commercial television than she's ever had, suddenly her desires have changed. I take her shopping and she wants everything she's seen advertised.

"The little purple pills called Nexium work best," she parrots.

"We're doing our best to limit her spending and we still need your help," my sister says, after my mother orders several hundred GORE IN 2000 T-shirts. I give my sister money for the cruelty-free vitamin supplements she wants. In addition Bob and I give my sister our old cars, because she and Elliot need reliable transportation to take Mama to her physical therapy and swim class.

"I'd rather be out of money than out of time with Casey," I tell Bob when he complains about having to replace our cars.

Bob, who rides his bicycle to work whenever possible, is better at making do without a car. I, however, immediately buy a green Volvo station wagon, which Casey considers the biggest toy he has ever had. As soon as I pull into the garage, he climbs into the front seat and spends the next twenty minutes experimenting with the various controls.

"This is a drink holder," he says as he pops it in and out.

"Make sure you turn all of the lights off before you get out," I say. I leave him alone in the car. The door leading from the garage to the inside of the house is open so I can hear him, and I have the keys. He isn't going anywhere.

I lie down on the living room couch, glad that he's happy. Who cares that I might have to readjust the car seat later?

Bob comes home with a Volvo sedan the following week.

"It came with this," he says, holding up a video.

"What does it do?" Casey asks.

"It explains how the car works," Bob says.

"Casey, why don't you get into Dad's car?" I say. Casey heads out to the newest car. I turn to Bob, "Why are you telling him about the video?" I pronounce the word *video* as if it's poison.

"I wasn't inviting him to watch it," he says. "Besides, I thought we were going to let him watch on special occasions, like the moon landing."

"After he turns six. And a new car isn't exactly a moon landing."

Bob shrugs. I consider the situation. Maybe this is a special occasion. I remember how excited I was when I was ten and my mother brought home a new Chrysler station wagon.

"Go ahead and let him watch it," I say.

Bob puts the video on when Casey comes inside. I stand in the doorway watching. It's a simple instructional tape, explaining each feature of the car and how it works. There are no sex role stereotypes, no violent scenes, and no suspense whatsoever. It has the same tone as my mother, colorless and boring.

The next day Casey asks me if he can watch it again when Bob is at work. I know I'm in trouble when I acquiesce. I lie down beside him, tired and guilty.

It reminds me of how I felt my freshman year when the campus doctor thought I might have an undetermined ailment and wanted to run some tests.

"You seem kind of anxious about this," the doctor said. "Take these."

I left with a prescription for Valium. It worked really well. I floated around for a few days, and by Saturday night, I figured the pills would be just the ticket to make my unwanted date that night tolerable. I knew that would be the beginning of my end. I sold the rest to the girls in my dorm. I guess they hadn't seemed anxious enough to get their own prescriptions.

I put the video back on the shelf out of sight. Casey doesn't mention it again, but he understands the workings of Bob's car better than Bob does.

"Dad, the button on the left controls the rear defroster," he tells Bob the next time the windows are fogged up.

When Camden asks Casey if he's seen the video *The Iron Giant*, Casey answers enthusiastically, "No, but I've seen a really good video called *Knowing Your S80.*"

"Now he has a better chance of fitting in," I tell Bob later.

"I don't think a Volvo video is going to do the trick," he says.

• • •

I DON'T OBJECT when Bob shows Casey some commands on the computer, too, and soon Casey is programming the screen saver, changing it from a beach scene to a desert one, manipulating the mouse, learning the color code and commands.

He plays around with it when he's with Bob, but only for a few minutes at a time. I consider putting a limit on it, but Bob doesn't think it's necessary.

"At least he'll be able to help you when you're having computer problems," he says. "You won't have to call me at work all of the time."

I nod absently. I don't really care that much. So many things used to seem so important. There was so much to get worked up about. Not anymore. I feel like I'm on Valium again, except without the good feelings, just the numbness.

At night I begin to have sleep problems. One night, after lying in bed for an hour, I'm still not the slightest bit sleepy. Bob is snoring loudly.

"Are you are asleep," I ask in a voice even louder than his snoring.

"Huh? What?" he mumbles.

I nudge him gently. Then not so gently.

"What time is it?" he mumbles again, but his eyes are still closed. He sounds annoyed.

"Not that late," I lie.

I give him a kiss and run my fingers across his chest wondering if this will quell his irritation at being disturbed. He's awake in no time, or at least I think he's awake. I remember hearing about this woman who managed to have sex and cook a big meal in the middle of the night without knowing it, because she was actually asleep the whole time.

I give him another kiss. He kisses me back and starts making his way down the length of my body. He must be awake, because he seems to know what he's doing. Of course, we've been married so long, I'm sure he *could* do this in his sleep. After a while I climb on top of him, hoping the exertion will eventually create the soporific effect I need. But no such luck, and when we're done, Bob is instantly snoring again.

I want to wake him up again to talk, although I'm not sure what I want to say, and even if I knew, I'm not sure Bob would say what I needed to hear from him.

I get out of bed to make a snack, wondering how I'll function without enough sleep. I wander into the guest room and grab the remote. Jay Leno is interviewing Bruce Willis. I switch to channel 12. But no matter what I watch, I feel overstimulated with all of television's flashing lights and noise. What used to put me to sleep is doing the opposite now.

If only I had C-SPAN. That would put me to sleep. I watched it when I was in Eugene with Mama and slept through half of it. Then I took her for a walk in her wheelchair. I pushed her along the paved walkway by the river and it occurred to me that I could finally walk with her at a speed I liked. She seemed to like it, too. I still half expected her to say, "What a splendid day it is!" But that's what the old Mama would have said.

I turn off the set, pick up the first Harry Potter book, and start reading.

"I CAN'T HAVE anything new," I tell Georgette. I'm sitting in her cushiony chair with my legs curled up against my chest. She gives me a crocheted blanket, pink and purple. She probably crocheted it herself.

I tell her how I've read the first Harry Potter book over and over. I never understood why anyone would bother to read any book a second time. I've never minded watching reruns over and over, but that's different. The beauty of reading Harry Potter over and over is that it puts me to sleep rather quickly now. I didn't know that books could serve the same purpose as TV, the purpose of numbing out the world.

"You're grieving," she tells me.

"But my mother hasn't died," I say.

"A part of her has died."

"But that part could come back."

Georgette nods, but there isn't the usual sparkle in her eyes, only sadness.

10

Cocktail Hour

Mama is spending the night. Maybe by having her with me in Portland, I'll learn to enjoy this new, differently abled mother more and give my sister a much needed break at the same time. In the morning I pull Mama's wheelchair up to the table, positioning her so her good ear is closest to Casey.

I give him a stack of books he received at his fourth birthday party last week.

"She'll be happy to hear you read," I tell him. "Just use a loud enough voice."

He picks up *Go, Dog. Go!* and reads like a champion.

"That's nice," she says, her voice so flat that I'm surprised he picks up the next book and keeps reading. When he's finished, he turns to me.

"She doesn't seem interested."

"I know," I say, thinking that *Hop on Pop* isn't exactly a compelling story. But the grandmother Mama used to be would have been positively glowing with pride and enthusiasm at this child who is barely four years old and reading like a pro.

Casey puts his books away.

"You can try playing a game with her," I tell him.

He sets up Chutes and Ladders, a game Mama will be able to play with her unparalyzed hand. She is a dull companion for him, although she's more animated with him than she is with anyone else.

"She's moving the piece the wrong way, Mom."

"Be patient with her," I say, and I realize that if he's noticed how impatient I am with her, I've set a horrible example.

He moves her playing piece, the African American girl with the green dress, and continues playing, but I suspect it's only because he loves games so much.

"I'VE DECIDED TO enroll Casey in a Waldorf preschool," I tell Bob. Mama has gone back to Eugene and September is closing in on us.

"Isn't Waldorf some sort of cult?"

"Why do you say that?"

"They think kids shouldn't be taught to read until they're at least seven, or something about whenever their first adult teeth come in."

I think about Casey's teeth. He has yet to lose any of his baby ones but he can read the word *toothpaste.* "Well, at least they don't believe in kids watching television, and the preschool is supposed to be really sweet. It's called Little Waldorf."

"I guess you don't want him to go back to Pine Ridge."

"I would get post-traumatic stress if he did."

BOB'S RIGHT ABOUT the Waldorf school's ideas on reading, but I'm not bothered by it. The teacher there is named Leslie.

She shows Casey around and explains the school's philosophy to me. Her voice is soothing as she describes the simple tools and fabric the children use to create little hideaways in the room.

"Bright colors are overstimulating," she says, "and clearly defined games keep children from living in the dreamlike state they are supposed to experience at this precious time in their lives." I nod pleasantly. The sound of her voice makes me want to curl up on the rug and go to sleep. I look around the room. In lieu of games and puzzles there are faceless dolls on the shelves. "Without faces, the children are better able to imagine the dolls to be the way they want them to be," she says.

I'm not sure Casey will care for the dolls one way or another, as much as I would like it to be so. I got him a dollhouse last year and he tried to play with it, but after a while he confessed to me, "I don't understand what to do with it."

I notice a box of plain wooden blocks on another shelf and feel more hopeful. Casey sees them, too, and heads over to play with them.

He starts the following week in September.

"Just have fun," I say, giving him a hug and a kiss the first day.

He waves good-bye and happily makes his way over to the blocks. He will spend the morning singing, building, painting, gardening, and cooking. The snacks are all homemade.

THE TEACHER LIKES CASEY. "I can tell that he doesn't watch television," she says, after he's been going for two weeks. We are standing by the door while the children play outside. "He listens intently to the stories I tell and he's very peaceful. He doesn't mimic the cartoon characters the way the other children do."

"Are there that many children here who watch television?" I ask.

"You'd be surprised how many of our children do," she says.

I nod. I had expected that I would finally be meeting parents like me, except they would be more centered and less neurotic than I am. They would be the type of parents who grow their own herbs and don't think twice about their decision not to own a television.

"What was I supposed to do except put Erin in front of the television?" Jennifer tells me. "I was sick all weekend, so I got a bunch of videos."

We're waiting outside the classroom for our kids. It's October and I'm dressed for the cool autumn weather in a turtleneck and sweater.

"I'm just afraid that once I start, that's what Casey will expect," I say. I feel more comfortable telling Jennifer what I think because of the school's philosophy.

Jennifer nods. She has grayish hair pulled back into a short pony tail and she's wearing purple pants like the hippies wear at Portland's Saturday Market. "That could happen," she agrees.

Brenna, who is listening to us, says she lets her kids watch Winnie the Pooh videos when she needs a break.

"What would be worse? Screaming at my kids or letting them watch television?" she says. "It's harder when you have more than one screaming child."

She has a point, I have to admit. Casey can play quietly by himself without worrying about anyone pulling his hair. But at least Brenna would never consider putting her kids in front of the television when Casey is at her house. "When you have friends over, you are supposed to play, not watch TV," she says.

Brenna's boy, Adrian, is becoming a good friend to Casey.

They've played together several times already. Adrian's playroom has a little stove and a miniature table with chairs all made of natural wood, the way it is at Little Waldorf. I worried that when Adrian came over to our house, Brenna wouldn't want him playing with Casey's plastic bananas and oranges. But, unlike me, Brenna is flexible and easygoing. And she has a great next-door neighbor, too.

"If I need a break and I don't want to rely on Winnie the Pooh, I just take my kids next door and Shauna watches them, and we've both agreed not to have the TV on when our kids are together."

"I don't think my neighbors would go for that," I tell her.

CASEY IS AT Little Waldorf three hours a day, three days a week. I'm making the most of my time while he's away. I take long walks, eat out with friends, and get my work done quickly. Sometimes I even clean the house a little. I'm no longer worried about Casey when he's at school, and I've discovered public radio. It doesn't have commercials and there's nearly always something interesting on, once the classical music portion is finished.

I listen to *Talk of the Nation* before picking Casey up from school, and on the weekends, Bob and I listen to *Wait Wait . . . Don't Tell Me! Michael Feldman's Whad'Ya Know?* and *Prairie Home Companion*. When Casey is around, I leave it on only for certain shows. His teacher Leslie would disapprove of ever having the radio on when Casey is around, no matter what the program. "Young children shouldn't hear disembodied voices," she would say. I take comfort in knowing that there are people with even more extreme views than mine.

Besides, I read in the book *The Plug-in Drug* that radio, unlike television, still allows the listener to use his or her imagination. It must be true, because I keep imagining what the people on the radio look like. Ira Glass of *This American Life* sounds like he's in his early twenties and wears an earring and maybe has a piercing or two elsewhere as well. Terry Gross I see as a tall, sophisticated brunette with a warm smile. When I finally get the public radio magazine in the mail after pledging, I'm disappointed. These people are all wrong.

"That's why they're on the radio," Bob explains to me after I have seen what Garrison Keillor looks like.

Now I understand why phone sex on those 1-900 lines is so popular. It's easy to make people into what you want when you don't have to see them.

By December I'm finally able to reach my goal — set four years ago — of watching two hours a week of television. Even in the evening, I'm not escaping into the guest room anymore to watch sitcoms while Bob is with Casey. Sometimes I go over to Kendra's if I need to get out of the house, but mostly I'm better at being at home.

Casey is figuring out how to play the songs he sings at Little Waldorf on the piano. They are tender songs, the type of songs that keep children in the so-called land of the imagination, according to Leslie. I close my eyes while he sings to me, his voice sweet and clear. "Over in the meadow where the bluebirds sing."

Then he plays the first line on the piano. I'm impressed at how quickly he finds the right keys, and being the overzealous mom that I am, I try to show him the proper way to place his fingers on them.

"I like doing it the other way," he says after my little demonstration. I back away because I'm pretty sure that's what a good parent would do. He isn't ready to learn technique right now. But after a while, I discover that he's interested in learning about the different scales and the different keys songs can be played in.

"You just played that song in the key of F," I tell him. "See, there was a B-flat in it." I point to it and he smiles.

Encouraged, I show him the rest of the scales. "C is the easiest," I say. "It's all white keys."

He plays around with what I've taught him. I'm not sure what he'll remember. But within a couple of weeks, not only has he figured out how to play all his favorite songs from school, but he's learned how to transpose them. This is truly remarkable, even if I do say so myself.

"Listen, Mom," he calls to me. I'm sitting on the couch across from him.

"I'm going to play this song in the key of C, F, G, and D," he says. "First, I'll do it in C."

"That's C, all right," I say, and I wish my mother were here to applaud him.

I remember messing around on the piano when I was little. "What do you think, Mama?" I would yell out. "It's the Winston cigarette commercial song."

"Sounds just like it," my mother would say.

"Now I'll play you the Kool cigarette commercial."

Guests would come over and my mother would try to get me to play for them.

"Wait till you hear her play the Marlboro song," she would say. "She just loves commercials!"

Eventually my mother signed me up for piano lessons and I took them for years but never advanced beyond "Für Elise." It might have helped if I had actually practiced. I took the piano books home each week in my piano book bag and I brought them back the next week, still in the bag untouched.

My mother never made me practice, and I suppose the teacher didn't care as long as she was getting paid. Playing the piano just couldn't compete with *The Dick Van Dyke Show*.

But Casey doesn't need *The Dick Van Dyke Show*. I listen to him now, comfortably transposing his song, finally playing it in the key of D, just as he said he would.

"Great job!" I say. He beams.

"You play something, too, Mom. Play the recorder!"

I hesitate but he looks so enthusiastic. I pick up the recorder I got from Amber.

"I'll have to learn how to play it," I tell him, "and I don't know if I'll be able to play anything that's not in the key of G."

He smiles. "G is a good key," he says.

I'VE JUST GOTTEN off the phone with my mother. She hung up before I could tell her about Casey's incredible musical ability. She hung up before I could say much of anything and she didn't even say good-bye. I pictured her lying in the special hospital-type bed my sister bought for her and in the middle of our conversation, simply moving the receiver aside the way she might move a cup of coffee out of the way or a plate of crumbs.

I'm missing the mother I knew before the stroke. My sister continues to lay her healing hands on her and I continue to pay for the acupuncturist to poke her body in hopes of rewiring her brain. The occupational therapist says she's making progress. I'm still hoping that she'll somehow become more like the mother I once knew.

Casey and I are in the living room. Bob won't be home for another two hours. I don't really want to pay attention to my child's explanation of a song he's figuring out how to play on the piano. This is the time when Olivia's *101 Dalmatians* video would sure hit the spot, but I don't want to drug my child in order to get the escape I need. But what else can I do? And then it occurs to me. I can drug myself. I glance at the clock. It's two p.m., already well into happy hour in Texas, and sitting in the highest cabinet above the stove is a bottle of Absolut. I reflect on the fact that Casey hasn't nursed for over a year. I can do whatever I want with my body now. Maybe this is what women really mean when they talk about getting their bodies back after weaning. They want them back to freely abuse them with alcohol and drugs.

I'm already feeling happier even before I get the bottle down and open it. I pour a shot into a fancy highball glass, and I sit down in the living room. After one sip I feel the effects instantaneously. I am my father's child. He liked vodka, my mother always said. I still have vivid memories of sitting in his lap watching *The Three Stooges*. He'd laugh when Moe would grab Curly by the ear and I would wince.

I remember watching scary movies with him, too, mummy and werewolf movies. We would sit in a big black leather chair together, and when the werewolf started to transform I would bury my face in my dad's chest and he would say, "It's not real."

I pull out a John Grisham novel, *The Street Lawyer*, a perfect book for people who watch a lot of television. It has plenty of dialogue and a fast pace. I turn to the first page and am instantly hooked. Casey continues to play the piano and talk about what he is doing. I sip my cocktail and utter "uh huh" every now and then without even losing my place in the book. I'm in heaven. The vodka is giving me what I need most, the chance to be worry-free, to not care that much about anything, to finally let go.

I think about what Georgette would say. *Couldn't you learn to do that without alcohol? No,* I'd tell her. I don't think I could learn to get this feeling or *lack* of feeling without alcohol. Maybe some people can reach a higher state of consciousness without drugs, like the Beatles said they did when they went to India to learn how to meditate. But I'm interested in reaching a lower state of consciousness, and I don't see how I can do that without drugs, especially if I don't have television.

Casey is telling me that he's going to change the rhythm as well as the key this time.

"Good," I say vaguely, and that's all I need to say. It's such an easy life. No wonder my parents chose it. There's nothing to worry about, or if there is, you don't notice. I remember the way my parents laughed when they were drunk. My mother had a full-bodied laugh. My parents were never mean drunks. They missed a lot, is all.

I sip on my drink, a little at a time. An hour passes before I finish it, before Casey begins to move onto something else. No harm done, I think to myself. I've had my fun and everything is fine.

Except that when night falls, I can't sleep. It feels as if I've eaten chocolate cake, with six cups of coffee to go with it. I can feel my heart beating faster than usual.

I get up to make a snack. I try to do it quietly, but Bob wakes up.

"Why are you up?" His eyes are barely open.

"For kicks," I say. "Go back to sleep."

I take a warm bath, but that doesn't help either. Nothing helps. It doesn't seem fair really. I hardly ever drink because I'm so afraid of ending up like my mother. I've given up so many vices: sugar, coffee, and television. Now it seems that if I want to get a good night's sleep, alcohol will have to go, too.

IN SWEDEN, NORWAY, and Finland, marketing to children under twelve is prohibited, but in the United States the average child sees 40,000 commercials a year. My niece Amber was telling me about a commercial that annoyed her. She's staying at our house for her spring break. It seems necessary to have her here now, with Mama unavailable. She's family, the young and healthy version of family.

"It was for Aleve and the woman with the headache acted so stupid."

"What's a commercial?" Casey asks. I'm sprawled out on the living room couch and they're sitting next to me.

"It's an advertisement they show on television." I remind him of the ads we've seen in magazines and in the newspaper and on billboards.

"I've seen a lot of commercials now, ever since Grandma moved in," Amber says.

"Are you glad you watch more television now?" I ask her.

"I like *The Simpsons*," she says.

"*The Simpsons* is great," I say. "How did you feel not having a television before, Amber?"

"It was fine."

"You know, Casey, some kids watch so much TV that they don't get to go to the zoo, play games, or just lie around and cuddle together. Does that sound fun?"

"No, it doesn't," he says.

"When you're ready, we'll watch some television, but not more two hours a week." I try to be matter of fact about this.

"I already watched *Knowing Your S80,*" he says.

"That's right," I say. "You see, there are some good things to watch."

I consider giving him other examples but am hard-pressed to think of what they are right now.

The more I stay away from television, the more my taste is improving. I want quality or nothing at all. Perhaps the same will happen for Casey. Dumb shows won't hold his interest for long. Maybe he'll only watch the PBS series of the civil rights movement that Bob has on tape.

I hand Amber the instructions to a new game called Enchanted Forest. Games are Casey's passion now. For Christmas he got more than his share to add to his growing collection. European games like Harvest and Snowstorm, games that are supposed to teach kids to cooperate instead of to win, and competitive games like Monopoly Junior and Sorry!

I liked games when I was a child. My sister and mother wouldn't play them with me, but my brother usually would, although this had its drawbacks.

"You just took five hundred dollars from the bank, didn't you?" I would shout.

I knew it was pointless to complain to my mother.

"He's younger than you. That's just his way of trying to keep up with you."

Later on, when my mother would suddenly find herself short of cash, she would make similar excuses for his stealing.

"He's having a hard time."

In the past few days, Amber has taught Casey to play every new game he has, including some of the games Bob and I already owned: Monopoly and Yahtzee.

"It's amazing that he can do the math required for these games," she tells me.

"Well, you help him."

"Hardly at all," she says, and I know she's telling the truth. Math has come even easier to him than reading, and he's a natural at it.

I nod absently at Amber. I can't help but think that once again Casey has another way in which he's different from his peers at Waldorf, and everywhere else for that matter.

"Aren't you glad he's so good at these games?" Amber asks, probably noticing my lack of excitement.

I smile. "Of course I am."

Mostly I'm just glad she's here. Bob and I can play a game or two every day with Casey, but we have our limits. Given the opportunity, Casey and Amber can stay with it for hours, as long as I used to spend watching a *Mary Tyler Moore* marathon. If only I could convince Amber to move in with us and spend the rest of her life playing these games with him.

As soon as Amber leaves, our house feels lonely, so Casey and I go to Rebecca's. Kendra and Hannah had arrived a few minutes before we did. I didn't know they would be here, but I'm feeling pretty good, not jealous or weird. We've been chatting away and our kids have been playing well together, the three of them.

Kendra is telling us how she can't understand why Hannah wants to wear high heels and refuses to wear her tennis shoes anymore.

"I don't know where she learns these things!" she says.

"Oh, girls are just like that," Rebecca says.

I smile all cheery and agreeable, wanting to be a part of this little trio, not some critical bitch.

Bob arrives after a while to take Casey to his swimming lesson.

"Are you coming, too?" he asks me.

"You go ahead," I say. "I'll just stay here and walk home later by myself."

Rebecca calls Camden and Hannah into the living room as soon as Bob and Casey are gone.

"I'm putting the movie on now," she tells them.

I watch Hannah and Camden sit down contentedly in front of the set. Rebecca and Kendra look noticeably relaxed, and I can tell it's a familiar routine for them. I feel strange. I've been cramping their style. I suspect that Kendra spends lots of time over here with Rebecca, chatting away while their kids stay in the same place, quiet and peaceful. They probably want to show me what I'm missing by being so pure. I'm the virgin and they are wild ones having all of the fun.

"Gosh," I say. "I better get going. I want to have a nice, long walk." I stand up and stretch my arms and bend my knees as if I'm getting ready to work out.

"Oh," Rebecca says, not all that friendly, and that's when I'm sure that they had planned to have the video on all along and would have started it sooner had I not shown up with Casey. I feel like smashing their television. And just when I thought I was becoming more mature.

"I'll see you all later," I say, and hurry out.

I INVITE KENDRA out the next night in order to feel better about our friendship. Bob and Quinn are watching the kids. She and I are taking a long walk together. I'm expecting to clear things up, talk about my feelings as if we're on *The Jerry Springer Show* without the yelling. But Kendra has other things on her mind.

"I've fallen in love with someone else," she tells me, as soon as we're away from her house.

"You're kidding," I say. "Who is it?"

"I met him on the set of *Jolie,* the last play I did. He played the part of the greedy headhunter. Do you remember? His name is Logan and we've been e-mailing each other ever since."

We are near the top of the hill above our houses and we would be able to see all the way to the coast range if it weren't cloudy. I suddenly forget all about the other day at Rebecca's. I've been watching so little television lately that I'm starved for real, authentic drama. This is better than an episode of *Dynasty.*

"What's he like?"

"He's depressed like me," she says, as though this is good news. "I gave him some of my Wellbutrin."

"Have you slept with him?" I ask, trying not to sound too eager to hear the answer.

"No," she says.

"Well, remember that if you do, and you eventually end up together, you'll never be able to trust that he won't find someone else again and keep it a secret from you." I remind of her of the Meryl Streep movie *Falling in Love.* "They were both married, but they didn't do anything about it until they had each left their marriages."

Maybe someday I might actually refer to books or even real-life experiences while trying to help someone. I think it could happen. Already I'm beginning to make up stories in my head to entertain myself. It's a lost ability I'm regaining.

"I'm not planning to sleep with him," she says. "Do you want to see his e-mail to me?"

She pulls a folded up piece of paper out of her jeans pocket. She's blushing.

"You've got to be careful with that," I tell her, pointing to the e-mail. I read it over a few times. It's not that exciting. Mostly he talks about his dog and how sad she looks when he leaves her each day. I'm thinking that maybe the dog needs Wellbutrin, too. "Promise me you'll call me before you do anything stupid," I tell her.

"I will!" she says.

11

A Lovely Offer

Bob and I are staying at a resort less than an hour away from home called the Skamania Lodge. We have cable and pay-per-view movies, but we brought two copies of the fourth Harry Potter book, which just came out. I've been without TV completely for almost a full month.

Kellie is at home with Casey. I miss him, but this is my attempt to be more present with Bob. Bob is trying, too. I've agreed not to call Kellie and ask about Casey or call Kendra and ask about her love interest. He's agreed not to talk about how much everything costs, including the new earrings I just bought at the hotel shop.

We took a long walk in the woods and now we're stretched out in a giant bathtub reading our Harry Potter books and talking. "Let's order room service later for dinner," I suggest.

"And for breakfast, too."

Anyone at the front desk would think we were having nonstop sex the way we're holing up in this room. Who would suspect two adults of plowing through J. K. Rowling's latest masterpiece? Not that I haven't thought about having sex since we settled into this bath, but I've never enjoyed doing it in the water. It always seems like it will be exciting, but it never is. I glance at the bar of soap and consider using it in a sensual manner with Bob, but it's a deodorant soap, which means it isn't naturally scented or even fragrance free. Forget it.

I lean back against Bob's chest. I do feel relaxed, amazingly enough. I don't have to worry about whether Casey is eating his spinach or if I'm going to get enough sleep. I don't have to concentrate on the housework I'm avoiding either. I can just lie here and talk to Bob and read about Harry Potter's experience at Hogwarts.

A FEW DAYS after we're back, Casey turns five. He'll be starting kindergarten in less than a month.

"We could keep him in a Waldorf school," Bob suggests. I know he's saying this because, whenever possible, Bob would prefer not to make changes. The exception is with our computer, which he's constantly trading in or upgrading.

"If we did, he wouldn't be misunderstood about not watching television," I say.

"That's right," he says.

"But Brenna says parents aren't welcome in the classroom. That's the Waldorf way."

Bob says he's not concerned about that because Leslie was wonderful. But how can I be sure about the rest of the teachers there? What if Casey ends up with some nut for a teacher, someone like the guy in Jonestown who separated children from their parents and brainwashed them all to commit mass suicide? We wouldn't know it until it was too late, because parents aren't allowed in the classroom.

Mostly, though, I'm not sure that I can be a true Waldorf parent. If I put him in a Waldorf school, I would be finally admitting that I'm truly different, a nonconformist and proud of it. I'm not ready to admit that yet.

Our neighborhood school would certainly be an improvement over what I'd known as a child, but it is also on my last-resort list. I had enjoyed teaching there, and it's in walking distance, so we would be helping to stop global warming. I knew it was politically incorrect to abandon it, a public school. But, even with all the extra support the parents provided, it was still too prison-like, and my child, being small, might be bullied by the inmates. Moreover, without knowing the latest cartoons, he would be a complete misfit there.

My friend Sarah suggests I find out about a so-called free school called Willow Creek. I call only out of curiosity and someone named Alex answers.

"Tell me about your classrooms," I say.

"We don't have classrooms," he says.

"What are your teachers like?"

"We have no teachers per se. Your child will be our teacher as much as we will be his."

"Does anyone get paid to be there?" I ask.

"Maybe you should examine your capitalistic interests."

I PROBABLY *SHOULD* examine my capitalistic interests. I know only that the school I like the best will require the most capital from us.

"I want him to go to Martin Smith," I tell Bob.

"Don't only rich people go there?"

"It's not just for rich people," I tell him. "One in five families receive financial aid or scholarship money. And we're really lucky even to get on the waiting list."

Casey had been required to meet with a group of seven other children while the teachers observed him in a classroom setting. I presume this was so they could see if he was the type who threw things at the other kids and stole their crayons. I'd done my best to unobtrusively prepare him for the meeting.

"We're going to play a new game called school game," I said.

I dumped the stuffed animals out onto the carpet.

Casey grabbed his favorite monkey, a spider monkey. He was thrilled that I was willing to play with his stuffed animals.

"We need eight students," I said.

"Little Bear can be the teacher," he said, pointing to his favorite bear.

I held Little Bear up and made it talk. "Good morning. What's your name?"

"I'm Spida," Casey made the monkey say. This was a good sign, because half the time when someone said hi to him, he didn't answer. It was these basic social niceties I wanted him to master before he went to Martin Smith to be observed. Some parents work hard to get their kids to learn the alphabet. I just wanted Casey to smile and acknowledge that others exist.

CASEY DIDN'T GET accepted until two weeks before school started. He was on a waiting list until the admissions director probably tired of my weekly phone calls asking about possible openings. Finally, in desperation, I consulted the psychic that Leila had mentioned when I'd interviewed her for child care.

"He will be accepted the third week in August," the psychic said. We were talking on the phone so I don't know if she was looking into a crystal ball or staring at tea leaves.

On August 17, the admissions director called. I would have

been stunned at the accuracy of the psychic, except that she also had predicted that I would receive a large amount of money from a dead aunt on the same day, and that didn't happen.

I go to the parent social a week before school starts. I assume that parents at this school must really value education for their children and that they will understand why it's important to limit television viewing.

"We don't really watch TV," I tell Lauren. She has a boy named Grayson who will be in Casey's class.

"We don't either," she says. "Well, except videos."

"We really limit it, too," Alice tells me. "We never watch it during dinner, and Bennet can't bring his Game Boy to the table."

Stacey, a skinny mom with thick glasses, says, "Hampton just watches cartoons on Saturday, *Pokémon* especially, and then after school he likes *Arthur.*"

A woman named Mary Beth lets out a sigh when she hears this and says, "My daughter Carolyn won't fall asleep unless she's watching a *Rugrats* video, so I had to put a set in her room."

I'M MOSTLY SURPRISED about the part that television will play in the classroom. Every Friday all the kids gather on the carpet and a big screen set is rolled out in front of them.

I ask the parent-teacher liaison about it at the open house the day before school starts. She's a tall woman with an elongated neck and face. Her name is Erica and she frequently dresses in bright orange. I drop by her office and act casual and friendly, as though I'm just a little curious about it.

"We only have it on after lunch recess on Fridays. It gives the teachers time to relax with the kids."

I nod politely, sweet and supportive. I want her to know that I'm a grateful parent, the kind teachers like. I'm not about to criticize those who are about to be responsible for my child. I don't mention that for $12,000 a year in tuition, maybe watching television isn't what I expected.

"It's all good stuff," she adds reassuringly. "*The Magic School Bus* and *Arthur*."

I smile and imagine Casey saying what he used to say when he was two: "TV, we don't need TV!"

He doesn't remember saying it, any more than he remembers watching the Volvo video. That night I try to put a positive spin on the situation.

"On Fridays, you're going to get to watch television at school," I tell him. "And because it's such a great school, you can be sure that they'll show only good programs."

We're in his room going through his chest of drawers, picking out clothes he can wear to school. I've carefully hidden the striped T-shirt with the stains on it so he won't be able to wear it there. He has made a stack of shorts.

"Does everyone watch it?" he asks.

"I think so," I say.

He goes back to work and doesn't say anything else. I relax a little. Maybe he won't leave the classroom. Maybe he won't stand up and tell the teacher that he's not interested in becoming a television zombie. I remind myself that I've never used those exact words around him, and I don't think his teacher at Little Waldorf did either. But that's what we both were thinking.

• • •

Bob is on the phone with Rebecca. "Camden wants to see Casey this weekend," he says to me.

I shake my head. "We're booked up this weekend. Tell her I'll call her back to schedule something."

Bob says something to Rebecca and hangs up the phone.

"What's wrong with Camden? They're best friends, after all."

"Camden's not important right now."

"I'm sure Rebecca would appreciate hearing that."

"We have to concentrate on school kids. And I'm not going to be picky."

I'm still upset about the get-acquainted conference we had a couple of weeks after school started. The teacher Judy said that Casey keeps to himself at recess. It was like a flashback to the Pine Ridge preschool nightmare, except he isn't dumping out toys, at least.

"He's shy," Bob explained to her. "I was that way, too. I used to hide under the table when company came over." Judy looked at Bob curiously, scrutinizing him. *What kind of nutcase was* he *as a kid,* she must've been thinking.

"Maybe it would help if he had some playdates," she said. "Then he might join in at recess."

We invite over Bennet, an energetic boy, and he and Casey spend most of their time building things out of LEGOs and blowing them up. When Hampton is here, he teaches Casey what a light saber is. "It's from *Star Wars*." Another classmate, Kyle, describes a car crash he saw on channel 6. He demonstrates the crash using Casey's Brio train.

"It was really cool," he tells Casey.

I start to interrupt them and say *Sounds awful,* but stop myself.

I make playdates fun. I pull out a puppet theater and train set. I make fun trays of snacks with fresh strawberries, slices of cheddar cheese, and chocolate chip cookies. I bring out the "grow your own rock" kit that Bob's parents sent and messy art projects. I let them use our couch cushions to build forts. When it's nice outside, I take the kids to the zoo or we hike through the woods.

As if this isn't already enough, I move in with the big artillery. Casey and I discover a giant treehouse by the creek near our house. It's a little rickety, so I put Bob to work fixing it. At first I consider showing Casey that I can use a hammer so he'll see that women can use these tools, too, except that I actually can't, at least not well.

"Just add a roof and another platform or two," I yell up to Bob. "I want it to be like it was on the Swiss Family Robinson movie."

Bob's mouth drops open, but he keeps working.

It takes a lot to compete with television.

By the time our next conference rolls around, I'm exhausted, but hoping that my efforts will have paid off.

Judy is waiting for us as we venture into the classroom and sit in the small chairs set up for us.

"Well, he's doing better," she says. "Kids seem to like him and they really like coming over to your house. I hear them talking. 'You're going to Casey's. Lucky you! You'll really have fun there.'" She smiles. "You've done a good job with the playdates."

She pauses and swishes her tea bag around in her cup. "He seems friendly in class, too, but he still doesn't join in at recess."

"We'll keep working on it," I tell her.

I'm so tired of working on things.

But already a strategy is forming in my mind. I'll come to recess to help him join in. I'll have playdates at school on the playground, maybe on the weekends. I'll have group playdates there.

I start to mention these ideas to Judy, but I hesitate because she might think I'm overly involved. Who in the hell would think that?

"Now, about his academic work . . ." Her eyes widen as she pulls out his tests. "I'm sure you know by now that he's exceptional. I believe that he's the brightest child I've come across in my twenty years of teaching."

I nod, thinking that maybe we'll get away from here without being tortured.

"But there is something that concerns me." She picks up his notebook. "In this assignment, the kids are supposed to think of something that begins with each letter of the alphabet and then draw a picture of it." She flips through the pages. "Casey has drawn only roads," she said. I look at the page for H and see Humphrey and a perfect representation of the street. I turn the page and see Irving Street winding up into the hills.

"I think he's a little stuck on roads. I have trouble getting him to draw something else," she says.

"He definitely gets really focused on things," I say. "First it was puzzles. Then it was LEGOs. Now it's roads and maps. But I can help him make a shift if you want."

That's me, always ready to help. Or as Bob would say—overcompensate, hover, and suffocate.

Judy smiles in a patronizing way. She doesn't want my help. She doesn't necessarily even want him to change. She just wants there to be something wrong with him.

"Maybe it would help if he watched videos," she says. "We were having a class discussion about the best movies, and he didn't have any favorites."

I turn to look at Bob to see if he's surprised. He's deliberately avoiding my gaze.

"Here's a list of videos the kids are watching," she says. "Watching them could help him at recess, too. A lot of the games the kids play are based on television shows and movies."

I stare at the list, my worst fears realized. She thinks he needs to watch television to fit in. I read the list. *Toy Story* and *A Bug's Life* are at the top. I want to ask her if she has considered sending a list home to other kids, a list of all the things they could do with their time besides watching television.

I tuck the list in my purse and smile politely. "You know, I think Casey just needs a little more time to make friends. That's how it was at his preschool, and he was happy there," I say, trying hard not to sound defensive. "And he says he's happy here, too." I want to add how amazing that is considering what his teacher is like.

BOB AND I WAIT until we're in the car before saying anything to each other.

"She doesn't understand him and she doesn't want to learn more about him from us!" I say. "And what's so bad about drawing roads anyway?"

"I don't think you're being fair to her," he says. "She means well."

I look at the list. I have already seen a lot of these movies and don't feel he's ready for any of them. I hand the list to Bob.

"*Toy Story* is obnoxious," I say.

"Then forget about it!"

"But will he feel left out if he doesn't see it?" Always the same question. And never a clear answer.

In the evening, I sit next to Casey on the couch and show him the list.

"These are movies that some of the kids in your class have seen."

"I know. The teacher asked us what our favorite movie was."

He says this matter of factly and doesn't seem upset in the slightest.

"I told you we were going to wait until you're six before we started watching movies, but if you're interested in watching any of them now, you can," I say. "That way you'll know what the kids in your class are talking about when they discuss movies."

He reads over the list. "No thanks," he says.

"It's okay if you want to watch them," I say slowly and loudly, as if I'm talking to a slightly deaf person. He looks right at me to show me that he understands, or maybe he thinks I've become hearing impaired now. I consider complimenting him on his good eye contact.

"I'm not really interested in them."

I stare at him. I've never been very good at taking no for an answer.

"What if we go to Powells and I pick out the book versions of these movies and we read them. Would you like that?"

"Okay," he says, "but not now." He points to the Portland map on the coffee table. "I want to see how Hamilton Street connects to Shattuck."

AFTER I DROP HIM off at school the next day, I head to Powells. Casey gave me directions. "Turn left on Barnes Road," he said. "It will lead to Burnside after you come to Miller Street." His fascination with roads has its benefits.

Powells is a giant new-and-used bookstore, adored by book lovers everywhere. Naturally, I rarely set foot in it.

When I get to the children's section, I try to find the Disney books on my own, but in the end I have to ask for help. A petite woman with short, cropped hair and red glasses shows me the shelf I need.

"Thanks," I say, embarrassed that I have asked to see the lowest of the low when it comes to children's books. I want to tell her that I prefer *Charlotte's Web* and *The Trumpet of the Swan*, but I stop myself. I'm trying to get out of the habit of always explaining myself. Bob used to ask me, "Who are you trying to impress?" "Everyone," I finally answered. He stopped asking me after that.

The woman leaves me alone, and I quickly pull the books onto the floor and spread them out in front of me. I get out my list and start checking off what I find. It's not as easy as I thought it would be. There are at least three versions of *The Lion King* and four of the *101 Dalmatians*. After flipping through the pages of *Pocahontas,* I can see why I have been sheltering him. Did Pocahontas really dress like that?

Next to the Disney books I notice an assortment of books based on television shows, *Power Rangers* and the like. Maybe these books would have made me read more as a child. I would have ordered the continuing adventures of *The Partridge Family, Bewitched,* and *Batman*. But I doubt they would have helped me to pick up a real book and start from scratch getting to know the characters. That takes energy, more energy than I had.

I place a large stack of books on the check-out counter. I wish I had thrown a copy of *A Farewell to Arms* on top so I could appear intellectual. I look at the guy in front of me. He has a goatee and a ring through his tongue. He glances up at me, and I feel compelled to say something.

"This is a first for me, buying a bunch of Disney books," I explain. "You see, my kid doesn't watch television and I thought I'd give him a chance to see what the rest of the world is watching."

The guy, who is in his early twenties, doesn't care. He probably doesn't have any kids, and even if he did, he probably would put them in front of the television so he could finish reading his classic copy of *Fahrenheit 451*.

"Would you like a bag for these?" he asks.

"Yes, please," I say. It isn't raining, but I want to hide my cache from anyone I might happen to meet on the way to my car. I might as well be buying a dildo and handcuffs from the porn store down the street for all my concern.

When Casey gets home, I try to act excited about the new books.

"See, there's Simba," I say, pointing to the little lion cub on the first page. I flip through a few more pages. "And that's his evil uncle, Scar."

He glances at the picture of Scar battling with Simba's dad. Then he pushes the book back toward me. I've seen most of these animated movies with my nieces and so I figured I'd be able to make these books sound exciting enough, but he's not that easily swayed.

"There's a Disney Web site, too," I tell him enthusiastically, leading him to the computer. He climbs into my lap. "This is *Beauty and the Beast*," I say. He uses the mouse to turn the pages on the screen.

"Do you like this story?" I ask him.

"It's all right," he says with little expression. He almost sounds like my mother, and he's generally a pretty animated guy.

"Do you want to see the movie?"

"No, that's okay," he says.

• • •

I CONSIDER FORCING him to watch it, but when I mention this to Bob, he looks at me as if I've suggested I give Casey castor oil.

"None of what you're doing is necessary," he tells me. Casey is in the living room out of earshot, studying a map of Flagstaff that Bob brought home from AAA.

"It's a part of our culture," I say. "Maybe he needs to be exposed to it."

"You are exposing him to it! You just bought twelve mindless Disney movie books."

"I didn't get him a Pokémon book. He's missing out on the chance to share a common interest and he might have more friends if he did."

"He's shy," Bob says, "and he likes playing games meant for eight- and nine-year-olds."

"He wants to look at roads," I say. "I don't even know any nine-year-olds who want to do that."

I set the books on the coffee table. I'll make sure we read a few more of them, but decide not to mention the movies again. Who knows what's right? It's too soon to tell. Parenting is a big gamble and you never know what choices will end up being the best ones. I might as well let him study maps.

I'M SPENDING THE NEXT week trying to get Gore elected. I could have volunteered for the campaign sooner, but I wasn't nervous enough until I saw the latest polls in Oregon. Moreover, even my mother is campaigning. I'm in Eugene visiting her.

"Elliot takes me downtown and I register people to vote," she says in her usual unenthusiastic manner.

I look at my sister and she nods.

"She's registered more than a hundred people."

I study my mother in her wheelchair, and then I see it. Behind her bland expression is a glimmer of the old Mama, the Mama who was filled with so much drive and passion. I give her a hug. Maybe some of the passion is still there. What else would make someone sit outside for hours registering voters?

"I'll do my part this week, too," I tell her.

She hugs me back a little with her one functioning arm. My sister looks down at her proudly.

"The acupuncture is helping," she says, "and so is the aroma therapy we started last month."

WHEN I BRING Casey home from school on the monumental Tuesday, he looks surprised when we walk in the door.

"Why is the television on the table?"

"We're going to find out who the next president will be, and the best way to do that is by watching television."

This should prove to everyone that I'm not a radical anti-TV freak. I have a television right in the middle of the kitchen table. I hand him his old wooden puzzle of the United States and explain the electoral college to him. Actually I'm explaining it to myself, too.

"Oregon has only seven electoral votes," I say, "but every vote counts this time."

Channel 10 is the public television station and seems like a safe choice to get the returns.

"There aren't any commercials on this station," I tell him. I plan on switching back and forth to the other stations as needed, but I don't bother to explain how the remote works. It won't leave my hands.

We watch the map on television. "Gore's states turn blue, Bush's red," I say. Casey dutifully places red and blue stones respectively on each state of his puzzle. I smile at him and visualize blue.

When Bob comes home, I'm thrilled that we're now having a true family television experience. Thankfully, Gore is doing better than I expected.

"California is worth fifty-four, Casey," I tell him as soon as the state is called. He puts a blue stone on the state. I switch back and forth between the stations moving quickly past an ad for Mazda to make sure OPB is on top of things.

As soon as Florida is called for Gore, I scream and jump up and down with Casey and Bob. The phone rings and Sarah is screaming, too. We are in heaven!

CASEY'S FIRST BIG television event was not what I had expected. I thought he would see a neat and tidy transfer of power, how well our system works. I had planned to show him how television can be very useful for limited periods of time. I had expected to have it on for a long night and possibly a long morning, but then I assumed I would put it back into the guest room where it belonged. But after three days, it's still sitting on the kitchen table, an oversized centerpiece, and I'm as glued as ever to the continually developing election news. I keep Casey's puzzle where he left it, on the carpet a few feet away from the television. Casey has placed two stones on Florida, a red one too shiny and menacing for my taste next to the blue one that should rightly stay put.

"Has Oregon been called yet?" Casey asks me each day when I pick him up from school.

"No, and Florida hasn't been decided either," I say. "Tonight

I'm going to put the television back upstairs. We can listen to National Public Radio. It doesn't have any commercials."

I'VE BEEN SO CONCERNED about Casey having friends at school that I haven't tried to make any close friends there for myself. But I like Lauren. She is Grayson's mom, and she has a younger boy, Jake.

"I nursed both my boys until they were three and they both still sleep with us," she says proudly. Lauren is tall and regal looking with strawberry blond hair that falls past her shoulders. She's in her thirties and can still wear her hair long and have it look sexy.

"I nursed Casey until he was three and half," I tell her.

We're waiting outside the classroom for our kids. She smiles at me and I think that maybe we'll be friends. It will be the way it was with Kendra in the playgroup. I figure after we finish talking about the benefits of breastfeeding and cosleeping we'll move on to more personal topics. When she whispers to me that she's try-ing to have one more baby, I feel closer than ever to her. I offer to take her volunteer shift in the classroom that she has been trying to fill.

When it's her turn to be in the classroom for me, I decide to confide in her, too.

"Judy is concerned that Casey's not joining in," I say hesitantly. "When you're outside at recess with the kids, will you please keep an eye on him and let me know what you think?"

I smile nervously and expect her to smile back and tell me how she understands, how she'll do her best. But she doesn't.

"He's fine, I'm sure," she says offhandedly, and I realize too late that I've made a mistake in confiding in her. Maybe I seemed too vulnerable and intense, a terrible combination really. Whatever the reason, I can tell that she has no intention of helping me or Casey.

The next day when I see her, she says hi to me in a superficial tone of voice and walks quickly past me. She starts talking to Janie and Stacey. I catch bits of their conversation.

"Did you hear the way Sam spoke to his mother?" Janie says. "His mother should have been at the last parenting workshop."

"The ones who need to go never do," Lauren says.

I imagine them talking about me, discussing how uptight I am. Lauren will tell them how Judy is concerned about Casey so maybe there *is* something wrong with him, and they would listen to her because she looks like a queen. As the days go by, she gathers more followers.

"There's a clique forming at school," I tell Bob, "and I'm not included."

"I'm sure you're imagining things," he says. He's probably remembering the time I thought Sarah was mad at me and not returning my calls, when she was really just visiting her mother in Illinois.

But I'm not imagining this. Within a few weeks, Lauren and her friends are greeting each other with warm embraces and returning casserole pans to each other. At first there are just five of them, but by January, two more have been added, including Andrea. Andrea used to say hi to me, but as soon as she was accepted into the clique, she followed suit and became stuck up, too. I watch them stand around in tight little circles talking quietly after we drop off our kids, discussing the other kids and parents who merit their disapproval. "Mary Beth sure is putting on a lot of weight," Wendy murmurs.

I am devastated when I hear about Lauren and her parties and how all the kids loved the chili that her husband, Jonathan, made. These are missed opportunities for Casey to play with his classmates. I feel like I'm in high school all over again, except that this time I'm actually coming to school every day to deal with the misery instead of staying home to watch game shows.

"Maybe too many people found out that Casey doesn't watch television and they think I'm too extreme," I tell Bob. "I should never have told Lauren that Casey didn't watch videos."

Bob doesn't buy the TV explanation.

"Don't worry so much," he says. "It doesn't matter."

I talk to Sarah about it instead. She comes over while Casey and her oldest daughter, Courtney, are at school. She brings along her curly-haired twin girls, Claire and Audrey. They have big brown eyes like their mom and their sister. Sarah is one of those natural beauties with perfect skin and luxurious golden brown hair. When she goes to her hairdresser, he always takes a picture of her for publicity purposes. Last year when she got a facial, the owner asked her to appear on some television show to promote his skin care products. This sort of thing happens to her all the time.

I point the twins toward Casey's Brio train set in the other room.

"I'm sure there are some real bitches at your school," Sarah says. "It's like what I grew up with on the north shore of Chicago."

"It's nothing like Little Waldorf. There, if any one of us were having a problem with our child, we would have asked each other for help and gotten it. Here, if you ask for help, people wonder what they can do to keep their kid away from yours. I heard that's how they got Weston kicked out."

"They got a kid kicked out?"

"Well, he was aggressive, and his mom was impossible, so it wouldn't surprise me. But it was brutal the way it happened. The rumor is that Lauren and her clique led the effort to get him removed, and his brother had to leave, too."

I offer Sarah some leftover split pea soup that Bob made. While she's eating, I pass her the class phone list. I've color-coded the names using Casey's markers.

"These are the snobbiest moms," I say, pointing to the names in red. "Lauren, Wendy, Janie, Julia, and Stacey are the main ones. Their offspring are in pink and baby blue. The kids Casey likes are circled in green. If he has a chance with them, I've put a purple check mark beside their names. Grayson, for example, likes him a lot, but his mom is the number one snob and won't invite him over, so there isn't a purple check."

I get Sarah another glass of ice water and sit back down next to her.

"So, how do I move into the red group?" I ask her. "What am I supposed to do?"

Sarah studies the names for a minute. She doesn't ask me why I've actually color-coded the class list. Nothing I do surprises her anymore. Once when we were downtown together and I needed ski clothes, I banged on the door of REI after hours and persuaded the manager, who was still inside, to let us shop. Sarah backed away, mortified.

"It doesn't help that Casey is so smart," she says seriously. "They're probably jealous. You'll have to work on diffusing that somehow."

"But I've never said anything about how smart he is."

Sarah looks at me with a patient expression on her face. "It's not exactly something he can hide."

I consider this. Maybe that's true. I think back to when Lauren saw Casey reading the yogurt container on the teacher's desk the first week of school. He asked me why it was fat free. I didn't consider it a big deal. I assumed that most of the kids at this expensive school could already read and write or they wouldn't have made it through the torturous screening process.

"I've tried all the usual techniques with these moms, techniques I read about in *How to Win Friends and Influence People*. I listen well, take an interest in what they're doing. I'm helpful and empathetic. But nothing works. I think it's me," I say.

"Maybe you should wear diamonds and pretend to be a Republican."

"No, they're not like that. They don't wear diamonds and they all voted for Gore. They're rich, but in a low-key way. It's nothing showy, but it shows, at least to them," I say, "and there's something about me that just isn't right. I think it's because I'm from Texas."

"Or maybe they discovered what you've done to your class list."

I laugh. "What should I do?"

"Find out where they shop," Sarah suggests, suddenly excited. Although Sarah has never begged a manager to keep a store open after hours, she loves shopping far more than I do. I like getting the things I want, but I don't like to spend much time doing it.

"These women are probably the type who pick things up in foreign countries, or they walk into resale shops and buy hand-me-downs that give them what they think is an original vintage look," I say.

"Let's take a look at what's in your closet."

At Sarah's suggestion, I start wetting my hair down first thing in the morning and blow-drying it just a little, even if I don't have time for a shower and am planning to exercise right away. At Little Waldorf, it had been fine to just wear a baseball hat in the morning to keep your hair from sticking out everywhere. At Martin Smith, even if you are in workout pants ready for a run, your hair needs to be in place.

I start running instead of walking and begin lifting weights twice a week, something I've never done in my life. So much for the maternal goddess look I had begun to feel comfortable with. I need power now and there is one power look shown in every commercial, every ad, repeated over and over. I may not be exposed to TV much now, but I still know the look.

"YOU AREN'T HAVING an affair, are you?" Bob asks me as I stand in front of the mirror admiring my legs. I've dropped six pounds in a month.

"Don't be silly," I say. "I'm doing this for the women at Martin Smith."

"You want to sleep with the women there?"

I turn sidewise and pull what's left of my abdomen in.

"If only it were that simple," I say.

Bob picks up the color-coded class list on my dresser.

"Don't you think it's time for you to get a full-time job?"

"Getting into this clique is a full-time job!" I shout. "And I'm volunteering in school, visiting Mama, and continuing to make our house playdate central! Isn't that enough?"

"Of course it is," he says, and he tosses the list back on my dresser.

"Do you think I come across as a little too uptight?"

"You think?" he asks, not bothering to hide the sarcasm in his voice.

"I'll have to get off caffeine again."

"You drink less than half a cup of tea in the morning."

"If I'm going to be popular, I have to appear relaxed." I take a deep breath and practice looking mellow in the mirror.

"Why do you care what they think of you? If they're really as terrible as you say, why would you want to be in their group?"

I roll my eyes. "It's for Casey," I say. "Otherwise I wouldn't give a rip. Besides, even if I got in the clique, I wouldn't become like them. I would never exclude anyone else. I would never become snobby, and I would always be wary, knowing that they could dump me at any time. I wouldn't be naive."

"Sounds like a lot of fun."

"It's for Casey," I repeat. "And at least I'm not watching much television. I have better things to do with my time."

As it turns out, Casey's task of fitting in isn't as hard as mine is. Mostly he just needs to learn to play tag, I discover.

I watch the kids at lunch recess after I finish helping out in the classroom.

"We're playing the cheetah game," Carolyn says, "and Andrew is it."

"Sounds fun," I say, and I let Andrew chase me around the swing set before he tags me. When I'm it, I catch a small red-headed boy in a matter of seconds. "I'm going to get you next time, Casey."

Casey looks nervous. He has been watching the game from the sidelines.

"It's fun," I say.

That night I tell Bob that Casey and I are going to play a new game with him. "It's called the cheetah game," I say. Casey looks excited now, all of the nervousness gone.

When Bob is it, I'm unexpectedly thrilled. I dash up the stairs, and Bob gains on me. I duck into the bonus room, my heart pounding as he pursues me. Now I know why tag is so exciting. Played with the right person, it's a heck of an aphrodisiac.

"Do you think you're ready to try playing tag at recess," I ask Casey in the car as we are driving to school. I'm speaking in a nonchalant manner, just making conversation.

"Maybe," he says.

I want to tell him that his teacher thinks he's weird and that I'm a nervous wreck, and if he would just please play a fucking game of tag, I could stop worrying. But I don't say anything like that. I don't talk about the great virtues of having friends or getting exercise at recess either. Instead I do what I presume most of the parent books I haven't read warn never to do.

"If you join in a recess, we'll celebrate after school." I like the word *celebrate*. It makes it sound better than the bribe that it really is.

"Can I see five new roads?" he asks excitedly.

"Yes," I say.

FINALLY, CASEY HAS a best friend at school, a rowdy boy named Jacob. Jacob probably watches a lot of television, but I don't care. They play together at recess, running around pretending to be alligators. Wendy, one of the original members of the clique, thinks Jacob is too aggressive. She tells her son, who is in my opinion a mean little jock, to stay away from Jacob.

At school the latest weekly newsletter comes home. Near the end of it, there's a tiny notice about TV-Turnoff Week, a national project designed to get kids and parents to take a week off from television. "Maybe some of you will be willing to try to stay away from television for a whole day," Erica, the parent-teacher liaison, says in the newsletter. "Myself, I know I'll still be watching *The Drew Carey Show*."

I imagine her getting together with Judy to watch the show.

When it's time for our spring parent conference, I'm filled with dread. I wear a peach-colored cotton knit sweater set. I want to appear pleasing and feminine, open and relaxed, none of which I feel. I might as well be wearing combat boots or carrying a spear. As far as I can tell, these people are the enemy. They don't understand my child and they don't understand me.

"Would you like coffee?" Judy asks. She is sitting next to Erica.

"No, thank you," I say. I don't tell her how I have only just this week completed a caffeine-withdrawal program and that it's all I can do to restrain myself from hurling her cup of coffee in her face.

She gives Bob some coffee and introduces him to Erica. He shakes her hand and she gives him the same phony look she gives me.

They make an attempt to start off the conference on a positive note. They marvel at Casey's intelligence, his memory, his reading ability. "His math aptitude appears to be off the charts," Erica says. "And he's got a best friend, too," Judy adds.

Bob and I nod our heads and smile, and for a fleeting moment I think to myself that maybe everything is all right after all, that all of the little classmates who have been over to our house and all of the tag games have made a difference, that all is well in the world. But then she brings out a notebook. Like a prosecutor, she is trying to build her case against the accused. She flips through the three-ring binder and points to the maps and mazes he has made. "Mazes," she says. "It's all he does now during drawing time." I stare at the pages.

"Yes, but they aren't just maps anymore. He's progressed to mazes." I emphasize the word *progressed* as if to demonstrate the higher-level thinking that mastering mazes requires.

She smiles a pathetic smile. "It's just very unusual, that's all," she says slowly.

"We'd like to have him evaluated, because he's so unique." Erica pipes up. She looks like a giraffe in her orange pantsuit. "We want to see exactly how high his IQ is. We suspect it's phenomenally high. We want to see what his learning style is, too, and find out how we can best serve him."

I stare at her for a moment, wondering if it will ever occur to her to ask me how I think my child can best be served. I force myself not to overreact, remembering that I don't actually have a spear.

She looks so fucking calm. She wants it to seem as if she has just suggested we try a new restaurant. I am not supposed to act like she has suggested something outrageous. But my already frayed nerves betray me and my voice is unnaturally high when I finally speak.

"Do you think he has some kind of disorder?" I ask.

She looks uncomfortable.

"I'm not qualified to say."

This is not a good answer. I want her to ask me if I think she looks like a giraffe, so I can tell her that I'm not qualified to say.

"We just want to know a little more about him. We already know that he has a great mom who is doing a great job with him." She reaches out across the table and I'm afraid she is about to pat my hand, so I pull it away.

I smile one of my fakest smiles, even faker than the one she is giving me.

She hands me a list of three names of psychologists.

"One of them will suit you, I'm sure."

"They want to label him and drug him," I tell Bob as we are driving home.

"You don't know that," he counters. "She said he was exceptional, the brightest kid she's seen in twenty years."

I look upon him with pity. "You really don't know how to read between the lines."

Sometimes television alone isn't enough to provide the necessary escape from the disappointments of life. It's still absolutely necessary, but it isn't enough. The problem is that I expected perfection, a picture-perfect family, a blissful existence. Even if there was a problem, I expected a quick solution.

What was I thinking? That after escaping into a box with antennae for most of my life I could wake up and know how to cope with life and raise a child flawlessly? Yes, that is what I thought would happen. That being fully present in each moment would be a profound and wonderful experience. Never boring. Never tedious and never too challenging. It would always be joyful and meaningful. My intense grasp of life would make me and my offspring superior to all others who are passively glued to a big screen, their lives devoid of the richness that ordinary life has to offer.

But maybe escape is what it's all about. Maybe television and alcohol are necessary in order to cope with disillusionment. My mother would have agreed. At least the mother I used to know. I finish the beer I started drinking as soon as Casey fell asleep. I'm halfway through watching the movie *Sabrina* with Harrison Ford, but I'm too upset to enjoy it.

When the movie is over, I call Rebecca and Marcus. Marcus is a psychologist and it's time for some free advice.

"I need to talk to your husband," I tell Rebecca.

"Are you drunk?"

"Yes," I say.

A few minutes later, Marcus answers in a groggy voice. "What time is it?"

"Do you think there is anything wrong with Casey?" I ask.

"Well, his mom is nuts," he says.

"I'm sorry I woke you." I tell him what the teacher said. "What sort of disorder do you think they are looking for?"

"I haven't the foggiest."

I hang up and get on the Internet and peruse the pathologies. There are so many that, after an hour, I have only covered obsessive-compulsive disorder, ADHD, autism, and oppositional defiance disorder.

"Maybe they think he has Asperger's," I say to Bob. "He has a photographic memory and he likes doing mazes." Bob has fallen asleep and doesn't answer me.

I call Marcus back, waking him up again.

"Do you think he has Asperger's?"

"No, definitely not. He has a great sense of humor, and so do I, which is fortunate for you right now."

I call him back three more times in the next couple of hours.

"Should I just sleep on the couch next to the phone?" Marcus asks.

"If you like," I say.

I feel as if I'm in college again taking Abnormal Psychology. I remember that my professor's name oddly enough was Dr. Strange and he warned us the first day of class that we might find it difficult to learn about mental illness. "Some people imagine that they have everything they read about. That's why we will start out studying the worst possible disorders, schizophrenia and split personalities, and end up the term with the study of the healthy personality. That way you will at least leave this class thinking you are normal."

Perusing the Internet is as dangerous for me as was Dr. Strange's class.

I say goodnight to Marcus at one a.m. and head to the guest room, too uptight to sleep. I put in *Notting Hill* to distract myself from Tourette's syndrome and bipolar disorder.

THE NEXT DAY I stare at the three names on the list of psychologists. On impulse, I look up the first one in the school directory. Just as I suspected. She is a Martin Smith parent. I mark through her name. I want someone removed from the school, someone independent from its politics.

That night, I decide to call the other two and listen to their voices on their answering machines. First I call the only man on the list. He sounds okay, but something isn't right about him. Of course something isn't right! He's a psychologist. He probably had a screwed up childhood and has spent the rest his life trying to get over it. I call the last name on the list, Nicole.

She doesn't have a child at Martin Smith and she sounds nice. Her voice is sort of like Barbra Streisand's. I imagine she could leave a singing message, too. I will let her do the evaluation.

We schedule it for the summer. That way Casey will be six, and IQ tests are more accurate at determining intelligence at that age, Nicole says. It's reassuring that she doesn't mention pathologies, and I refrain from asking her which ones are more likely to show up after age six.

I call Marcus and invite him and Rebecca to dinner.

"It will be our treat," I say.

"Are you trying to make up for keeping me awake the other night?"

"I'm sure you get lots of calls like that," I say.

"Our number is unlisted," he reminds me.

"Well, we're taking you to a fabulous restaurant," I say.

We have a reservation along the river at the Minuet. It's not an overly fancy place, and since we live in Oregon, we could get away with wearing jeans. But Rebecca is wearing a sexy black dress and Marcus has donned a silk button-down shirt. This is a monumental change for both of them. I am sitting across from Marcus, biding my time, making small talk for as long as I can stand. Finally I get to the point.

"I want to know what will be on the test they're going to give Casey," I say when we have finished with our salads. Marcus pushes his plate away.

"I don't really know," he says. "They might have him draw a

self-portrait, that sort of thing." I consider Casey's drawings from art class. Some of the people have large feet. I'm sure large feet mean something is off, I say. Bob points out that Casey actually has large feet for his size and the self-portraits that he was required to draw in art class are actually in pretty good proportion.

I take a few sips of my wine, remembering that it will probably keep me awake all night. But I don't care. I have to stop myself from nervously tapping my foot under the table.

"I don't want them to find a disorder," I say. "What else is on the test?"

I'm leaning forward now.

"Even if I knew exactly, I wouldn't tell you."

"Why?" I'm taken aback by this. We're all friends.

"It's unethical."

I consider this for a little while. Unfortunately, I don't consider it for long enough, because the next thing that pops out of my mouth is something I immediately regret saying.

"If you just let me see the test, I'll give you a blow job."

Bob is choking on his drink. Rebecca's mouth drops open. This is not a classy moment, and unfortunately there's no way to take back what I've said. I try to recover quickly, because if there's one thing a TV child can do is change the station lickety-split, distract the viewer, sometimes even get a big laugh. I can pretend to be someone with an off-the-wall sense of humor like the folks on *Saturday Night Live*. I turn to Rebecca.

"I'll make it a three-way, if you like."

"That's okay," she says, her voice flatter than usual.

"Wait just a minute," Marcus says. "Don't I get to at least consider this?"

Rebecca jerks her head around to stare at him. "No, you don't," she says.

I'm trying to breathe and think of what to say next.

"I was only kidding, of course." I exhale and try to look convincing, calm and easygoing. To me it seemed like a perfectly fine deal. Marcus is attractive and kind and I need his professional expertise. I simply offered what I thought he would like. Unfortunately, the fact that I'm happily married to Bob seemed to have flown out the window. But surely everyone will think I was kidding. They would never believe that I was completely serious.

"Ellen," Rebecca says, "when we go out to dinner, I would prefer if you didn't offer sexual favors to my husband." Her tone of voice isn't altogether hateful, I notice, and I'm hopeful. She's drinking red wine, and I quickly pour the rest of my glass into hers. Maybe if I get her drunk, we'll remain on speaking terms. Maybe if I get her really drunk, she'll forget about what I said.

"Oh, I don't know if it was such a bad thing to offer," Marcus says.

"Marcus!" Rebecca jabs him in the ribs. Bob remains perfectly quiet, too quiet.

"Right," Marcus says, turning to look at me. "Ellen, thank you for your lovely offer, but I must decline." He takes a gulp of his drink. "But I could talk to some of my less than ethical colleagues. I'm sure I could find one of them who would take you up on your appealing offer."

"Please don't," I say, my face feeling hot now.

Maybe watching *Seinfeld* wasn't the best way to learn couple-date protocol. I order more wine and spend the rest of the evening filling Rebecca's glass and paying attention to her, hoping that everyone really will think I was just kidding.

12

Forest Friends

By Casey's birthday party all appears normal between Marcus and Rebecca and me again. Well, mostly normal. I've assured Bob a dozen times that I'd much rather give him a blow job than Marcus, and much to Bob's delight, I'm a woman of my word.

"So, you're not really that attracted to Marcus?" Bob asks as I push him up against the refrigerator after Casey has gone to bed.

"I would tell you if I was," I say, and I'm telling him the truth. Bob could handle it. Several years ago I was obsessed with a man I worked with named Wyatt. After agonizing about it for days, I decided to confess everything to Bob, rather than Wyatt, which was a good choice.

Later that same night Bob slipped off my nightshirt and said, "Just pretend I'm Wyatt. What would you want Wyatt to do?"

I told him, and then I forgot all about Wyatt.

THE SITUATION WITH Rebecca is a little more awkward. We are at her house and she's helping me prepare for Casey's party.

She has put on the green elflike costume I borrowed from Kendra's theater group. The idea is for the kids to hike through the woods near our house and "Forest Friends" will jump out at strategic points along the way in an entertaining fashion. I have talked Rebecca into being one of these Forest Friends.

"Do you think I look sexy as an elf?" she asks.

"It's a kid's party," I say. "Sexy isn't exactly the point."

She poses playfully in the mirror. She has a body like a centerfold model even though she never exercises or diets.

"I had a three-way once," she tells me.

"Really," I say. "When was that?"

"In college. It was with a married couple."

"Was it fun?" I ask her. I'm wondering how it happened, if everyone agreed to do it ahead of time. Or maybe it just happened spontaneously one night after dinner. They decided to skip dessert and have sex together instead. Or it could have happened after the drugs they were taking took effect.

"The woman was really nice," Rebecca says. "She was a massage therapist, so she was really nurturing and sensual. It was her idea."

I want to ask her more questions but I'm still feeling guilty about the other night.

"I'm sorry I said that to Marcus."

"No, it's okay." She pulls off the top half of her elf costume, revealing a black lacy bra lined with red. "Marcus and I talked about it, and we really weren't that offended. We decided we might even like it, the three-way, I mean." She is bending over now to take off the little elf skirt.

"You and I could wear matching lingerie," she says. "Marcus would love it. Do you like what I have on?"

The elf skirt is on the floor and she is facing me, wearing French-cut panties, lacy with red trim like the bra.

"Really cute," I say. I try to sound casual.

She eyes me curiously.

"Bob would never go for us having the three-way, would he?"

"I don't think so," I say, but I'm wondering what she means. Does she want Bob to join in at some point or does she want to know if he would mind if I did it with them? "He's pretty into being monogamous," I say truthfully.

She picks up the skirt on the floor. "Oh well."

"Oh well," I say, and we don't say anything else for an awkward minute. She folds up the elf outfit before she finally breaks the silence.

"So I have to wear the elf costume for the party?"

I nod, welcoming and sort of not welcoming the change of subject. After all, I'm over forty. How many more offers for three-ways will I get?

CASEY'S BIRTHDAY PARTY involves a cast of ten, two other elves in addition to Rebecca, a forest nymph, a garden fairy, and a nature goddess, who ostensibly watches over the woods. We have invited every kid in the class and spent the past month getting ready for this theatrical extravaganza.

"Aren't you getting carried away?" Bob asks me.

I ignore him. He doesn't understand that the party is my salvation, my declaration that my child and our family are as thrilling as Disneyland and we don't need television and video games to be this fun. This party is a fabulous expression of our creativity inspired by nature, not Madison Avenue. There are no Pokémon or Powerpuff Girls decorations purchased from Target, with separate party favor bags for girls with toy lipsticks and eye shadow. Casey and Mindy from next door have painted a large birthday banner and party bags filled with origami butterflies, organic chocolate treats, and sprigs of cedar.

As the party plans unfold, I am a whirlwind of energy, dampened not even by Bob's chronic whimpering.

"Wouldn't a simple hike in the woods be enough?" he asks desperately.

I shake my head and hand him the script I've written. "You'll need to gather everyone together at strategic points along the trail."

Amber, as the youngest elf, is perched high up in a hemlock tree. "Be sure to give each child a tiny cone when they pass by," I tell her. "And you need to practice climbing down from this tree in less than sixty seconds."

"Are you sure you want her going up that high in the first place?" Bob yells. "It's over a hundred feet up."

"She's fine," I say. "Just worry about your own part in this."

I turn to Kendra. "Remember to sing 'Oh What a Beautiful Cedar' to the tune of 'Oh What a Beautiful Morning.' "

Kendra has scribbled notes on her hand. I glare at her. "All scripts must be memorized. Just like it is in your plays."

"It's the drama she likes," Bob says to Quinn.

I glare back at Bob. He doesn't realize what I've accomplished. I never would have created live theater if I were still watching so much television. Or maybe he does realize it and he wonders if it's entirely a good thing, the unleashing of all this energy.

BY THE TIME Casey and I have found a place in his room for each of his new toys, the day for his evaluation has arrived. We're still talking about the birthday party.

"So, did you absolutely love it?" I ask him for about the tenth time.

"It was the best party in the universe!"

"Well, the fun isn't over," I say. "Now you get to do something really interesting."

Casey looks excited. "What is it?"

"You're really lucky," I say. "Next year Erica and Judy want to make sure you get the perfect first-grade teacher for you, so they want to find out more about you. You get to meet with an expert, so be sure to do the best you can."

I tell him how fun it will be to answer all the expert's questions. The best part about my being an actress is that Casey actually falls for my lines. He doesn't know what an evaluation is, and as far as he's concerned, school is wonderful, his teachers are the best, and he's the luckiest kid in the world.

In addition to cutting out all caffeine, I've completely given up alcohol. No more little sips here and there every now and then when we are out to dinner. It's a deal I have made with God. Both substances keep me awake, and the propositioning incident with Marcus, and Rebecca's follow-up proposition, are still fresh in my mind.

I'm in the psychologist Nicole's waiting room trying to appear relaxed and centered. As I sit in a chair writing thank you cards to the cast of Casey's party, I try not to think about how Casey is doing in the next room.

After a couple of hours, the door opens and Casey and the psychologist are both smiling. I quickly stack the cards I have written and look in the crack behind the cushion to make sure I haven't left any behind. Then I think that maybe this makes me look like an obsessive-compulsive in front of the psychologist. Having spent too much time online studying disorders, I'm noticing every possible quirk in my personality, and there are so many of them! I try to look unconcerned about the couch. Then I wonder if she can see the handwriting on the cards I'm holding. Maybe she knows how to analyze handwriting. I cover up the top of the card. Then I wonder if that makes me look paranoid. I've got to get out of here.

"I'll see you tomorrow," she tells Casey.

"Bye," I say loudly, hoping he'll catch on and say good-bye, too.

He does and I grab his hand. We head to the parking lot. Day one is done, for better or worse. Now as casually as possible, I must begin my cross-examination.

"What did you get to do?" My voice is so singsongy and artificially cheerful that I'm surprised he doesn't comment on it.

"Well, I got to make up a story about some pictures."

"Tell me about it."

He describes a series of pictures, and it occurs to me that if I were to take assiduous notes, I would have some valuable information that another neurotic mom might want.

THE NEXT DAY the evaluation lasts a little less than two hours.

"I think he was getting a bit tired," the psychologist says at the end.

I looked concerned, and she adds, "It's perfectly normal for a child this age."

I nod, hoping that when this is all over with, she won't suggest drugs for me.

"I'll call you when I have my results," she says.

I WATCH *Four Weddings and a Funeral* and *Good Will Hunting* every night until I finally hear from Nicole. Bob and I meet with her in her office.

She explains the series of tests Casey has taken. I stare at the various numbers and graphs. I'm listening, trying to be sure I'm hearing everything, something about his amazing ability to remember a long series of numbers backward and forward. I am frantic, hoping she isn't about to drop a bomb. But after several minutes, I can't listen any longer. I have to cut to the chase and see if I'm getting it right.

"So he has no disorder of any kind?"

"None whatsoever," she says.

"Then he's perfectly normal?"

She looks at me curiously, and I'm pretty sure that she thinks I'm the one who's not perfectly normal.

"He's highly gifted," she says. "And that means that he is quite different from his peers." She hesitates for a moment. "And he knows that he's different."

"But we don't make a big deal about his intelligence," I say defensively.

"You don't have to. He's figured it out and he likes himself. He has a good self image."

I smile, but her words still haven't sunk in, probably because I don't have a good self image. Maybe I should have spent my childhood making mazes and learning every street in Portland.

"So he doesn't need any therapy or special help or medications?"

"Not that I can see. He's a little introverted, but nothing abnormal." She looks over her report. "But you need to learn about gifted children." She hands us a list of books and points to her favorite. Then she finishes the rest of the evaluation, but I don't hear much of what she is saying because I'm too flooded with relief to pay attention. She gets up and motions us toward the door.

"He's a charming boy. You're very lucky."

I am almost breathing normally at this point. I hold hands with Bob as we walk out to the parking lot.

"He is different," I repeat to Bob, "and it's not easy to be different."

"Maybe it's just not easy for you. He likes himself the way he is, remember?"

I'm sure I've been insulted, but under the joyful circumstances, I overlook it. I go directly home, not wanting to talk to anyone else just yet. Casey will be back from Camden's house in a couple of hours. Maybe I can finally calm down or even focus on something besides Casey for a while. I look around the living room. I could organize the books on the shelf or maybe I could write or drop by the newpaper office.

I head upstairs instead and pick up the video holder with Matt Damon's face on it. I laugh out loud. No wonder I like this movie. I thought it was because of Matt Damon's physical magnetism, but maybe it was the character he played instead, a boy with a brilliant mind who was different from all his friends.

I call Bob at work. "Maybe Casey wouldn't have become so different if he had been watching every Disney movie ever made since he was a baby."

"I'm sure that's true," Bob says. "I think it's for the best."

I'm not so sure. I hang up the phone and put the video in. I see Matt Damon in his cheap apartment surrounded by books. I let the flickering lights and music wash over me and stop worrying about everything.

. . .

IT IS ONLY WELL after the fact that I'm able to discuss the ordeal with someone besides Bob. I call my mother to tell her she was right about Casey. I long for a good argument with her about how best to educate the gifted. She was always good at arguing. "He's a fine boy," she says in her minimally responsive way.

My sister, who's listening on the extension, pipes in, "Of course he's brilliant! It runs in the family."

I wonder if genius and rudeness go together.

The week before school starts, I decide to tell Gina about Casey's evaluation. Gina is the biggest gossip at Casey's school. I figure if I tell her, everyone will know by the time school starts.

Gina says, "Of course, he's really bright."

"Yes, well, the main thing is that he doesn't have any kind of disorder. They don't want to give him therapy or put him on drugs." This is the point I want to get across so she can disseminate it to everyone else.

"Well, don't you want him to do more accelerated work in math?"

"Only if he wants it. I'm just glad he's happy."

I don't expect her to understand. She is constantly badgering the teachers to give her child harder work. But Casey learns as easily as he breathes no matter where he is. I didn't put him in school so he could master advanced mathematics in the first grade. I put him in school primarily so he could learn to chase kids around on a playground and make secret codes with his classmates. I don't care if he reads the classics before he's ten, whatever the classics actually are. I want him to feel a part of his community. The only problem is that television is the central focus of his community, which is why I keep asking myself if he would be better off watching it.

I ask Casey, too, before the summer ends.

"Do you want to watch one of those movies on the list yet?"

"I'm okay, Mom."

"Well, let me know if you change your mind."

As the school year starts, I learn that Casey is not the only one who has been evaluated, and most haven't had such reassuring results.

Bennet's mom, Alice, is standing in the parking lot telling me about her oldest son, Frederick.

"He's ADHD," she says. She reaches into her purse for her keys. I ponder her choice of words. She didn't say he has ADHD, but that he is ADHD.

"I'm so sorry," I say.

"We're going to have to medicate him."

"Can't you just do behavior management and therapy? The teachers should be open to trying that."

She jingles her keys in her hand. "They've done all of that already. The counselor has spent hours and hours with him. So have the teachers. They won't let us stay at the school if we don't medicate him."

I can imagine that the parents of the kids in Frederick's class have been difficult. Some are probably like Lauren, telling everyone that the rest of us shouldn't have to be around kids like Frederick. They've probably complained and pressured the teachers and administrators to do something about him. I remember what Catherine, another parent, once said: "Kyle's mom wouldn't let Houston come over until he got on medication."

It reminded me of what my best friend DeeDee told me when

I was ten. She said I wasn't allowed at her house because I wasn't clean enough. I played in the creek, and her mother said that my clothes were filthy. Plus, the one time I was allowed over, I thought it would be fun to jump on the mattress of her new bed. She said her mother hated that.

I tell Alice that I hope everything works out. I don't know what else to say. Between 20 and 30 percent of grade school kids in public schools have been diagnosed with ADHD. Private schools are supposed to be worse. I wonder if Alice would think that something is really wrong when so many kids have to be drugged.

Maybe at some point Casey will be considered abnormal because he isn't on some drug or another, just as he is considered odd because he hasn't watched five thousand hours of television yet. And what about the adults? Catherine thinks she has ADHD as well.

"I took some of Houston's medicine, and I was lot more focused," she said. "Now I have a prescription, too."

Moms are the latest group targeted for ADHD drugs. Last month I took a survey, which was part of a drug advertisement in *Time* magazine. "If you answer yes to four or more questions, you might have ADHD and should talk to your doctor about taking this medication," the ad said. I answered yes to three of the questions. If I evaluated my behavior under the influence of too much caffeine, I would have to answer yes to at least four, if not five of the questions. I wonder how I would do on the other drug surveys.

Kendra says she won't give up her antidepressants. "They help me be less angry, and Quinn says I'm much better on them." I think about what my mother used to tell me when she taught women's studies. "Our sexist, patriarchal society has always wanted its women to be drugged. It keeps them powerless," she would say, her speech often slurred from the alcohol and drugs she herself was taking.

"I'm really sorry," I tell Alice again.

I walk back to my car. I'm glad Casey doesn't have to be on drugs to go to school. I'm glad he isn't like all the kids who can't think of anything better to do than sit in front of a PlayStation. And yet, at the same time, I feel sad that he isn't like them, too, or more truthfully, that they aren't like him.

BOB IS STEPPING into the shower when I come home. I tell him what Alice said about Bennet's brother having ADHD.

"Do you think I have ADHD, too?" I ask him. "I watched a lot of television, and every kid we know with that diagnosis did, too."

"You didn't watch as much as little kids today do, and they've got video games, also." He raises his voice above the sound of the water. "But, no, I don't think you have ADHD." He says this in the same slow, condescending tone he uses when he is reassuring me that I don't have a mounting brain tumor or new strain of Lyme disease.

I wish I could have said something to Alice a long time ago when Frederick was a baby, the way Kendra did to Olivia about nursing. That's when I could have said, "You might want to consider not exposing your baby to television and video games if you don't want him to have ADHD later on." But what can I say now? I can't tell her to throw her set out before she gives that child a single capsule of Ritalin or whatever drug it is. Besides, maybe his brain would get better or maybe it wouldn't.

I know only that I've gotten better. Maybe someday I'll be able to take a *Time* magazine survey and not answer yes to any of the questions in the ADHD drug ad.

I CALL MY SISTER. She doesn't think I have ADHD either, although she agrees about the way I am on caffeine. Next she launches into her own explanation for the increase in the disorder. "The planet is so polluted with pesticides and chemicals that all of these so-called ADHD children have been poisoned. Toss out the soft drinks and candy and give them fresh air and wheatgrass juice, along with eliminating television. Then they might have a chance."

I go back downstairs. Casey is reading a book.

"What's the name of your book?"

"It's called *Dinosaurs before Dark*. It's really exciting."

I sit down next to him on the couch and kiss him on top of his head. I'm glad he's okay, a little quirky perhaps, but okay. "Casey is the profile of the absentminded professor," Nicole said in her evaluation of him. I guess that's why he can barely keep track of where his coat is sometimes, but he can tell you exactly what he just read or which numbers you just dialed. His mind is often someplace else, maybe figuring out a new route to school, but it's a good mind nonetheless.

The culture of a drug for everything makes me nervous. I think of my mother even before the stroke and how acutely aware I was of the early signs of decline, the sluggish speech, the slower gait, the shrinking muscles buried under too much fat. Even when she was in her thirties and forties, she needed a few drinks just to drive home from work each day. I remember tagging along to her classes sometimes and stopping at the liquor store with her afterward. They would give her a cup of ice to go with her bottle of scotch so she could drink on the drive home. DRIVE FRIENDLY was a Texas slogan featured on bumper stickers everywhere.

I imagine if I were she, I would be drunk right now, sitting here watching Casey read. I would have that hazy feeling my mother had when I saw her after school each day.

Maybe that's how life feels for a lot of people. My cousin said antidepressants gave her a glazed-over feeling when she took them. She didn't even notice that she had lost her sex drive. It was her boyfriend who pointed out that they hadn't had sex in two weeks. She said she hadn't missed it. She had lost her passion, the highs and lows that made life stimulating.

I guess this is why I'm trying so hard to find simple pleasures in my life that don't accelerate my own decline and why I'm trying so hard to do the same for my child. If Casey learns to find happiness in ways other than staring at a screen, maybe in the future he won't want all the drugs that other people need because of the void in their lives.

I'm still holding out hope for myself. I haven't watched TV for three weeks now, not since *Good Will Hunting*. Maybe when Casey is in school again, I'll be able to work and play, just as he does every day, with no need for television.

The only problem is that everything in the world isn't exactly as it should be when it's time for Casey to return to school that second week in September.

Sarah calls to give me the news. It's a quarter to eight in the morning, and Casey is finishing his breakfast. Bob has already gone to work.

"Are you taking Casey to school?" she asks.

"Why wouldn't I?"

"Hasn't Bob told you? We're being attacked. The Pentagon and World Trade Center have been bombed."

I glance outside the sliding glass door, assuming by what she has said that our city is next. I remember that during the Gulf War, I did the same thing. I scanned the sky for bombs periodically.

I flee to the study, shutting the door behind me. I pick up my cell phone and call Bob while holding onto the receiver with Sarah on our land line. Panic is growing in me.

"Should I still bring him to school?" I ask. Bob in his usual calm manner says yes. He might as well be talking about the weather. No wonder he didn't bother to tell me anything before going to work.

As I get in the car, Gordon is loading Mindy and Luke into his car. "Do you think it's okay?" I ask.

"I do," Gordon says. We don't say anything else to each other, but what's left unsaid hangs in the air between us.

"Dad won't be going to Ohio today," I tell Casey as we back out of the driveway. I say this matter of factly and he's relieved that his dad's four-day trip has been postponed.

"Why?"

"The airports are closed," I say.

"Why?" he repeats.

"I need to listen to the news," I tell him, "and then I'll know more."

But I keep the radio off for his sake, questions buzzing through my head. I want to shelter him. I want to behave normally. I can make believe that everything is fine.

When I get to school, I'm told by some of the parents that the teachers have decided to talk to the kids, because some of the kids already know what has happened. "Did you see those planes crash into the buildings?" Sam calls to Jacob. I don't know why I thought I could shelter Casey.

The head of the school calls everyone into the library. I wish

I'd said something to Casey first. I make my way into the library and hear Arianna calmly and matter-of-factly explaining what has happened. "Your parents may be worried today about friends they know in New York. Be kind and patient with them and know that you are safe where you are."

I give Casey a kiss and race out to the parking lot. I must get to a television. My first impulse is to go to Sarah's, but her kids are with her and I don't want to have to deal with their feelings, too. I head to Kendra's house.

I don't know what it would be like to simply imagine the scenario with only a newspaper or radio imparting the information. With television, I'm there with the rest of New York watching the buildings fall, watching the people scream, seeing their faces in shock, the tears rolling down their cheeks. Reporters and news anchors are pouring out their thoughts before the viewers can even formulate their own opinions, before the reporters themselves can examine their feelings. It will take days, weeks before we can sort it out and separate what we actually feel from what the television is making us think and feel with its montage of the event, complete with music and logo.

I watch for three straight days until my head is pounding and I'm plagued with fear. I want to help diffuse the anger. I don't want us to retaliate. I wonder if I'm just afraid of confrontation or am I really a pacifist. Considering how many times I resorted to force in an attempt to control my brother, I'm surprised I feel so strongly about keeping the peace.

I pick up Casey after school each day and the television remains off when he walks in the door. When he's back in school on the fourth day, I'm startled to see commercials again, which the networks had kept off. The stupidity of the ads is striking. A four-year-old waits for his mother to make some sort of instant dinner. But at least the commercials bring the mundane back into our lives.

I finally cry when I hear a victim's mother tell about the last words of her son who was on the plane that went down in Pennsylvania. I cry not just for her, but for my own son. Funny, I thought it would be enough to help Casey to join in on the playground and learn to say hi more often to his peers and he would be guaranteed happiness and success. I had assumed the world around him would be a safe place for him to thrive. What a ridiculous assumption that was! I'm sad that I've brought him into a world like this.

I've fed Casey many uncomfortable truths, information about earthquakes, hurricanes, tidal waves. I tell him what I know about this latest horror, but I don't let him see the devastation spread across the screen, and he doesn't ask to see it. I tuck the latest issue of *Time* into the bottom drawer of my desk. I'll show him the pictures when he's ready.

I wipe my tears and call my sister.

"Don't cry just for the people killed here. Our country has been killing people everywhere for years! Call your senators! Contact Bush!"

I e-mail Bush and applaud him for his patience. "Please don't retaliate with violence that will lead to the loss of innocent lives," I plead. "Work together with other countries. Please don't get us into war."

I watch CNN and every other news station. We have signed up for cable again. It was my idea. I listen to the alternative radio station spouting off conspiracy theories. I go online to see what the rest of the world is saying about us.

I don't really stop watching and listening until the anthrax news comes on weeks later. I can handle news of bombs and guns and hijacking, but I can't begin to cope with germ warfare. As soon as I hear about microscopic dust, I know I have to turn off the news.

IN SPITE OF the strange beginning with 9/11, first grade is the best school year ever. Monique is a night-and-day difference from Judy. She understands Casey. The first week of school, she photocopies one of his mazes and passes it out to the other kids to do. Through this simple gesture of hers, Casey gains admiration from everyone. She gives me an extra copy at the end of the day.

"He's so good at these mazes," she says enthusiastically. I wait for her to say something about how strange this is and have I considered therapy, but she just beams. "I'm so delighted to have him in my class."

The next day I bring her an African violet for the classroom. It feels good to want to be genuinely giving, and I plan to give her a lot. I'll even water her new plant, which she puts on her desk. I'll become the parent version of a teacher's pet, if there is such a thing.

Everything about first grade is better. There is no television ritual on Fridays or any other day of the week. That was just for kindergarteners, the group that needs it the least of all. When I pass by the kindergarten building, I never see Judy. I see Erica, though, and I smile at her tentatively. She smiles back and seems sincere. Maybe she did mean well in her own way, and she did make sure Casey was in Monique's class this year.

Casey has made another good friend at school, a bright kid, new this year, with unusual interests. His name is Diego and he knows as much about wiring and plumbing as Casey knows about maps. They play outside for hours together, creating intricate forts with doorways and bridges made of bamboo.

Diego watches TV, but he mostly watches shows like *This Old House* on PBS.

"Do you want to watch it sometime, Casey?" I ask cheerfully.

"No, that's okay."

Diego's mom, Mariana, is petite with short dark hair. She's from Peru and tells me she's glad that her child is bonding with Casey.

"Some of the parents have been a little bit snobby," she says hesitantly.

"Don't worry about them," I say. I don't tell her about my color-coded class list.

With Casey's old and new friends, I begin to feel more relaxed. Lauren and her little group are still exchanging ski vacation information, but another group has formed, a larger group born out of anger and angst, a dis-the-snobs group. Mariana and I join them outside on the playground while we watch our kids play after school.

Cathleen is best at articulating the crimes of the snobs. "They don't say hi and they ignore your phone calls when you invite their kids over. They treat us like we're invisible."

"I know what you mean," Isabel adds. Isabel is tall with curly brown hair and has a daughter who looks just like her. "Lauren won't let Lindsey play with Grayson," she says. "She said her son didn't need any new friends right now."

"What it is about them?" Teresa asks. "They're not that cute. They're not that interesting."

I refrain from adding my insults into the mix, mostly out of fear of it getting back to them, but I don't disagree either. Mostly I play it safe and make empathetic comments.

"That must have been really hard for you," I say to Isabel.

I begin to understand what my mother told me in the sixties

about the women's movement and the Black Power movement. "Members of oppressed groups need to talk to each other," she said. "That's how we discover that we're not alone. We begin to hold our heads a little higher when we do. That's what consciousness-raising groups are all about."

Alice, who comes from old money on the East Coast, offers another perspective on the women in the clique.

"Some of them think they're better than you because their grandparents started a potato chip company or an oil refinery. It's nothing to be that proud about. Don't let them get to you, Ellen. You don't need them, and Casey doesn't either."

"But they only let their kids see the kids of the parents in the clique."

"There are lots of other children. Remember the kids who are on financial aid," Alice says. "You better believe their parents aren't in the clique and they would be happy to make playdates with your child."

"But don't you want to change these people?"

"You'd be wasting your time. They're too stuck up and insulated, and they aren't that fun anyway."

This is just what high school is like, a place where you use words like *stuck up*. We even have a fundraising dance, an extravagant affair at the Benson. When it comes around, I pick out the sexiest, most expensive dress I can find and pretend that I'm at last going to the prom.

I MEET WITH GEORGETTE, excited to tell her about my progress.

"I've moved past middle school and into high school. Instead of watching television, I'm learning how to function in the midst of cliques."

"And how does that feel?"

"High school is fucked up. There is no perfect pathway into a clique and cliques are not all they're cracked up to be." I take a sip of the chamomile tea Georgette had made me. She smiles and takes a sip of her own tea, a mixture of raspberry leaf and hibiscus.

"Mostly I've decided that I don't want to be snobby, and I could easily have become that way. I could have snubbed everyone who put their kids in front of TV and video games and acted superior to them."

"And now?"

"Well, it still doesn't solve the problem of what to say about Casey not watching television and my not being open about my feelings about TV."

"Do you think you can be accepting of them and still tell them the truth?"

"It doesn't seem likely," I say.

AT CASEY'S SCHOOL a guest speaker is giving a presentation with helpful tips for parents. We are sitting in a large circle and I'm taking notes. "Don't overschedule your child with too many activities, lessons, sports, and so on," she says. "Kids need down time, time to relax."

Wendy raises her hand to contribute. "That's why every day after school I let Kyle zone out in front of the television before I ask him to do anything else."

"I let Heidi watch *Arthur* and *Powerpuff Girls* every day," Marilyn adds.

Last week I was listening to *American Routes,* a public radio show. The interviewer asked some famous guitarist how she became so accomplished. "When I was a kid, I would be in my bedroom with nothing to do and so I'd get out my guitar and mess around with it for hours," she said. What started as a way to kill time for her turned into a profession. Maybe I should tell this group about it. Maybe the speaker should have stories like this to share.

But she doesn't. Perhaps she raised her own kids on television. But I don't think that's it. I think that she's a little bit like me, afraid of offending people.

"Let's break into smaller groups now, groups of four or five, to examine our children's schedules," she says.

Casey has swimming lessons and soccer. In the spring he wants to be on a baseball team. Bob and I never liked playing sports when we were kids, but Casey likes sports. There's nothing about Casey's schedule that concerns me. His down time is truly his, a time for his mind to wander, time to be with his own thoughts.

Kendra told me that the main reason she chooses to fill up Hannah's schedule with so many activities is because it's the only way they can keep her from watching television. "If she didn't have dance class and soccer, she would watch day and night."

Peggy's kids are usually watching TV downstairs when I come over, but she's quick to say, "They just got back from soccer and piano lessons." In other words, there's no reason to feel bad about our kids' TV watching as long as they have structured extra-curricular activities the rest of the time. It reminds me of the character Shirley MacLaine played in *Postcards from the Edge.* She makes this really healthy-looking smoothie and then pours hard liquor into it.

I actually start to say something about this to the group, but I stop myself. Peggy is the normal one. It's normal to watch television. It is normal to drug your children. I remind myself that I'm abnormal.

OLIVIA HAS INVITED us for Thanksgiving dinner and Bob told her we would be happy to come. He said this mostly because he doesn't want to drive all the way down to Eugene.

"But Mama will be disappointed," I say.

"I don't want a vegetarian Thanksgiving," he says.

"Actually, it's a raw foods vegan dinner this year."

"There won't even be mashed potatoes?"

"No, but Sapphire said she will grind up raw cauliflower to make a creamy, potatolike mixture."

"What about pumpkin pie?"

"Simon is going to make a raw crust from almonds. I'm not sure he will use raw pumpkin. He might just make it a berry pie. It can't be that bad."

But Bob wants nothing to do with it. I call my mother and promise to visit her the day after Thanksgiving.

"It will be fun to eat at Olivia's," Bob says. But I'm not so sure.

"The only rule I have is that the kids eat in the kitchen," Olivia tells me when I ask her what we should bring.

I nod, but I'm not thrilled about it. Even on television shows, the family eats together on Thanksgiving, the kids, the parents, the grandparents, everyone. It's the way it was with my mom, too.

I talk to Casey about the plan before we walk over to Olivia's, and he seems ready to oblige. He settles himself in a chair next to Mindy at the end of the kitchen table. I join the grown-ups in the dining room. Casey fills his plate and begins to dig into his sweet potatoes and green beans. He has barely finished his third bite when I hear the quick shuffling of chairs and feet and see a horde of children racing downstairs.

"It's time for the Pokémon movie," they shout.

I walk into the kitchen. Casey is alone, looking bewildered. The other children's plates look as if they have not been touched. Casey, unlike Bob, who can inhale his food in a matter of seconds, likes to take his time with his food. And now he's left to eat by himself.

"You just enjoy your dinner," I tell him, patting him on the back. I'm kicking myself. I should have known that a movie would have been the main attraction, the planned event for the kids. Thanksgiving is about Pikachu and friends.

I go back into the living room and try to eat, but the food, although cooked to perfection, is tasteless now. After a few minutes Casey comes into what is the designated grown-up area and makes an awkward attempt to sit on my lap. I get up quickly and head back into the kitchen to offer him seconds on sweet potatoes. "You'll have to stay in here now. That's Olivia's rule," I say, "and we're her guests."

I go back to be with the adults, and while they discuss Bush's latest fiasco, I sit there pretending to listen, trying not to feel sorry for my child, and for myself, for making my child this way. After several painful minutes, I get up on the pretense of serving myself more green beans. Casey is finishing his dinner.

"You are six now, so you are allowed to watch the movie. Shall we just go see?" He grabs my arm and stops at the top of the stairs. "But I don't want to watch it," he says. I quickly steer him back into the kitchen, not wanting to draw attention to us.

"Then you will just have to play quietly by yourself in here," I tell him. I grab a pad of paper and a pencil from Olivia's desk.

He starts making a maze, and I think about how much I would prefer to stay with him right now than to be with the adults in the other room. I wouldn't even mind doing one of his mazes, even though I find them tedious. If only it wasn't Thanksgiving. Holidays invoke all of my Hallmark sentiments about togetherness and tender family moments. Hasn't Olivia seen any of these schmaltzy commercials?

After dinner I talk to her while Casey is drawing pictures at the kitchen table. "He's not much into television," I say.

"That's great," she says. "I just wanted them all plugged in so we could enjoy our dinner."

Casey follows me into the dining room, where I'm clearing the dishes.

"Can we go home now?"

"Maybe they're done with the movie now," I whisper.

"They're going to watch *Meet the Parents* next," he says.

"Are they?" I say. I take Bob aside to explain and he offers to take Casey home.

"He's pretty worn out," I tell everyone.

My voice sounds strained, but they don't seem to notice. I help with the dishes, talking amicably with the guests, trying to be charming.

I keep wondering what would have been the right thing to do. I tend to believe in the old saying, "When in Rome, do as the Romans do." I haven't actually been to Rome, but when I went to school in Spain my junior year of college, I never set foot in the newly opened McDonald's in Madrid. I ate the tapas and drank the Spanish wine in a glass tumbler, standing around the counter.

I brushed off the American students, dated the locals, and slept with my Barcelona-born professor.

The problem, Georgette would say, is that as usual I'm not communicating my true feelings. But I know that's only because I don't want to sound like my sister. If I had brought cooked food to her Thanksgiving feast, she would have made a loud pronouncement in front of everyone. "I smell food that has lost energy and vitality. It will not be a part of our meal!"

At least I can take comfort in the fact that I've made progress with my other friends. Had it been at Kendra's or Rebecca's, I would have been myself. They would already know that I wanted the kids to run off and play rather than watch a movie, and they would have accommodated me, even if it felt inconvenient for them.

I carefully dry a blue ceramic salad bowl and ask Olivia where I should put it.

"I'll take it," she says. "You know, you really don't have to do this." I know she means it, too, because she's sweet and kind, one of the nicest people in the neighborhood. It's not her fault that I'm miserable. How was she to know that I didn't want Casey to inhale his food in less than five minutes in order to be one of the first kids to turn on the television and watch Pokémon? She just wanted a calm dinner party without a bunch of kids running around constantly fighting, the way I did with my siblings.

It's almost nine p.m. when I leave. "Thank you for inviting us," I tell Olivia.

I slip into our house quietly. Casey is just getting into bed. I lie down and snuggle next to him. "Were you okay with playing by yourself while the other kids watched a movie?"

"I didn't like it that much," he says.

"I bet you didn't." I kiss him on the top of his head. "Sometimes you might have a great plan when your friends are coming to our house, like having everyone play Yahtzee after dinner. Would you want them to reject the idea or go along with it?"

"I would want them to go along with it."

"Well, sometimes, that's the right thing for you to do at some-one else's house," I say. I'm trying to sound upbeat, but he looks annoyed with me.

"I didn't want to watch the Pokémon movie, if that's what you mean."

"But you could have watched it," I say. "You can watch two hours a week, remember? You can watch *Arthur*. Is that something you want to watch?"

"I have no interest in that show, Mom."

"How do you know?"

"I saw it in kindergarten on Fridays."

"Well, remember that if you're curious about any other shows or movies that kids are watching, you can tell me."

"I know, Mom," he says exasperated, as if I have just reminded him for the hundredth time to brush his teeth.

"HE IS NOT asking for television," I say to Bob. We are in bed together and Bob is trying to read an article in *Funny Times*.

"So why introduce it? If he wants it, he'll ask for it," he says curtly.

"But I've convinced him that it's not worth asking for and he's being stubborn about it." He reminds me of the way I was with my mayonnaise boycott.

"So what?" he says, and then he starts reading again.

I jump out of bed, pulling the covers partway off with me.

"Where are you going? It's late."

"I'm calling Sarah."

"Do you have to call her right now?" Our Thanksgiving is turning out to be less than he expected. His Hallmark vision of the holiday probably includes great sex after our child has fallen asleep.

"Yes, I do."

He sits up straight in the bed, but I'm already at the door. "You're going to talk to her about what happened at Olivia's, aren't you?"

I don't answer him. He doesn't understand. I have to talk about something until I figure it out, and I haven't figured it out yet.

I head to the guest room and shut the door behind me. Back when I was watching lots of television, it didn't matter that Bob wasn't good at listening to me when I was upset.

I think this is what it's like for recovering alcoholics. They give up alcohol and suddenly all of their relationships are under scrutiny. Tiffany used to say, "When I was drinking, it didn't bother me that my boyfriend never came home. I had my gin and tonics."

I creep back into the bedroom after talking to Sarah. Bob is still awake. He tries to snuggle up next to me, but I turn away from him annoyed.

Georgette would say that I'm not angry right now, as much as I'm hurt. She would say that I actually want to be closer to Bob. Maybe she's right.

"I'm sorry," he says. "You can tell me whatever you want now."

"But you'll be suffering." I draw out the word *suffering* in a melodramatic way.

"You're just better at talking than I am."

I hate when he says this. He makes it sound like he's an idiot, someone who can only speak in monosyllables.

Last month, when I was getting my hair cut, I read an article in *Oprah* magazine. It said that when you're upset with your spouse, you're supposed to remember a time when you felt tender toward him.

I told this to Kendra hoping it would help her with Quinn. "I can't think of a time when I felt tenderly toward Quinn," she said.

I close my eyes now and think of last weekend when Bob made me a peach pie and gave me a bouquet of roses just because I went across town to pick up his cell phone, which he had left at the optometrist. It was my favorite pie and he was really sweet to make it for me. I have to think about it for a minute or two before I feel a change of heart, before I feel like talking to him again, and then it's only because I have an idea.

"I think you just need girlfriend lessons," I say.

"Girlfriend lessons? Is this something you learned from Georgette?"

"It's my own idea. You'll like it." I put my arm across his chest. I am making this up as I go along.

"I want to teach you to act like a girlfriend," I say. "It will make you really sexy." I reach under his shirt. It's a Pavlovian technique, but it just might work.

"Okay, give me the girlfriend lessons," he says softly.

"You'll have to listen closely," I say. I move my hand down below his belly button. Surprisingly, I enjoy using sex in this way with Bob, as long as it's my idea. It's an art form really, and I take pride in whatever talent I have.

"A good girlfriend always acts like she's interested in what her girlfriend has to say even if she needs to say the same thing over and over." I toy with the top of his pajama pants.

"I can do that," he says.

"Of course you can." I move my hand just slightly under the waistband.

"If you want to be a really good girlfriend, you must never rush her when she's talking about something important to her."

I reach my hand under his pajamas. "You'll find it can be really fun to be a girlfriend."

13

A First Time for Everything

Mostly to prove that our TV-free life really is fun for all of us, I decide to throw myself into festive real-life activities, although my idea of a real-life activity is probably more elaborate than it is for other people.

I've had Mindy over all week, since winter break started. She and Casey are spreading large pieces of butcher paper across the kitchen floor and placing trays of tempera paint around them. I have given them an array of paint brushes and sponges to make colorful holiday wrapping paper. They are wearing long T-shirts of Bob's, which make them look like preschoolers again. If I didn't have paint all over my hands, I might grab the camera.

"It was nice to be at your house for Thanksgiving," I tell Mindy as I fill up a jar of blue paint and set it beside her.

"We liked having you over," she says, all smiles. She doesn't mention Casey leaving early because he doesn't like to watch television. She brushes her baby-fine bangs away from her face, leaving a splotch of green paint on her cheek. "I like being at your house the best."

We've been making things every day, and, as I have no real

artistic imagination, Casey and Mindy have generated most of the ideas. We have covered rubber balls with model magic clay, pressed sparkly beads into the outside of them, and added hooks on top.

"The rest of these ornaments will be presents for my grand-parents," Casey says.

He and Mindy have made origami ornaments, too, little white seals and shiny silver cranes. We have gone outside and clipped branches from the cedar trees to make wreaths.

I look around the kitchen and consider calling *Sunset* magazine to see if they want to feature us in the next issue.

"Don't you want to paint some wrapping paper, too?" Mindy asks me.

"I guess so," I reply tentatively, having never been comfortable painting anything but my face. I pick up a medium-sized paint-brush and cut off a section of paper big enough to wrap up a board game or a sweater. I don't know who will get a present wrapped up in this piece of paper, but at least if it looks childish and awkward, people will assume that Casey made it. This is a great comfort to me. I don't know what I'll do when he's older. Perhaps we should have more kids. I dip my brush in the paint and remind myself that I don't need to create a masterpiece. Casey seems to know this for himself already.

When I set up my first apartment in college, I went shopping for towels and bedspreads and dish racks. I went to JCPenney and spent less than an hour buying everything I needed. My room-mate said she could knit a throw blanket for us if we wanted.

I didn't understand. Why would anyone bother to make some-thing they could easily afford to buy? Anyone who watches a lot of television would be puzzled, too. You go shopping and everything is there, perfectly packaged and guaranteed to make your home look like every other home you see on television.

I paint a bright golden star and a silver dove on my wrapping paper and it pleases me. I show it to Casey and Mindy.

"It's really pretty," Mindy says.

"It's kind of fun," I say.

I'M EXCITED ABOUT all of our homemade Christmas decorations. I invite over Kendra, Quinn, Rebecca, and Marcus for dinner. We're having lasagna, and most of the kids have seconds before they disappear upstairs.

"I made the centerpiece myself," I say, pointing to the cedar and pine cone creation on the table. I feel like I'm six years old.

"Wow," Rebecca says, but she doesn't ask me how I did it. Maybe I should have let her assume Casey made it.

I head upstairs to check on the kids and let them know that dessert is ready.

"Just a minute, Mom," Casey calls out.

He's wearing a purple velvet robe and Camden and Hannah are wearing Casey's bathrobes over their clothes. Wands, decks of trick cards, and little plastic cups from a magic set are strewn about the carpet.

"We're going to perform a magic show for you in a little while," Casey says. His clothes look bulky, as if he has suddenly put on an extra ten pounds. Apparently, it takes several layers of clothes to do his tricks.

"I can hardly wait to see it!" I say.

The kids come downstairs again and we make a space for their performance in the living room. Bob gets out his camera and everyone pulls up a chair. We are all so easily entertained for the simple reason that our children are the stars.

"No one missed watching television," Bob says after everyone has gone home. "You don't have to worry about that."

"Yes, but do they like having us come over to their houses as much?" I ask. We are unloading the dishwasher together quietly so as not to wake Casey.

"What are you talking about?"

"Haven't you noticed that everyone suggests coming to our house? It's too hard for them to think about entertaining our child at their houses because he won't watch television and he refuses to play video games."

"Maybe they just like my cooking the best," Bob says.

"Well, that, too," I say, and laugh, even though I'm still upset. But I'm good at laughing when I'm upset.

I figure if I find a really good Christmas movie, maybe it would be a good thing to show Casey so he would have something to do at other people's houses. If he likes the movie I choose, he'll know that movies can be fun. If he thinks it's really fun and wants to see it over and over, I'll tell him that it's a special holiday treat, like Christmas lights. You enjoy them, then take them down and put them away until the following year.

I'm walking around at Blockbuster trying to stay focused on my task. I rummage through the videos on a display table at the front of the store. *Miracle on Thirty-fourth Street* is one of my favorites, but it would be a bad choice because Casey still has an unquestioning belief in Santa Claus. *Rudolph the Red-Nosed Reindeer* seems dorky and *Frosty the Snowman* even dorkier. I'm not sure he's quite ready for *A Christmas Carol*. A lot of kids his age have seen *The Terminator,* but I'm worried about the Ghost of Christmas Yet to Come.

"Do you want to watch a Christmas movie?" I ask him, even though I have returned empty-handed.

"Maybe next year," he says.

This is exactly what I expected him to say and I decide not to force the issue. I've programmed him so well, a little too well. This must be what psychologists mean when they say children internalize their parent's fears.

We end up reading Christmas books instead. I read *'Twas the Night before Christmas* and *How the Grinch Stole Christmas.* Bob reads a book about a nun and her Christmas tree.

After Casey goes to bed, I stay up to watch *A Christmas Carol* with Bob. It's the version with George C. Scott. I think of it as the one that intelligent people prefer. TV watchers look for distinctions like this in order to make themselves feel smarter.

"Next year he can watch this movie," Bob says when it's over, "or at the very least, *A Charlie Brown Christmas.*"

I recall the awkwardness of Thanksgiving.

"He has to watch something before that," I say.

"MAYBE HE COULD watch the winter Olympics," Bob says. "They're in Salt Lake City this year." We are sitting at the kitchen table, both of us looking at the newspaper.

"They happen only every four years," he says. "I think he'll like seeing what they're all about."

I show Casey the schedule of events. "Do you want to watch them?" I ask.

"Okay," he says, giving it back to me. Bob gives me one of his I-told-you-so looks, a look that says, *Well, of course a televised sport is the answer to everything.*

We decide that the figure skating pairs would be a good first choice. Hopefully there won't be any Tonya Harding–type incidents.

Casey finishes putting on his pajamas and curls up in Bob's lap just in time to see the first pair of skaters. They are dressed in blue satin with gold trim and they perform their first jump together with perfect precision. Casey's face lights up in utter joy and surprise.

I explain about the point system. "Will 5.7 be good enough for them to get a medal?" he asks.

"I'm not sure."

We watch as the first commercial comes on, except it isn't a commercial. It's a trailer for some sort of violent thriller. I see rising flames and hear frenetic music, like something from a Ted Nugent concert. I reach for the remote, which had been right beside me a few seconds ago. Now it's gone.

I jump up and instantly place my body in front of the screen in time to cover up a man with the gun who is entering a burning building. "Change it to channel 10," I shout to Bob, who has the remote. I don't want Casey to notice that I'm upset, although it would be hard to miss with my hysterical yelling and my body pressed up against the set. I fumble around for the button on the TV and change the station. The fire is gone, and in its place is a nice English drama on public television, dull and uneventful.

"I'll handle the remote," I say to Bob, snatching it from his hand.

Having watched so many commercials in my life, I know instinctively when it's time to switch back to a show.

"We don't need to see the commercials," I say nonchalantly to Casey.

But then I wonder if that will just make him curious about them. At the next break, I decide to let him see something relatively harmless. "This is a commercial for a store that sells beds," I tell him. No one can accuse me of completely sheltering my child.

"Does it make you want to buy the bed?" I ask him.

"Not really," he says.

"But if you were to see this commercial thirty more times, you would at least remember the brand name," I say.

We watch the last pair of the evening, a Chinese couple up for the gold, and then it's time for bed. His television experience has been all of twenty minutes. "You can stay up on Thursday night if you want to watch more of the Olympics," I say.

"I'd like to see the skiing," he says.

After Casey has fallen asleep, Bob and I have a less than amiable discussion about how to handle the remote.

"I'll be the one in charge of it from now on," I say, as if we are having a custody battle.

He says something about how controlling I am and I remind him of the 200,000 violent acts the average child will have seen by the time he turns eighteen.

"We could just tape the whole thing," he suggests.

"That won't be as exciting," I say. "Anyway, it's not just the violent movie previews and news clips that I'm concerned about." I explain that I don't even want him to see most of the so-called innocuous commercials. "He doesn't need some woman complaining about aging skin until she discovers that Neutrogena is the answer to her prayers."

Bob has turned away, so I set the remote on the shelf in a place where he won't find it. The day will come when Casey will be allowed to handle the remote and watch without us around. He'll get a chance to catch up with his peers on the number of bloody deaths he's witnessed. But maybe that day will be far away.

WE WATCH THE Olympics two more times before the torch is extinguished. Casey couldn't have made it into a habit even if that's what he wanted. But I'm glad he's had this experience.

I feel like one of the crowd when I'm talking to Isabel about it the next day at school. "Casey and I really liked the skiing. I let him stay up a little bit later than usual so he could see it."

"I let Lindsey stay up, too."

I'm just an ordinary parent watching a little television with her child.

I ALWAYS THOUGHT that if I ever got off television, I would finally read all of the great works of literature. I would go to the library and check out *The Great Gatsby* and *Pride and Prejudice*. Then I would make offhanded remarks about Mr. Darcy, whoever he is.

It has been two months since I've watched TV, and I'm still mostly reading the Harry Potter books over and over.

We are on our way home from school and Casey asks me if we can stop at the library. Maybe I'll finally check something out, too, instead of just watching Casey check out books.

"Monique read these three books written by an author I like," he says. "I want to see if I can find them."

When we get to the library, Casey locates his books easily and then grabs a few others from another shelf. "*Flatfoot Fox* and *The Grasshopper* are also good," he says.

He piles the books up on the counter. This week they're all fiction. Last month he picked out a book on cats. He wanted to find out more about the flame point kitten we brought home from the pound.

I ask the librarian to show me where *Jane Eyre* is, because Trillium said I should read it.

"Isn't that a classic?" I had asked Trillium.

"Yes, you'll like it," she said. "Please read it."

When we get home from the library, Casey sits down on the couch immediately and starts reading. I busy myself with the newspaper.

"You can read one of my books if you want, Mom."

"Maybe," I say. I consider reading the book I brought home from the library. I watch Casey already focused on his book. He is so different from the way I was. I learned to read easily and well enough, but I don't remember any trips to the library and I don't recall ever having a favorite author.

Books were mainly a source of guilt for me, like my piano lessons. I remember receiving books as presents, Nancy Drew ones from my Aunt Frieda and *My Father's Dragon* from my grandmother. I recall looking at the front and back cover of these books, but that was as far as I got. It was too much trouble.

Even magazines were too much of a bother for me. My uncle gave me a subscription to kids' *National Geographic* when I was ten, but when the magazine arrived, I rarely opened it, not even to look at the pictures. If he came over to visit my family, I would pretend that I had read every issue. "The koalas were really interesting," I would say, and hope that he didn't ask me for specifics.

I didn't read any books in earnest until I turned thirteen, and that was only because I was interested in sex. *Everything You Wanted to Know about Sex; Our Bodies, Ourselves; Naked Came the Stranger.*

These were books my mother had around the house that caught my attention.

At school, when it came time to give a book report, I often managed to get by without reading an actual book. I remember making it halfway through *To Kill a Mockingbird,* skipping to the end, and then relying on the movie before writing my report.

It has never been like that with videos. Even if I don't like what I'm watching, I don't think of fast-forwarding to find out what's going to happen next. I pick up *Jane Eyre* and set my newspaper aside. I move closer to Casey. He doesn't bother to look at me but he snuggles against me while he reads. I open my book to the first page. Casey is already on page 15.

So many kids Casey's age need reading tutors now. I asked a boy on Casey's soccer team if he was interested in having his parents read the first Harry Potter book to him. "We could lend it to you," I said.

"Well, I've already seen the movie and I don't think the book will get the pictures right."

I tried to explain to him that with reading you get to create your own pictures in your head.

"That's too hard," he said.

I knew what he meant. When Bob offered to get me the Wizard of Oz books, I told him not to bother.

"I just don't think they will follow the movie closely enough," I told him.

I read the first page of *Jane Eyre* over again and try to focus. Casey is now on page 20. The strange thing is that the parents of Casey's friends may have actually read a lot when they were kids, but they don't understand why their own kids struggle with reading.

Wendy also took Kyle to see the latest Harry Potter movie, even though they'd never read the book. She said, "When we got out of the theater, I told him that I hoped he could now see why books are worth reading. I'm also letting him watch lots of PBS videos of stories, so he'll want to read more."

I wanted to ask her why she doesn't offer him more fruit so he'll learn to like vegetables.

I put PBS on the other day when Casey was away and watched five minutes of *Arthur*. Arthur and his friend were sitting in front of a TV screen at home playing a video game. I guess I had expected more of public television than watching the characters play with a GameCube or whatever it was.

After *Arthur* was over, I watched what were actually mini commercials from the sponsors of the program. I flipped over to the Disney Channel and saw Pooh reading a poem to his animal friends. Piglet read the first line and then the narrator of the show said, "When you hear poetry, you are supposed to use your imagination, so let's use ours." I thought that at that point the kids should be told to close their eyes, but you can never tell TV viewers to close their eyes. Tell them to read, but don't tell them to turn the television off right now and start reading. Tell them what program is coming up next instead and why it can't be missed.

I changed the station again and found a Hooked on Phonics commercial. Parents and children who watch television are the perfect audience for these ads. I don't see them anywhere else.

I wonder if books about sex will be the thing that motivates kids to finally start reading. Probably not. There are so many sexual images on television now, in videos and on the Internet. Who needs to read about sex anymore?

I watch Casey deep in concentration, happy to be reading. I finally turn to page two in *Jane Eyre*. I have to believe that I can read a book like this.

AT CASEY'S SCHOOL at the end of the year all the kids will camp out in tents in the middle of the soccer field. I'm not sure why it's so important to have a bunch of six-year-olds stuffed into sleeping bags away from their parents, but it's a major goal of the school. Bob and I are at our teacher conference and Monique is explaining how important it is to prepare the children for this big event.

"Has he had any sleepovers yet?" she asks us.

"He spent the night at his babysitter's house while Bob and I went away for the weekend," I tell her. I don't mention that Kellie cuddled him to sleep and then he climbed into bed with her at one a.m. on both nights.

Monique smiles. "Well, this is different, and he needs to be ready. Perhaps you could arrange for him to spend the night at a friend's house. Someone from this class would be a good choice." We are in her classroom sitting across from a bulletin board with pictures of Australian animals. She's been raving about Casey and I was ready to get up and give her a big kiss until she started talking about sleepovers.

"He'll be fine," she says, sensing my anxiety. "The kids love our overnight. They eat pizza and watch a movie. He'll have a great time."

"What if he doesn't want to watch the movie at the school overnight?" I ask Bob after the conference. "What if he tells the teacher he's never seen a movie and doesn't want to participate?"

"I doubt he'll say that, because he'll be at school."

Still, Bob leads me upstairs to the guest room and hands me the Tigger video his sister Lynn gave Casey for Christmas. "He can watch this before the overnight."

I cringe. Maybe the whole idea is a big mistake. I think of Pandora and how much she regretted opening that box. "What if, after he watches the movie, he doesn't want to read?" I say. "What if he just sits in a corner whining and begging to watch one video after another, complaining all day that he's bored? We will have ruined him."

"Well, at least he'll be ready for the overnight. Isn't that what this is all about?" Bob says sarcastically. "Besides, it could be fun."

"But he already has fun. He's happy without television."

"And he still will be," Bob says slowly.

"Or not," I say. "It could be like using a vibrator."

Bob looks at me curiously.

"When have you used a vibrator?"

"I haven't, but I can tell that I would get really addicted to using one. It would be so intense, I would want to use it all the time, and then ordinary sex would no longer seem like enough. You'd be reduced to holding the vibrator every night until I couldn't take it anymore."

"Are you saying that the Tigger movie is like a vibrator?"

"Well, it could become like one," I say.

"Isn't there such a thing as occasional vibrator use?" Bob asks.

I set the video down and wonder why he doesn't understand.

"Who do you know who uses a vibrator only occasionally?" I ask.

"Who do you know who uses a vibrator?"

I ponder the possibilities. Rebecca maybe.

"Well, it hasn't exactly come up for discussion," I say, "but that's not the point."

"The point is that you couldn't own a vibrator and leave it alone."

I ARRANGE FOR Casey to spend the night with Andrew. "What about Camden?" Bob asks when I tell him.

"Camden doesn't go to his school. It has to be someone from his class."

"What about Diego or Jacob?"

"Janie invited him for this weekend. She said Andrew would be happy to have him over."

Casey and Andrew are not that close, and I suspect that Janie is only paying me back for what she feels is a debt to Bob and me. Her grandfather died and Bob made her eggplant parmesan, which I brought over to her last week. I'm scared to try to get close to her because she's friends with Lauren, the head of the clique. Even though she's being nice to me, I'm still uneasy with her.

We make the arrangements over the phone. She asks me what Casey can and cannot eat, and if he is allergic to anything.

"I thought they could watch a movie," she adds. "Would that be okay? It would something really benign, rated G."

"That's fine," I say. I don't tell her that it will be his first movie. I don't tell her that I haven't even been able to get him to watch a Tigger movie.

THE DAY OF CASEY'S overnight with Andrew, I say, "They'll want you to watch a movie, and it will be a good movie for you to see. You'll probably really like it."

He doesn't say anything. I keep my fingers crossed. It could work out okay because it's at someone else's house. I never wanted to eat almonds until my best friend's mother offered them to me.

Bob and I give him a kiss, and I try to act relaxed and confident.

"Have fun! See you tomorrow." I'm smiling and waving, but inside, I'm feeling ill. I'm not comfortable enough with Janie to tell her how I feel.

"Shall we go out on an exciting date?" Bob asks me as we drive away.

"I'm too nervous."

Bob puts his hand on my leg.

"I can help you forget about it."

"I doubt it," I say.

We manage to have a nice dinner but then I just want to go home. After having sex in the living room, simply because we can, I walk into the guest room, turn back around and walk out.

"We could read," I say.

Bob looks surprised. I'm surprised, too. Casey is away. I'm worried. This is a situation that begs to be filled with late-night television.

"Whatever you want," he says.

THE NEXT DAY we pick up Casey right after breakfast. I'm wiped out but wired at the same time. I stayed up reading and bothering Bob most of the night, waiting by the phone in case Janie called. But at least I didn't watch television.

"How did everything go?" I ask Janie.

"Everything was fine. They played a lot of games. He wasn't interested in watching the movie."

"Oh, I'm sorry," I say horrified. "I bet that was a problem for you." She must think we are such weirdoes.

"No, it really wasn't a problem," she says.

But I'm sure it was. They had a fun evening planned, which included a movie. Janie was probably counting on having at least one portion of the evening a peaceful, effortless time and my child didn't oblige.

I want to ask her more questions about the evening, but I also want to seem easygoing and relaxed. I imagine her talking to Lauren later, telling her I'm so overly concerned about Casey and maybe mentioning how he didn't even want to watch *Beauty and the Beast,* for God's sake!

I keep my voice even and attempt to sound curious, as opposed to agitated.

"Was he polite?"

"He was fine," Janie says.

I smile tensely, and before I can stop myself, I fire away three more questions about the evening. "How late did they stay up? Did he wake anyone else up in the morning? Was he finicky about breakfast?"

"It was fine," Janie says.

I give her a hug, which seems to surprise her, or maybe it annoys her. I can't tell, but I pull away abruptly.

"Thank you so much for having my child for his first overnight! Let us know when we can have Andrew over for the night."

"Oh, don't worry about that," she says too quickly, and I can tell that she doesn't want us to reciprocate. She will send her son over to the house of a less neurotic parent, a place where all of the kids will happily watch movies as planned.

On the way home I ask Casey if he had fun.

"I had lots of fun."

"Did they want to watch a movie?"

"Lewis did but I didn't and Andrew said he would do whatever I wanted."

"Did Lewis cry?"

"For a while, and then he played with us."

I pictured Janie and her husband, Jimmy, having to mediate arguments, find things for Lewis to do while the boys played checkers, and all because I had raised a child who was clearly averse to watching TV. I had made the evening harder for the parents and that can only make it harder for my child.

"Why didn't you just watch the movie, Casey?"

"I didn't want to watch it."

I nod and tell him I understand even though I don't understand him at all.

"I NEVER THOUGHT it would come to this, that we would have to entice our child into watching a movie." I'm being overly dramatic with Bob.

"What do you mean? You've brainwashed him from the day he was born!"

"I didn't think it would take!"

We are in the guest room again, passing the infamous Tigger video back and forth between us.

"We'll do it this weekend," Bob says. "You can tell him."

Casey is downstairs sitting on the carpet with colorful squares of paper beside him.

"I'm going to show you the Tigger movie so you'll know that there are some good movies out there," I announce to him.

"Not right now," he says. He's making an origami crane out of rainbow paper.

"You're going to need to watch a movie on your school overnight," I tell him.

"I know." He finishes folding the wings back. "Do you like it?"

"It's nice," I say.

In an advertising class in college, I learned why commercials work. For example, the jump-on-the-bandwagon technique was supposed to be powerful in persuading people. People want to do what their friends are doing, the professor said. But so far this technique hasn't convinced Casey.

He hands me his latest creation, and I set it on the coffee table.

"We can watch this movie this weekend with Dad." It's not really a question anymore.

"Well, okay," he says, at last.

Bob buys him the Tigger movie book from Fred Meyer, and Casey reads it in one sitting.

"What do you think?" I ask.

"I like it."

We make a plan to watch it on Sunday. I contemplate screening the movie before showing it to Casey, but I don't want to bore myself twice. At least I don't have to worry about it being too violent. It got rave reviews from three- and four-year-olds. I'm not even concerned that he'll no longer approach the classic Pooh stories in the same way, because for at least a year now the Winnie the Pooh books have been largely ignored.

We gather in the guest room. Casey and I sit at the foot of the bed a few feet away from the screen. Bob stretches out behind us on the bed, already looking bored. I fast forward through the previews until we hear the pleasant voice of a narrator and see a lovely view of Christopher Robin's room.

Casey seems happy. He leans forward a little when Tigger announces that he is going to find his real family. As the movie progresses, I expect my child to be completely mesmerized, his eyes glued to the set, as the seed for a future addiction is planted in his brain. I expect him at any moment to tell me that he can't believe I've deprived him of such a fabulous experience for so long.

But after forty minutes, he asks when it will be over.

"Just thirty more minutes," I say. Bob looks up from a book he has been surreptitiously reading.

Granted, the movie is proving to be even more boring than I'd expected. The plot is poor, the events unrealistic, and the characters predictable. Rabbit is annoyed too easily. Tigger is too bouncy. Pooh's life revolves around honey. Unlike other Disney movies, this one doesn't even attempt to hold an adult's attention. It's clearly intended to be played to a three-year-old in the family room while the parent busily washes the dishes or changes the cat litter.

As the climax approaches, Casey is at least paying attention. The characters are in danger of being covered by an approaching avalanche. But when it mercifully ends, the room is surprisingly the same and Casey appears to be free of any glazed look.

"Well, that was fun, wasn't it?" I say cheerfully.

"So I could watch this again this week," Casey says, "since I get two hours a week, right, and this movie is less than two hours?"

"No," I say, thinking of vibrators. "This movie is seventy-two minutes long, and besides, you only get one movie a week."

"So, next Sunday, I could watch it."

"If you want," I say.

"But if I don't, then I get to watch four hours the next week, right?

"No, it's not like that," I say. "It's never more that two hours a week, unless it's a longer movie."

I'm starting to regret our decision to watch this. I look at Bob, instinctively ready to dump any blame on him.

The next weekend rolls around and the vibrator phenomenon has not transpired as I had feared. In fact, the Tigger movie seems to have been forgotten.

"Please don't mention it," I say to Bob. "If he doesn't think of it, then we won't suggest it."

"Why would he think of it? It was a simplistic piece of drivel meant for a preschooler."

"It was a good first movie," I say.

Bob sighs.

"Well, at least he'll be ready for the school overnight."

It's TV-Turnoff Week. Kendra says that her school sent home information about it. "Quinn and I are going to do it with Hannah because I want her to know what real life is like for a whole week."

"Well, good for you," I say. I don't ask her why she doesn't want her to know what real life is like all of the time, because I understand. Real life is just too much for most of us to handle. That's why we don't expect our children to handle it either, not for more than a week anyway.

Kendra and I are taking a walk down to the store. She's telling me how her school does TV-Turnoff Week every year and how more than half of the families in Hannah's class participated last year.

"That's great," I say. "How are things with Quinn?"

"We're in counseling," she says. "And I've stopped seeing Logan."

I tell Bob what Kendra said about TV-Turnoff Week when I get home.

"Why don't we have it at Casey's school?" he asks.

"Erica didn't think the kids could handle more than a day without television."

"She's only the parent-teacher liaison. Why don't you talk to Sheila, and help start it in the elementary school?" Bob asks me. Sheila is the school counselor.

"If I say something, I'll draw attention to the fact that we don't watch."

"And we can't have that!" is Bob's response.

I ignore him. He doesn't understand that I feel different enough as it is, lately more than ever. I've been away from commercials for so long, I only hear about new products from my friends and neighbors who watch television.

BY THE TIME summer arrives, I'm even more out of touch. I'm at the neighborhood watch meeting at Lori's house. It's Saturday morning and we're sitting on her porch eating.

"How can we possibly live up to the standard Martha Stewart sets for us?" Lori complains.

I nod in agreement. I've seen Martha Stewart in the newspaper, but I've never seen her show. I don't feel tremendous pressure to buy her brand of sheets at Kmart either.

Lori goes on to complain about how bad McDonald's is for her children. "But my kids beg me to take them there. And I don't want them to get fat."

"Kids are fatter than ever," I say, and I grab a Krispy Kreme doughnut.

Yesterday at Fred Meyer, I saw a little girl begging for another box of Hostess Twinkies and, paradoxically, for a Barbie, who looks as if she has never eaten a single Twinkie in her Barbie-land life. The mixed messages are crazy making. Eat junk, diet, eat junk, diet. And even without the commercials, watching television burns about the same amount of calories as sleeping does. No wonder so many kids are fat.

I grab another doughnut. These are the first ones I've tried. Casey never asks me to take him to McDonald's, but I wonder if he could develop a taste for these things. I take a big bite. They're pretty good, although not as good as they're cracked up to be.

BY AGE SIX, most children will have seen six thousand hours of television. They may live with enlightened parents who take turns changing diapers and changing the oil, but television will be the primary authority in their home. TV teaches kids that girls and boys are polar opposites. Girls wear pink. Boys wear blue. Girls are supposed to play with Barbies. Boys are supposed to destroy them. Lots of Casey's classmates won't play with the opposite gender.

I'm thankful that Casey and Mindy are still friends. Today I'm taking them to a play. I'm discovering that plays are more exciting than television shows and movies. You never know what will happen. An actor could sneeze unscripted, stumble on a line, trip and fall. There are no retakes.

Casey and Mindy seem to understand this. They are as excited about seeing *The Boxcar Children* as I am.

"Have you read the book?" Casey asks Mindy.

"No. What's it about?"

"It's about some kids who don't have any parents," Casey says.

We are sitting on the third row and the play is about to begin. Casey and Mindy stop talking as the lights dim.

I take them up to the stage when the play is over.

"What would you most like to do if you were part of a play?" I ask them. I've been explaining what actors, set designers, directors, and lighting engineers do.

"I would be an actress," Mindy says, and she begins imitating Lizzie McGuire.

"I would be the lighting engineer," Casey says.

"That would be interesting," I say, even though a lighting engineer is about the last thing I would have wanted to be at his age.

I was like Mindy, always craving the spotlight. I knew I could have done as well as any of the children on television selling Snickers bars and Skipper dolls. I pictured myself eating Frosted Flakes in front of the camera, looking delighted to be working with Tony the Tiger.

Once I expressed my desire to my mother, who dismissed it evenhandedly. "I'm not going to trot you around from studio to studio for you to smile for the camera all day and night. It's a tough life filled with rejections." I thought about what she said. Wasn't my life already filled with rejections? Besides, in my fantasy, I wouldn't be rejected. I would simply appear on television coast to coast laughing and smiling. I would put away the money I made in a special account so I could buy whatever I wanted. When my mother said, "Let's see if we can find that bicycle secondhand," I would shrug her off. "That's okay. I'll use my own money."

My fame would not only attract the popular kids in my class, but it would help my mother, too. Eligible men would want to date the mother of the famous child star. They wouldn't mind the prospect of becoming the father of three children, and I, as the star, would of course be the favorite child. We would move into a clean, new, rat-free house with a swimming pool, and because I would have starred in so many commercials, we would have all of the products I had promoted and more.

"Child actors do not have normal lives," my mother would say. I pondered this. I was pretty sure my mother wasn't even trying to give me a normal life. Otherwise, she would have married again and she would wear polyester pantsuits and we would attend a church other than the Unitarian one.

Though my mother had no interest in my starring in commercials, she did have her own designs for my future stardom. When I was a teenager, she sent off for the Miss Teenage America contest forms. "You can be the one who tells them all off when you win." Her goal was for me to spread the feminist gospel to the widest possible audience.

I ask Mindy what her mother thinks of her wanting to be an actress. We're riding the light-rail on our way home from the play.

"She says I have to get better at reading. Actresses have to read a lot of lines."

"Reading helps," I agree.

"But I might want to be a singer like Britney Spears."

"Who's Britney Spears?" Casey asks.

"She sings *Oops! . . . I Did It Again.*" Mindy begins her rendition of the song, doing her best imitation of Britney, which isn't half bad.

Mindy wants to get her ears pierced and her hair lightened. Why wait? I can imagine the makers of lingerie saying, *Why not triple our sales by offering see-through underwear to grade school girls?*

Do you think we can convince girls to wear them? they ask each other. *What about their parents?*

Parents just want their kids to fit in.

"CASEY DOESN'T EVEN know who Britney Spears is," I tell Bob, after Mindy has gone home. We're in the front yard and I'm watching Bob put the recycling containers in a row along the curb.

"I wish we could all be so lucky," he says.

"Shouldn't I get him a teen magazine, so he can learn who all of the kid actors are?"

"No," he says quickly. Then he looks at me as if he doesn't know me.

I hate when he does that.

CASEY ISN'T INTERESTED in learning about the latest teen idols, so I decide to forget about getting him *Teen People*. I tell Bob that he's right after all. I make a big deal about it whenever I think he's right, so he won't notice all the times I think he's wrong.

I get Casey a subscription to *Chess Life* instead because I know he'll love it. This morning, Casey is at the breakfast counter eating oatmeal while reading a book on chess strategies.

"Mom, did you know that I used a skewer the last time we played?" I hand him a sliced banana and a bagel, too.

"No, I didn't," I say, hoping he won't explain to me what a skewer is until he's finished his breakfast. I tell him to take at least three bites of oatmeal and then he can tell me about a skewer. I probably should take the chess book away while he eats, but I'm being especially sweet to him right now because I'm about to take a long vacation without him.

14

Pandora's Box

Television is about throwing away anything that's old and getting whatever is new. Almost every ad and every show tell you that new is better, new is more interesting, new is what you need. Who cares about history? It's old. It's boring. It's about your parents, your grandparents, dead people. Wouldn't you rather hear about Teletubbies? Except that they're history, too, now. Forget them! Even the gay one. Who cares! And Pokémon? It's probably out, too. Get with it!

I'm thinking about history now, because I'm on a bus touring the English countryside with Trillium, who just turned eighteen. We are on a ten-day vacation together to celebrate her graduation from high school. Actually I'm fulfilling my end of a bargain I made with her when she was thirteen. "You can go anywhere you want in the world, if you don't drop acid before graduating."

We were at Trillium's hippie-style coming-of-age ceremony in Hendricks Park when I made the deal with her. Everyone had been going around in a circle offering her their blessings and guidance for a long inspired life, healthy partnering, and beautiful babies for her someday, if she desires children. I worried when it was my sister's turn to share her pearls of wisdom.

"I hope to be the one to introduce you to the mysteries of expanded consciousness," she said in a tone she probably thought an ancient priestess would use. Perhaps her friends thought she was planning a yoga retreat with her daughter in the Himalayas or some other benign and wholesome activity. But I felt certain my sister was envisioning something not so wholesome, such as a trek into the woods with her daughter and a mind meld of sorts occurring with the aid of some hallucinogenic substance. I wasn't sure when the desired initiation would occur, but I didn't want to take any chances. My sister had given our brother a joint when he was eleven and mailed him acid when he was fifteen. I didn't think her experiment with him had turned out very well. She had tried to get my mother to smoke pot, but Mama was too worried about losing her job. "I'll stick to my own drugs," she said, pointing to her scotch.

"I'm so disappointed in her," my sister told me. When my mother inadvertently ate a marijuana brownie and didn't even feel the effects, my sister stopped trying to get her high. "I guess she drinks too much to get anything out of it. And those were powerful brownies, too," she said.

In the end, it turns out my sister had no such plans for her daughter. "I only used cannabis medicinally during labor, and it has been more than a decade since I've experimented with psychoactive substances," she told me when she found out about my deal with her daughter. "Trillium doesn't need mind-altering drugs either. With a raw-foods diet, I'm able to coexist with higher beings naturally, and she is welcome to do the same."

I was hoping that, upon graduation, Trillium would choose a

nice, warm, tropical resort so we could lie around under palm trees reading paperback novels and eating fresh pineapple together. But she's a medieval literature buff, a fan of ballads and wizards. And so England and Ireland and a world of castles and ancient ruins beckoned her.

That's why we're on our way to Stonehenge and Avebury. Yesterday we spent all day at the British Museum. I found out the time when people first walked upright, when the first humans like us appeared, and when writing began. I looked at gods and goddesses from Africa and relics from the Stone Age, the Bronze Age, and the Iron Age and found out when these ages occurred. I learned when Rome invaded Britain and what distinguished the Renaissance period from the Middle Ages. Trillium already knew this, of course.

Her goals in London are far loftier than mine. I don't tell her that I want to see Notting Hill in order to see where Hugh Grant and Julia Roberts made their movie together. I would be embarrassed about being so shallow. Trillium expects to delve into the history of Avalon. I expect to meet people who are like the characters in Monty Python movies. My sense of the region is colored by seeing *Shakespeare in Love* three times. Trillium could recite her favorite lines from *A Midsummer Night's Dream,* because she's read it five times.

We arrive in Avebury. Our guide leads us out of the bus into a well-worn field with what remains of various structures used in pagan celebrations.

He points to an oddly shaped boulder. "This was once a ring-shaped stone. If a woman was having trouble getting pregnant, she was supposed to climb through it to increase her fertility."

He leads us to the place where people once gathered to dance and procreate. When he finishes talking, he tells us we can wander around on our own for a little while.

Trillium and I return to the base of the fertility stone, all that's left of it anyway.

"Does it feel powerful to you?" I ask. I'm stretched out on top of it and she's sitting next to me at the other end of it, her legs dangling down.

"I don't feel anything," she says.

But that night Trillium wakes up from a dream, her face flushed.

"I've been dreaming about so many men! All of these men wanting me!" She is sweating.

"I've been dreaming, too, but not that kind of dream." I take a drink of water and then set my glass down again. "I know what I'll write about next," I tell her.

I bring Trillium a fresh glass of water and remind her to be particularly vigilant about birth control. Then I scribble some notes in my journal before I fall back to sleep.

ON THE FLIGHT BACK I'm sandwiched between two sleeping teenagers, and however much I recline, it's not enough. I long for first class. The plane is dark and I don't want to turn on the overhead light, so I can't read. And so I stare at the TV, wide awake. I look enviously at my soundly sleeping niece in the window seat, her thin legs comfortably curled up against her chest, her head resting against the side of the plane.

I'm watching a fashion show, and it's in French. No matter, the mesmerizing effect is the same. The television has been on the whole way, as we crossed the Atlantic Ocean, to pacify the masses, I presume, and maybe to prevent terrorist acts. I watch without the sound. One emaciated body after another ambles down a runway, hips swinging in an exaggerated fashion reserved for models and prepubescent girls trying to look as if they have hips.

I haven't missed television. I've missed Casey.

Next time I'll come here with him and Bob. We'll go to other places, too, and Casey will appreciate the history. He's been learning about the origins of the Olympics in Greece and wants to go there.

Maybe he won't have gaps in his education. I listened to a Holocaust survivor on NPR. She spent years in concentration camps, and Terry Gross asked her how she caught up on her education. She said she hadn't. I haven't either, but my reasons aren't nearly as compelling.

BOB IS MAD that I'm once again making Casey's birthday party into a grand production. This year he turns seven.

"Are we heading to the river?" Bob asks me when he sees a canoe in the backyard. We are standing on our deck. It's July and we're planning to eat outside tonight. My nieces have arrived to make costumes. Casey and Mindy are painting party bags on the kitchen floor.

"I borrowed the canoe. It's just a prop, part of the set for the party. The first rehearsal is tomorrow." I hand him a script. He doesn't look at it.

"It's not too late," he pleads. "We could probably still reserve a couple of tables at Chuck E. Cheese."

I look at him with pity. "We already rented the Hoyt Arboretum. I've assigned parts to the kids." I turn to Casey. "Tell him about it," I say, thinking that whatever he hears from Casey will be easier to take. He won't want to disappoint him, at least not to his face. Bob hates when I do this.

"Morgan le Fay will show up after the play and lead the kids into the woods," Casey says.

"And how many of 'us' are there?" he asks, looking at me warily.

"You'll be in charge of only ten children, and I'll give you the easiest kids," I say.

"But you've invited everyone again, haven't you?"

"I'm sure that not everyone will come," I reassure him.

He stalks away, knowing he's helpless to do anything about our plans.

I follow him into the house. I doubt that Bob would believe me, but I really hadn't intended to make the party such a big deal. It started out innocently enough. I had returned from England ready to enjoy the summer with Casey. He was reading the twentieth Magic Tree House book, part of a series about a brother and sister who travel through time in a tree house, have adventures, and help save the world. As far as I know there hasn't been a Magic Tree House movie or cartoon yet. Maybe the author has been approached. I imagine her saying to NBC, *I don't want my book ruined by your industry, my characters made into toys to sell at Burger King.*

I asked Casey if he wanted to have a Magic Tree House party.

"Great idea!" he'd said immediately.

I looked into his eyes and saw myself, someone capable of imagining elaborate scenarios, without regard to the hours of work, the exorbitant amount of money required, and the number of people needed to make the vision a reality. But it was the joy in his face that let me know we would have another fabulous party.

I try to explain this to Bob. He has gone into the study and shut the door. I open it cautiously.

"This is what families do who don't watch television," I say.

"This is what high school theater departments do!" he says.

He could be right. How would I know? I wasn't in theater in high school. I was at home watching *Three's Company.*

"The point is that everyone expects a big party now. It's a family tradition!"

"I just don't think it's normal," he says.

"Well, of course it isn't."

I TALK TO GEORGETTE about it. It's early afternoon, and I notice that she has painted the room we are sitting in pink. She says pink will help me experience deeper levels of love for myself and others. I'm wondering what she wears when she paints. I can't see her in sweats and a T-shirt, but she can't wear flowing dresses all the time.

"Bob thinks that maybe I'm trying too hard to make sure that Casey is happy and popular. He thinks I'm trying to compensate for the lack of television in his life."

"Sounds like Casey is pretty happy," she says. "But what about you? What about the little girl within you?"

Georgette loves talking about my inner child. I had trouble understanding exactly what she meant at first. I just knew I was supposed to nurture her. But what was I supposed to do? Take her to tea parties?

Once Georgette gave me a little doll made out of cloth with shoulder-length hair and green eyes like mine. "Let her serve as a reminder for you to take better care of yourself."

I tell Georgette that maybe I do go a little overboard sometimes, but that I have a lot of energy now.

I wait for her next insight. But she doesn't seem to have one other than something about my creative force and how she hopes I will keep finding lots of channels for its expression.

• • •

Casey's first-grade teacher has been moved up to second grade. There is nothing to explain, no fear of being handed a list of movies for Casey to watch. She knows Casey and we know her.

I'm a veteran now, determined to make the most of this year and not to worry so much about Casey's social life and mine. The party was a great success and Casey seems happier than ever. I vow to try to be easygoing, or at least as close to easygoing as can be expected.

The first week of school gets off to a surprisingly good start. It's not something I can put my finger on. I just notice that everyone seems a little nicer.

When I ask Janie about her trip to Japan, she actually meets my eyes and talks to me about it for five minutes.

Wendy gives me a kiss on the cheek when she sees me.

I look around for the tight circle of snobs, but it's nowhere to be seen.

After I walk Casey into the classroom, I stay and chat with Isabel, as soon as I'm able to get her alone.

"Something's different, isn't it?"

"It's because Lauren isn't around. Grayson's brother, Jake, started preschool."

I glance in the direction of the preschool. Lauren is standing around in a circle of new moms.

"I think she's starting a clique over there," Isabel says. Lauren is dressed in a short black skirt that would look good on a teenager.

"She's pretty decked out," I say.

"She also has a new job."

I look at the second-grade parents and notice that everyone seems to be more relaxed. Maybe with Lauren more or less out of the picture, the other snobs can afford to be nice to everyone. Maybe the dis-the-snobs group will disband eventually, too.

I want to tell Georgette that I'm graduating from high school and moving into adulthood. I think about calling her, but then she would tell me that it's time to forgive everyone there, not just the snobs, but the kindergarten teacher, too. "Forgive them and you open your heart to more joy," she'd say. I like the part about joy.

I sign up to help out in the classroom once a week. After saying good-bye to Casey, I head to the track to run every morning. When I first started running, I didn't have a partner and reluctantly decided to go it alone. The strange thing is that as soon as I actually embraced the opportunity for solitude, I ended up with unexpected company.

Now there are five of us who show up on a regular basis. I enlist their help in starting a chess club at school. None of us actually plays chess, but why should that stop us?

"Who will be the teacher for the chess club?" Casey asks me when I've finished making the arrangements. We're at home and I've been working on it for an hour.

"We're getting Byron," I say.

Casey gives me a hug. Byron is the best chess instructor in town. We met him at a toy store and watched him play chess against ten kids at once.

"He's a grand master," Casey says, smiling. I smile back at him. Starting a chess club is something I'm doing not because I care whether or not Casey's good at chess but because I've decided to honor what he already loves doing. Casey seems to know this. I'm sure there are lots of articles in the parent magazines I haven't read about doing this very thing.

"Where do you get all of this energy?" Isabel asks me the week after the chess club starts. We're waiting for our kids to finish.

I want to tell her that it's because I've stopped watching television. I want to tell her how hard it is to stop watching at first, because the more you've been watching, the more likely you are to be depressed. And when you stop, you get even more depressed before you start getting better. But you do get better, lots better.

THIS YEAR WE'RE GOING to Arizona for Thanksgiving with Bob's family. No Pokémon movie. No raw foods dinner. Bob's sister Lynn will be there with her son, Emerson, who is two years older than Casey. I tuck a few of Casey's favorite games into his suitcase, including a travel chess set.

Emerson, as it turns out, likes chess almost as much as Casey does.

"This is a great set," he tells Casey after they've finished their first game. "I'm glad you brought it." We're in a restaurant that Bob's sister owns sitting at three long tables that have been pushed together to accommodate everyone. It's the day before Thanksgiving.

"Now, wait until you see what I've brought with me," Emerson says, and he reaches into his backpack and pulls out a tin container.

"These are Yu-Gi-Oh! cards," he says. "Have you seen the cartoon?"

"No," Casey says, but he looks interested in the cards.

"Well, it's a game, and it's as hard to play as chess, but I can teach you."

Lynn is sitting beside Emerson. Her water glass is inches away from his cards. "Why don't you go over to that table in the corner, you guys, so you'll have room to spread out your cards?" We're in the party room and have the place to ourselves.

I consider suggesting the boys do something else, but Emerson has just played Casey in chess. Besides, it's not like he's asking him to sneak into the broom closet to look at ads for escort services.

They head to a small table in the corner of the room. I can tell that Casey is listening intently to Emerson, picking up cards, studying them.

"All the kids at school are into it," Lynn says to us. "Casey is a little young, but by next year, he'll be totally into it."

I glance over at the table, wondering if she's right. Casey never got into Pokémon, and it was all the rage.

An hour later, they're still deep in conversation.

"Casey picked it up pretty fast," Emerson says to me when they finally come back to our table.

On the car ride back to our hotel, Casey tells us about the game. It's as if he has picked up a foreign language, a language I'm not interested in learning.

"Do you want to play sometime?" he asks me.

I think of the torturous hours I put into learning how to play chess, Backwords, and SET.

"I'm sure it's a great game," I tell him, "but I think I'm going to let this be something you do with Emerson and your friends."

"Can we see Emerson first thing in the morning?"

"Of course you can," Bob says, with more enthusiasm than I expected.

A FEW DAYS AFTER we return to Portland, a package arrives in the mail. "This is an early Christmas present," it says. "Open now."

Casey is upstairs. I show the package to Bob.

"Pandora's box has arrived," I say.

"It's from my sister," Bob says. "I'm not going to keep it from him."

"Once he opens it, there's no going back. He'll want to watch the cartoon. He'll want spend loads of money on the cards," I say. I am channeling a Southern Baptist preacher, warning his followers of the sinful world. Bob looks weary.

"You can't be sure of that."

"Did you know that kids nag their parents an average of nine times when they want a new toy? And so far, that's what we've been spared! Casey walks into a toy store and he doesn't ask for anything!"

"We can make some sort of agreement with him," he says.

Casey comes downstairs before I have a chance to ask Bob what sort of agreement he has in mind.

"Is that package for me?" He's looking at us expectantly.

"Go ahead and open it," I say, bracing myself for the worst.

He rips it open and, as expected, it's his entrance into the land of Yu-Gi-Oh!

"Wow," he says, and then he doesn't say anything else for the next hour. He carefully sorts through the cards and creates what he calls his best deck. Bob and I look on mystified.

"Well, at least he'll have something to do with the neighbors," Bob says under his breath.

I whisper back, "I wonder when he'll ask to watch the cartoon."

AT SCHOOL, CASEY discovers that there is a Yu-Gi-Oh! lunch once a week.

"Milton and Rajeev from fourth grade told me about it," he says. "We aren't allowed to bring out our decks anytime except in this room once a week."

"A lot of these kids are in chess club, too," the teacher's assistant tells me when I ask her about it. "They're both games of strategy."

She's even better at rationalizing than I am.

WE ARE AT Rebecca's and Casey is explaining his deck to Camden.

"Well, I've seen the cartoon," he tells Casey, "so I know who Blue-Eyes White Dragon is."

"I haven't," he tells Camden.

"Do you want to see it?"

"No, not really."

Rebecca and I are sitting on her couch vaguely listening to their conversation. She looks surprised. We walk into the kitchen.

"He has no interest in the cartoon?"

"I guess not," I say.

She smiles as if she's in the know. "Well, I bet he'll want to watch it soon."

"You might be right," I say, allowing her to think she's right. Maybe she is. I don't care. I'm too busy enjoying Casey's foray into mainstream America. After not understanding the first thing about Buzz Lightyear, he's finally engaged in a commercially certified kid activity. He's speaking the language of some of his peers, and it's not an altogether abhorrent language. Granted, the pictures on the Yu-Gi-Oh! cards leave something to be desired. Some are hideous and gory with names like Snake Fang, but since he doesn't watch the cartoon, the pictures remain inanimate.

"You can watch the cartoon if you want," I tell him when we're on our way home.

"I have no interest in watching the cartoon, Mom. I just like playing the game."

Maybe I've discovered the key to keeping him from other things as well. *You can start having sex if you want,* Bob and I will say when he's a teenager.

I know, Mom, he'll say, exasperated.

The issue of the decks themselves is harder to brush off in the world of political correctness. I assume the cards are made by a large and greedy corporation that lures children and parents into spending endless amounts of money. But I can live with that. At least he's not hooked on television and video games, and that seems like enough of an accomplishment.

"You'll have to buy the packs yourself," Bob tells him when he asks for more. It's after dinner and Casey has spread his cards out on the carpet in the family room. Bob is sitting in the chair next to him explaining one of the biggest differences between chess and Yu-Gi-Oh! "You don't need to keep buying chess pieces, so anyone can afford to play. I still want you to be able to find stuff to do with kids who don't play Yu-Gi-Oh!"

"I'll always find something to do with my friends," he says cheerfully.

"We're going to give you an allowance, and you'll get to decide what you want to spend it on, including your own cards," Bob says.

AFTER A COUPLE of months Casey still has shown no interest in watching the cartoon even though his friends talk about it a lot. I buy him a subscription to a player's guide.

"Now you'll be able to keep informed about new cards." I hand him his first issue.

He studies it with the seriousness of a stockbroker. He figures out which cards to buy and which ones to trade for something better. I help him deconstruct the creepy ads. "Here, they've exaggerated the action figure's body. Real men don't look like this," I say, "unless they take steroids." I explain what steroids are.

"He's learning to manage his money," Bob says in what he

probably thinks is an upbeat tone. "That's good." He makes up a chart for Casey on the computer and offers him a special savings plan with interest, which he calls the Bank of Bob. They are both excited about it, Bob especially. He hopes to teach Casey what he has never been able to teach me.

MY NEW WORKING theory is that kids who are brought up with very little television will be able to entertain themselves in a creative manner even if they are introduced to television later.

"Even when it's freely offered to them, they won't be interested in it," I say to Bob. We're lying in bed and I'm expounding on my so-called theory.

"I don't think it always works that way," he says, pushing the covers aside. "When white people introduced alcohol to Native Americans, a lot of them became alcoholics."

"Yes, but if they had been brought up understanding the potential dangers of alcohol, they might not have ever tried it." I pull the covers back up.

"What about all the people who learned about the dangers of cigarettes but still grew up to smoke?"

"I never smoked," I say smugly.

"The point is that we don't know that Casey won't become a couch potato at some point in his life," he counters.

"No, we don't." I turn away from him, irritated.

I wonder why I share my theories with him. Mostly he just argues with me. Of course we don't know what Casey's future will be, but so far it's better than I had thought it would be.

I had, for instance, expected Casey's imagination to plummet with each new Yu-Gi-Oh! card he acquired, but I was wrong. In fact, he's started designing his own Yu-Gi-Oh! cards, drawing detailed pictures of superpowered beings. "This one has five hundred life points," he told Camden yesterday.

I thought Camden would laugh at Casey's homemade entities, but he didn't. He proudly got to work making his own cards on our kitchen table beside Casey, and they incorporated them into their Yu-Gi-Oh! game. Then they spent another couple of hours building their own LEGO creations, completely different from the ones shown on the boxes. Afterward, they played an imaginary game with their BIONICLES, which are these bizarre, insectlike robotic LEGO creatures they both love.

"I WONDER IF Casey will want to see the BIONICLE movie," I ask Bob.

"Well, he's yet to care about the Yu-Gi-Oh! cartoon, so why would he care about the BIONICLE movie?"

Bob is mostly concerned that Casey has inherited the theater gene from me after all. We've just finished dinner and Casey is in the living room reading part of the BIONICLE script he wrote about Takua and Jaller finding the sacred mask of light.

"How's it going?" Bob asks.

"I'm getting ready for my BIONICLE show," Casey says proudly. "I'm the director and I've invited eight of my friends to be in it. We're going to do musical performances, too." Casey has been taking violin lessons and has decided to incorporate a few numbers into the show. His classmate Andrew is playing the cello and Jacob is playing the piano.

He pulls out a bent piece of yellow construction paper. BIONICLE SHOW ON SATURDAY, it reads. TICKETS FOR SALE, $3 TO $8.

"These are the posters I've made to put up around the neighborhood," he says.

"Do you think eight dollars might be a little high?" Bob asks. "That's the front row, Dad."

Bob looks ill. The birthday parties were enough of a stretch for him. I want to be like Samantha on *Bewitched* and make him a martini to ease his pain and helplessness, but he doesn't drink martinis. I give him a kiss instead.

A FEW DAYS BEFORE the production, Casey agrees, under Bob's influence, that if he's going to hit up his neighbors, he has to donate a portion to the homeless. I consider surreptitiously paying the neighbors to sit through the show.

Bob, resigned to the inevitable, sits down at the computer with Casey, and they use the latest in digital technology to make programs featuring a photo of each child in the performance with a written description under each picture.

Casey dons a suit and tie on the day of the performance. "I'm the director. I think I should look my best," he says. I can't help but think of Michael J. Fox on *Family Ties*. It's scary.

The BIONICLE show ends up being a huge success, in part because Gordon, our next-door neighbor, brought a pitcher of daiquiris.

"Enjoy," he said. I looked at him nervously. It was one p.m. How many people were going to start drinking? Every grown-up in attendance apparently.

15

"I'm Fine, Mom!"

Catherine and I are at Stacey's house and we're setting up art projects for the Valentine's Day party at our kids' school. I'm using Stacey's paper cutter and lots of pink construction paper and trying to work creatively with the parents in Casey's class.

"Why don't they do TV-Turnoff Week at Martin Smith?" Houston's mom, Catherine, asks Stacey. "My daughter's preschool does it every year."

"I don't think Martin Smith kids need it," Stacey says. "Television isn't really a problem for our families. My kids just watch cartoons."

"Of course, he's getting exposed to thousands of ads," I say bravely.

Stacey scoffs. "Hampton is not influenced by them."

"I don't know," Catherine pipes in. "Houston told me he has to have the PlayStation he saw advertised on channel 6."

Hampton, who is on the couch, comes alive. "No, actually, it's the new PlayStation 2 that they sell at Toys "R" Us. I'm sure that's the one he wants."

"Hampton, go finish your reading," Stacey says.

The next day I send off for some information about TV-Turnoff
Week to give to the school counselor. The kindergarten teachers
might not have wanted to embrace the project, but Sheila is delighted to do it. She is far more adventurous than I suspected, and
more aware of the issues, too.

"Would you like to talk to the classes about it?" Sheila asks me.
We're in her office, which makes me paranoid. I imagine the other
parents will think that I'm here because of some problem with
Casey. It's like being at a clinic for STDs.

"I think I'll be happier just working behind the scenes, if it's
okay with you," I say.

I remember Georgette telling me that I'm a natural teacher,
that teaching was supposedly part of my path, but I'm not ready
to be out in the open yet, even if it is my divine calling or whatever
she said.

I print out neon-colored stickers for the kids to wear that read,
I'M TV-FREE TODAY. I make copies of pledge forms to hand out to
the kids. Each child must promise not to watch television or play
video games for a full week. Family members have the option of
signing the pledge, too. Casey happily signs it.

"This will be really tough for you," I joke. He laughs.

"You should have seen Murphy today. He tore the pledge form
in half and said he would never do it, no matter what his mom
says."

I give Sheila articles about television and video game addiction
to send home to parents. Maybe Diego's mom will make some
new rules and then I won't have to worry about Casey not fitting
in with Diego and his classmates. Maybe Jacob's and Andrew's
moms will make the same decision. It could happen.

Sheila says we need to be positive and encouraging with parents.

"If we can get them to cut back, even a little, we'll be making progress," she says. She refers to a study in the TV-Turnoff Week literature that says kids who watch ten hours a week or less do much better in school than kids who watch thirty or more hours a week.

"We need to be supportive of parents and offer them alternatives," she adds.

We fill up the bulletin board with the kids' pledges and pictures they've drawn of all the activities they plan to do during the week instead of watching television and playing video games: riding bicycles, playing board games, painting, and hiking.

I listen to parents talk among themselves. "We've always limited television and video games. I'm glad the school supports our decision," Cathleen says.

Others aren't so enthusiastic.

"We're not doing it. I've got a two-year-old at home," Marcie complains. Andrea and Julia nod their heads to show that they understand that it's impossible to care for a two-year-old without television.

I remain especially quiet as some parents only reluctantly agree to join their children in making the pledge.

"He'll be miserable without his video games," Leo's mom says when the week begins. That proves to be the hardest part for a lot of kids. They miss their video games more than their television shows. I am hard-pressed to find a single boy in Casey's class who doesn't have a GameCube or PlayStation or whatever they use, and as the months go by, it doesn't seem to be getting better.

"Maybe if Casey played video games, he would have more friends at school," I say to Bob. We are eating cherry pie à la mode at the kitchen counter.

"He has friends."

"But he could be friends with kids like Kyle and Grayson. Then he would be more popular."

"I think he can choose his own friends now," Bob says as patiently as he can, trying hard to remember his girlfriend lessons. "Besides, he told me that Kyle and Grayson are mean when they're together. Maybe you should listen to him. He doesn't need to be with a group of kids he doesn't much like and who can't find anything better to do than play video games."

He takes another bite of pie. "Anyway, weren't Kyle's and Grayson's parents in the clique you talked so much about?"

I'm surprised he remembered who was in the clique. It impresses me that he actually listened to me.

"They were, but Casey's friend Diego likes Grayson, so shouldn't Casey learn to like him, too?"

"No, he shouldn't. He said he doesn't care who else Diego likes. He's not like you."

"I know that," I say, and I'm thinking how much Bob isn't like me either. He would never color-code the class list for possible friendships, and neither would Casey. Frankly, I don't know anyone who would, but that's beside the point.

"He fits in enough with his BIONICLES and Yu-Gi-Oh! cards," Bob says. "He has great friends who play soccer and chess and violin with him. He doesn't need to get addicted to video games." Bob is sounding like the zealot now. I finish my pie and take my plate to the sink.

"But maybe it will be the way it is with TV and movies. He doesn't ask to see them, but at least he's experienced them."

"Or maybe he would try them and get hooked."

"But then we would tell him that he can have only two hours

a week," I say. Bob gives me the rest of his pie. He's probably lost his appetite because he's so annoyed.

"He won't want to stop playing until he gets to the next level, because if he stops, he'll have to start all over the next time. That's how the games are designed."

I start to think that maybe Bob has been secretly playing them. Maybe he plays them when he's out of town on business staying at the Marriott. Maybe that's why he looks so tired when he comes back, tired and agitated at the same time.

"What makes you so sure about this?"

"I just wouldn't do it. Besides, it's his choice anyway, and he doesn't want to play them."

When I volunteer in the classroom the following week, I watch Casey rush outside to play soccer with his friends at recess. He seems perfectly happy.

"I've almost beat Tekken 5," Kyle says to Andrew. Casey doesn't seem to care that half the time he has no idea what his classmates are talking about.

Rebecca says she understands the video game issue more than her friends who have girls do, because girls aren't as drawn to these games. She and I are talking while our kids play in Camden's room.

"Camden isn't the same kid after he's been playing with the Xbox at his cousin's house," Rebecca says. "It's all he thinks about. And he looks like something from *Night of the Living Dead*. That's why I'm not getting him one. It's enough that he has a Game Boy."

"But if you took him over to another kid's house, would you tell the parents that you didn't want Camden playing video games?"

"Beatrice and I did that. We agreed that when our guys are

together, we won't let them do video games, because otherwise that's the only thing they would do."

Rebecca is making spaghetti sauce while we talk. I'm watching her and wondering why we got off to such a difficult start in the beginning. I'm not jealous anymore if she sees Kendra, and she seems to have forgotten that I ever propositioned her husband. She and I have come to appreciate how great it is for our kids to have each other.

Camden would prefer to play with Casey more than with any of his friends who own PlayStations. Maybe Diego is the same way about Casey. I still wish Casey's friends at school and on his street hadn't all gotten into these games. It reminds me of what Sarah said about her sisters. The first one got implants, and six months later, the second one had, too.

"Pretty soon normal breasts in my family are going to be considered abnormal."

OLIVIA IS HAVING a party for the neighborhood to celebrate the publication of Janice's new cookbook. Bob has made a spinach quiche and I've brought organic strawberries. Casey piles up his plate with pizza and blueberries and sits on the couch to eat it.

When he's done, I tell him to go see what the other kids are doing. He wanders into the next room. I'm talking to Lori, who is telling me about her kitchen remodel that has been going on for two months.

"Did you see the last episode of *Trading Spaces*?" she asks.

"No I haven't," I say, not mentioning that I haven't seen any of the episodes. "Tell me about it."

She starts describing the house they showed, but before she can finish, Casey is whispering in my ear. I excuse myself from my conversation with Lori.

"All the kids are playing video games in Luke's room," he says.

I glance around the room hoping to see some kids who are not in Luke's room. There are none. I wonder what games they might be playing, hopefully not Grand Theft Auto, but I'm not in the mood to check it out and I'm not in the mood to leave.

"Talk to Dad about it," I say, pointing toward the door. Bob is talking with the old man down the street who gives us giant zucchini every year.

Casey walks away and I go back to talking with Lori. A few minutes later, Bob tells me that he's taking Casey home. I watch the two of them go and consider that Bob doesn't care for socializing and is probably thrilled to latch on to any excuse to leave a party early.

When I get home Casey is putting on his pajama top. I sit on the bed next to him. "You know, you might actually like video games," I tell him. "Maybe you should try playing them. Some of them are not that different from the computer games Dad's shown you, like Tetris. And remember how you had no interest in movies? Now you're okay about them."

"Mom, the video game they were playing was awful and I didn't want to play it."

"I'm sure it was," I say. "But it could be like chocolate cake. It's okay to have a piece of it every once in a while."

I give him a kiss on his forehead and tuck him in.

Bob brings me a glass of water and sits down next to me on the couch. He was listening to me talk to Casey.

"Who are you and why are you trying to coax our child into playing video games?"

"I'm sorry," I say, thinking that the chocolate cake comment went a little too far. "I just wonder how many more of these neighborhood get-togethers I have to endure where my child asks me to take him home as soon as he's finished eating." I take a sip of water.

"If you're looking for a perfect answer to these situations, you're never going to find one," he says. "If he actually did join in with the other kids and play video games, you'd be upset that he was being exposed to dehumanizing depictions of gunslinging maniacs. You would go on and on about how much you regret it."

I stare at him. This isn't what I want to hear, probably because there is a grain of truth in it. Probably a whole ocean of truth in it. But I don't want to admit it.

"I'm sure there's another way to deal with this," Bob says finally.

"Well, we better think of it soon, because I don't like it when you desert me."

I LOOK THROUGH the back section of the weekly newspaper. I surf the Web. Once again I'm trying to find a group of parents like me, but there isn't a place for me to meet anyone who is doing something as radical as watching little or no television and forgoing the Xbox.

I study the resource list that came with the TV-Turnoff Week literature. There's a media literacy organization in the Portland area and they're offering a workshop this month. I give them a call, although I'm not that enthusiastic. I assume that the workshop will be all about working to change media images — showing Latinos as lawyers, Native Americans as CEOs—rather than cutting back on television itself.

I think about how my mother taught me to be media literate. I would be watching *Bewitched,* and she would yell, "If Samantha wants to act like a mortal, she should be running her own advertising agency instead of waiting on Darrin!"

This was her way of enlightening me. Mostly, though, I felt it was her way of being rude. Of course, the shows I watched *were* sexist, but they were my world and I wasn't interested in her critique of it. Besides, did she actually think her comments were going to affect me? Did she actually think she could be a stronger influence on me than television? It doesn't matter how many times you discuss media stereotypes. If you are continually exposed to them on TV, you internalize them.

Even as I remembered my mother's words "Makeup is just another product imposed on women by Madison Avenue," I covered my skin in Revlon's products. Even though I was raised by a single parent, it was as if I had two parents: my mother with her feminist lectures and television with its rigid sex-role programming.

Olivia tells me, "I'm not afraid to let Luke know that some toy he wants is a piece of junk." But my question is why would you want to spend so much time having to be so negative, when you could prevent the problem from even existing in the first place by not watching? Why wouldn't you throw an abusive boyfriend out of your house, instead of simply complaining about him? The problem is that television is part of the family and it's not easy to get rid of a family member.

THE WORKSHOP IS on a Saturday, and I've freed up the entire day. I take a seat next to an African American woman in her twenties with bright red toenails. The instructor is named Carl. He's my age, with brown hair and the same sort of forehead as my husband. His voice is gentle and he carries himself in a way that tells me he is at home in his body. He and his wife became interested in teaching media literacy because of their seventeen-year-old son, their only child.

"It all started when we gave him a Game Boy when he was eight. He became so addicted to that thing, we fought over it constantly. By middle school he was hooked on the most horribly violent video games you can imagine. His grades fell. A couple of years ago, we offered him five hundred dollars to get rid of his Nintendo, which he had bought for himself. Bribing him was the only thing that worked." He pauses and looks around the room at each of us.

"We were naive. A lot of parents have no idea where their kids are headed."

He shows us a commercial for Coca-Cola, a baby polar bear holding onto his first Coke as if it's a bottle of milk.

This is aimed at babies and toddlers. "Is Coke good for babies and toddlers?" He reads the ingredients to us.

"Television isn't good for babies and toddlers either." He cites the recommendation by the American Academy of Pediatrics that children under two shouldn't watch any television. "But new programs are being created every day aimed at this very young audience. Look at the Teletubbies. Someone worked hard to figure out what babies would want to watch."

I think about what he's saying and imagine the creators of the show sitting together over coffee, brainstorming:

So, what do babies like? a guy in his twenties with a goatee asks.

How about showing big breasts? the man next to him says.

No, the formula companies won't like it and they could be sponsors. And we'll get complaints from the Christian right, the producer says. *We need big, close-up faces and soothing, happy voices to make babies pay attention.*

Babies like to see things bounce around, the guy with the goatee says.

Like breasts?

Forget the breasts! the producer yells.

I'd like one of them to be gay. Can we make one of them gay? the youngest member of the group interjects.

Carl shows a clip from *Teletubbies.*

"Mostly, this show is teaching one thing. It's teaching babies to like television. It's getting them hooked."

I nod my head in agreement with this man. Why have I been so afraid of simply telling the truth? He makes it look so easy.

He shows another commercial. This one is for Little Debbie snack treats. A little girl is throwing the treats into her shopping cart when her mother isn't looking.

"Television commercials teach kids to do whatever it takes to get the products these companies want them to buy."

He shows commercials aimed at women. One features a woman in her twenties complaining about her lifeless hair. Another one shows a slightly older woman complaining about her aging skin.

"The important message in all of these ads is that you're not good enough the way you are. Companies selling cosmetics want you to feel that way. They want you to believe that you will only be good enough if you buy their products.

"And it's not just the commercials. It's the embedded advertising, the messages in the shows themselves. Some are downright blatant, some are not."

I think of Kellie, who has been watching *Extreme Makeover.* "They take someone unattractive and give them plastic surgery and whatever else is needed to make them 'hot,'" she told me when she was over at our house the other night. She stood in front of the mirror in the bathroom. "I'm thinking about getting surgery for my nose and blepharoplasty for my eyes. After that, I'm going to get porcelain veneers for my teeth and liposuction for my thighs."

I stared at her in disbelief. She is twenty-seven, strikingly beautiful, and she has a minor in women's studies. I raise my hand and tell the instructor about her.

He nods knowingly. He's heard it before he says. "It's not just women like your son's babysitter who are being manipulated by these programs. Men aren't exempt from the damaging influence of these shows." He passes around an article about how teenage boys are becoming obsessed with working out, developing eating disorders, and wanting surgery just like teenage girls. "And not surprisingly, teenagers who watch more than two hours of television a day are 35 percent more likely to have had sex than those who watch less than that. In fact, the average teenager views 14,000 sexual references a year on television."

Carl talks about the news media. "Only a handful of companies own virtually all of the television stations, and every news story has a bias," he says. "You can sell the public an unnecessary war and make people feel helpless to do anything about it, because being passive is the nature of the viewing experience."

After the workshop is over, I wait until everyone leaves. I help Carl move the chairs back, stalling for time. Then I tell him about my dilemma with Casey and video games.

"I think it's fabulous that he doesn't want to play video games. Be thankful. I wish I had done the same with my son."

It's Sunday morning and I'm sitting on the couch with the newspaper beside me and a glass of ruby red grapefruit juice. I squeezed it myself.

I pick up the Living section and read the advice columns, and because it's Sunday, I turn to Miss Manners. She is advising a young woman on how to graciously decline her mother-in-law's offer to redecorate her new home.

I glance at the photo of Miss Manners and it occurs to me that maybe Casey just needs some helpful tips in etiquette, some polite ways to deal with social situations involving television and video games.

Casey is in his room building a LEGO dirt crusher. I sit down next to him, scooting a pile of pieces over to one side.

"Here is a multiple choice question for you," I say.

He looks up from his creation, happy to oblige. I find that I can talk about almost anything with him if I do it in a quiz format. It's a gimmick, but I was brought up on gimmicks and game shows, so it works for me.

"Here's the question," I say to Casey. "If you are at a party with a group of kids and everyone wants to play a video game, and it's rated E for everyone, what should you do?

    A) Suggest everyone play something else

    B) Play the game

    C) Find something else to do by yourself

    D) Ask the parents to make everyone do what
       you want instead.

"I think D," he says.

I shake my head, although his answer doesn't surprise me in the least.

"No, that's the one thing you shouldn't do," I say. "You can't ask the parents to make everyone do what you want. A, B, and C are okay."

He looks unhappy about this. "What if the parents don't mind making everyone do something else?"

"Trust me. The parents might not show it, but they mind. They want to have kids over who are easy and flexible."

This seems like a hard truth, but he might as well know it.

"But what if the parents offer to make everyone do what I want?"

"Then you need to say, *No, I don't want to spoil everyone else's fun. I'm fine.*"

He picks up some LEGO pieces absently, and then looks up at me with a gleam in his eye.

"What if they suddenly switch the game to something rated T for teen?"

"Then you need to tell them that you are not allowed to play games like that."

He looks relieved about this. He rummages through the pile of LEGO pieces beside us. I smile at him. I'm glad we're able to talk together. I'm like one of the Cosby parents, helping her child find the answers, except I'm three-dimensional.

"You don't have to do what everyone else is doing," I say. "You can tell the truth, that you're not big on television and video games, but I want you to be polite about it and be willing to let others have fun doing what they want as long as it's safe."

CASEY SAYS THAT Jacob's sleepover is going to be a Teenage Mutant Ninja Turtle party complete with a Ninja Turtle video.

"We'll find out about ninjas," I tell Casey.

I consult an expert.

"Ninjas are so passé," Rebecca says. "I'm surprised there are still ninja parties."

"I think his teenage brother was into them," I say.

"The movie is rated PG," I tell Casey. "It could be violent, but you're old enough to see a PG movie. Do you want to go this party?"

"I do."

ON THE DAY of the party, I remind Casey about the etiquette I taught him.

"Should I bring a chess set?" he asks. "That way if some of the kids are playing video games I can play chess with someone."

"That's an idea," I say, and his face brightens.

"Milton from chess club is coming. I'll call him to see if he's interested in playing a game with me."

Casey picks up the phone. "Do you want to play chess with me at the party? I'm not much into video games," he says.

He comes back into the kitchen.

"Milton says he will!"

He tucks the chess set, his Yu-Gi-Oh! cards, and a book into his backpack.

At the last minute, I consider going to the video store to check out the ninja movie while he's at the party, but I refrain. I'm loosening up. I'm like the religious fanatic in *Chocolat,* who in the end goes out with his secretary.

"He'll be okay," Bob says after we drop him off.

"I know he will," I say, and I'm telling the truth.

"Do you want to stop and get a video?" he asks.

"I'm okay either way," I say, and realize that I'm telling the truth about that, too.

CASEY COMES BACK from the party with a couple of prizes. "I made the most words out of the letters in *ninja turtle,*" he says, holding up a plastic trophy. I ask him about the movie.

"It was pretty violent," he says, "but it had a happy ending."

After that he doesn't mention the movie again. He doesn't ask to rent a ninja video nor does he ask to see a ninja cartoon. He doesn't even run around the house with a sword shouting, "I'm the Shredder."

"Did you play chess at the party?"

"I played with Milton and once with Perry while the rest of the kids played video games."

"You could have played video games, too, you know."

"I know," he says, "but I was fine."

I study his face for a few seconds and know that he's telling the truth. He's absolutely fine. He isn't concerned about fitting in. It dawns on me that maybe that's because he hasn't been inundated with thousands of commercial messages and shows telling him that he has to be a carbon copy of everyone else. Maybe the psychologist who evaluated him was right. He likes himself the way he is.

A COUPLE OF DAYS later Jacob calls to invite Casey to a movie on the weekend.

"Which movie?" I ask.

"My choice," he says.

"Do you want to go?"

"If it's a good movie."

I look through the newspaper's Arts and Entertainment guide. There is one movie that looks fun. Bob and I could see it with him. If he likes it, he could see it with Jacob later.

"Does this sound good?" I read the description for *Finding Nemo* to Bob. He shrugs.

"It looks a lot better than a Winnie the Pooh movie at least."

I explain about Jacob wanting to take Casey to a movie.

"So you want to take him to the movie first, before you let anyone else take him?"

He makes me sound so overprotective.

"I always wanted to be the one to take to him to his first movie in a theater."

We get in the car and I'm truly excited. All of this work as a parent, reading to my child, singing, playing musical instruments together, eating dinner as a family, has been well and good, but what I've wanted just as much is to sit in a dark room next to my son in front of a good movie.

The theater is crowded but we still find excellent seats, eight rows back in the center. Casey has a perfect view. As we settle in, I think of the countless movies that lie in our future together, and I'm thrilled at the prospect of seeing them.

Bob comes back with popcorn and a bottle of water for each of us. We're early enough to see the commercials, and I'm suddenly glad for the media literacy training I've had. I've already explained to Casey in detail how commercials work, the different ways in which they manipulate their audience. Yesterday I was singing the Izzy's Pizza jingle to him to illustrate how these songs get stuck in your head.

"Izzy's is pizza plus a whole lot more."

"Stop it, Mom! I see what you mean."

Casey gets it all right. I think of what Carl said at the workshop. At age eight, children can understand how advertising works and deconstruct it.

Britney Spears bounces onto the screen to promote Coca-Cola. I don't say anything about the sexual innuendos, but I figure I can talk to Casey about it later on. The beauty of having a kid who hasn't been exposed to thousands of commercials is that he doesn't need a lot of deprogramming and he doesn't like soft drinks besides.

The movie is far better than I expected, enlightening and funny, mostly because I am so much like Nemo's father. He is the parent who can't let go. When he tells little Nemo's teacher about his son's fin, I know that Bob is thinking of me. I steal a glance in his direction and find him staring at me, nodding his head knowingly. I smile.

"I think Jacob will really like it when I see it with him on Sunday," Casey says after the movie.

"I do, too," I say, and I'm feeling confident and relaxed, which is definitely more than Nemo's father could say for himself.

16

Leaving TV Land

I am on the track with Isabel and about to go see Sheila to plan for next year's TV-Turnoff Week. It's only December but Sheila has big ideas to discuss with me. I decide to tell Isabel where I'm going this morning after our run.

"I think it's great that you're doing that," she says. "I've needed a reason to tell Lindsey to turn the damn thing off."

I smile. I'm being myself, and like Casey, I'm starting to be okay with who I am.

Yesterday Marcie asked me if I like *Judging Amy*.

"Actually, I don't watch much television," I told her. "Is it a good show?"

I run an extra lap before saying good-bye to Isabel. I brush the hair away from my face, and as I walk away from her, the ground feels solid underneath my feet.

Sheila says she heard positive reviews from lots of parents last year about TV-Turnoff Week. She wants to do it every year.

"I want to include a media literacy piece this year and I need your help," she says. "And I'd like to at least mention you in the parent newsletter."

"That's fine," I say, throwing caution to the wind. We're sitting in her office and I'm still sweating from my run.

I imagine some of the parents talking about me. I think about what Georgette said the other day. "I believe you'll find that when you stop judging others so harshly, you'll stop being afraid of their judging you. In fact, you won't invite their judgment." Maybe she's right. I think about what Isabel just said this morning. She liked what I had to say. She was nice, even appreciative.

Telling the truth might not be so bad after all. Maybe I can stop worrying about what others think of me and actually be of some help. I could be like Jane Eyre's friend, Helen. I smile to myself because I'm thinking of a book instead of a movie or TV show.

This must be what coming out is like, except that I've been in the closet about television. When the truth is out, you discover that most people already knew whatever it was you were hiding.

"Casey has never watched much television, has he?" Sam's mom says to me when she sees me in the first-grade classroom gathering pledges.

"Not too much," I say.

I call Carl for some more information on media literacy for Sheila. We meet at a coffee shop in his neighborhood in Southeast Portland. He orders a scone. I order a lemon ginger concoction that is supposed to stimulate my immune system.

We sit by the window looking out on Hawthorne Boulevard. He gives me a CD-ROM about media literacy to show to the school counselor. I tuck it into my purse.

"I'm glad you called," he says, "because I have proposal for you, if you're not too busy."

I take a sip of my drink. "Tell me what you have in mind."

"What our organization needs is a support group of sorts for parents like you, parents who are raising their kids with little or no television and video games. Is this something that you're interested in leading?"

I stare at him, at a loss for words, but only for a few seconds.

"Since the day I had Casey, I have been interested in a group like that," I tell him.

He smiles. "Then maybe you wouldn't mind teaching the workshops either?"

I take another sip of my lemon ginger drink and feel my immune system becoming stronger already. I look straight at him and flash him my finest smile, the one I wear on those rare occasions when I'm truly happy, except that it's no longer so rare anymore.

"I would love to teach these workshops," I say.

Epilogue

I am in front of an audience of sixty or seventy people at the downtown library giving a presentation. This is my first televised presentation, albeit it's for an obscure cable-access station, but I'm on television, nonetheless. It seems fitting somehow.

"One fourth of all children under two have television sets in their bedrooms and one third of all children under six have them," I say. I pause to give myself time to relax, hoping the audience will think I'm doing it for dramatic effect. I've been giving workshops and leading the parent support group for the past year, but having a camera in front of me is more intimidating than I thought it would be. Maybe I actually wouldn't have liked starring in commercials as a child.

I scan the audience, which is made up mostly of parents and grandparents and the people I coerced into coming tonight, such as Sarah. She's sitting in the front row, looking fabulous in a new Saks purchase, a chartreuse dress that shows just a hint of her implant-free cleavage. I guess she wanted to be sure I wouldn't miss her. She gives me a thumbs-up sign. When it's time for the camera operator to cut to the audience, he'll probably zoom in on her first and ignore the blandly dressed library goers around her.

I make eye contact with Kendra, too, who is sitting two rows behind Sarah. She smiles and gives me a little wave. She came to one of my first media literacy workshops last spring and has come, on and off, to the parent support group.

"I wish I had done what you did with Casey from the beginning," she told me the other day.

"Well, I probably went a little overboard," I said. "I'm sure Casey still would have been fine if I'd let him watch a little more TV. And it might have helped if I'd been a little less neurotic about the whole thing."

We both laughed, and I thought to myself that it's all worked out for the best, for both our families. Casey's hasn't become hooked on television and Hannah watches less than ever now. Kendra got rid of one of their television sets a couple of months ago.

"As soon as we did, Hannah started reading more and helping me cook dinner."

I'm starting to see that a little goes a long way. Some people have to throw their television sets out and go through massive withdrawal to save their family. Other people are conscientious and balanced right from the beginning, effortlessly limiting the hours their children watch.

"We've never been into TV much," a mom told me during TV-Turnoff Week this year. "We might watch a movie together every now and then, but that's about it." Her son, Ryan, is smart and cheerful, and as even-tempered as his mom. Like Casey, Ryan learned to talk early, but his mother never barricaded herself in a room to watch *Seinfeld*. "I've always preferred reading," she said.

I mention the latest statistics now, letting the audience know about the rise in obesity, diabetes, and ADHD, and how these problems are correlated with watching too much television. I mention the detrimental effect TV watching can have on language acquisition, reading, and academic performance. People in the audience are nodding their heads. They're a pretty savvy group, I assume, but I'm on television and I want to reach all those people sitting on their couches, too.

I remember what Georgette said when I went to see her last night because I was nervous about giving this presentation.

"You will reach a lot more people if you come from a place of compassion and understanding," she told me. "Remember that we are all doing the best we can."

I recalled the times when Casey was fussy and knew she was right. Back then, the only person who managed to get through to me was a woman I met at the dry cleaner's who had a gentle approach. "You might try a bouncy motion instead of swaying," she said when Casey was losing it. I jumped up and down with Casey on the bed when I got home and he stopped crying.

I guess every family has to discover what works best for them in regard to television. Who am I to judge? It's not a black-and-white matter, as much as I wish it were, and the issues are always changing. Soon enough, Bob and I will have to decide what to do about the Internet with Casey. Do we block the ads for erectile dysfunction or explain to Casey what erectile dysfunction is? We'll have to figure it out, and God knows what else will come our way.

But at least we won't be alone anymore. In the seats behind Kendra I see some of the friends I've made this past year, people who have been right here in Portland, doing the same thing I've been doing. I just didn't know it.

It's been almost a year since I've watched more than two hours of television a week, with a few exceptions. Most weeks, I don't even bother. Without television my thoughts and values feel more my own and I get to the heart of things faster. Instead of escaping from my feelings for days at a time, I talk to Bob more, and he's become a pretty good girlfriend, and a smart one, too, at times.

I've come to see that he was absolutely right when he said there

isn't a perfect answer with this issue. There will be pluses and mi-
nuses either way. So why spend my life fretting over every decision
I make, about video games or anything else?

The funny thing is that I was so busy trying to raise a child who
would be all the things I was not that I didn't notice I was filling in the missing pieces of myself and learning to forgive people
at the same time. Lauren and her clique and Casey's kindergarten teacher certainly didn't do anything worse than I've done at
some point, and I most likely offended them, too, in any case.
Georgette's right. Forgiving people has made me a lot happier.

I finish my presentation on what I hope is an inspiring note.
I tell everyone how important it is to talk about this issue. "Let's
help each other find alternatives to television and video games for
our children. It's too hard to do it alone."

I smile and attempt to look relaxed, and fortunately I don't
need to try that hard.

"It's never too late," I say. "Television is but one piece of the
picture, not the only one, and kids are pretty resilient. Most of us
turn out okay anyway."

I think to myself that, in the end, I've turned out okay, too.

IT'S EARLY EVENING when I come home. I say good-bye
to Kellie, who has been watching Casey. He gives me a hug and I
sit next to him on the couch. I show him a bumper sticker.

"What do you think? We offer them at the workshops."

He sets his book down and smiles. "I like it."

I go outside and put it on my car, just as Bob is pulling into the
driveway. He gets out of his car and stares at the bumper of my
Volvo station wagon and smiles.

TURN OFF TELEVISION. TURN ON LIFE, he reads aloud.

"Do you like it?"

He laughs. "Only a zealot would put that sticker on her car."

"I know," I say, "but she's a forgiving, understanding sort of zealot."

"The best kind there is," he says, and he kisses me gently on the lips, lingering for a second or two, before he turns to go inside.

I stand in the driveway looking down at the houses below us. It's getting dark now and I can see an unnatural glow coming from each one. I think of my husband and child waiting inside for me, the three of us so close and connected to each other. I say a silent prayer of thanks before I turn to go inside.

Acknowledgments

Many thanks to—

My husband, Bob, for his endless patience and understanding, not to mention his excellent cooking. I am yours forever.

Our fabulous son, Casey. Without you, I would probably still be watching reruns of *Family Ties*. You are my joy and inspiration!

My nieces, Moksha and Isha, for their dazzling insights, hard work, and endless energy. Better girls have not been made!

My sister and brother for their unconditional love and support, and our parents, who lived life with passion and creativity.

Rachel Owen and Kellie Raydon-Feeney for listening to me talk endlessly about this book and encouraging me, sometimes begging me, to finish writing it already! And for Rachel's twelve-year-old daughter, Rose, a talented writer in her own right.

My friends in Casey's first playgroup for all of the serendipitous moments we shared in the trenches of new motherhood.

Nick Rothenberg at Northwest Media Literacy Center and Robert Kesten at the Center for Screen-Time Awareness.

Michael Denneny, who believed in my manuscript from the start and found me the perfect agent.

Margaret Ruley, the perfect agent, at the Jane Rotrosen Agency, who enthusiastically accepted my book and brought me to the best publisher imaginable.

The brilliant Amy Gash at Algonquin, the best publisher imaginable. Thank you, Amy, and everyone at Algonquin!

Casey's teachers, who continue to inspire him, and teachers everywhere, who enthrall their students daily (without television). Thank you!